Bahá'í Children's Classes
and Retreats: Theme #1

God and the Universe

Dr. Randie S. Gottlieb

Published by
UnityWorks LLC

God and the Universe
Teacher's Guide with Lesson Plans for Ages 8-12

ISBN 978-0-9828979-1-1

© 2007 UnityWorks LLC, revised 2012

All rights reserved. No part of this book may be reproduced or transmitted in any form or by any means without prior written permission from the publisher.

UnityWorks hereby grants permission for one children's class teacher or Bahá'í school to copy student handouts as needed. Handouts are also available for downloading from: www.UnityWorksStore.com.

The small fee charged for our materials helps to cover printing costs, the development of new products, and the maintenance of our website to make these resources more widely available. If you find these items useful, please let others know about them. Thank you!

Available from: www.UnityWorksStore.com

Quotations from the Bahá'í writings reprinted with permission of the National Spiritual Assembly of the Bahá'ís of the United States and the Bahá'í Publishing Trust of Wilmette, IL.

Special thanks to my husband, Steven E. Gottlieb, M.D. for his support and editorial assistance.

Appreciation to my sons, Jordan Gottlieb for cover design and pre-press work, and Jonathan Gottlieb for musical transcription.

Cover illustration, Kamal Siegel

Clip art images taken or adapted from:
The Big Box of Art from www.Hemera.com

All websites and references listed are correct at the time of publication.

Published by UnityWorks, LLC
www.UnityWorksStore.com
Yakima, Washington, USA

Dedicated to our first grandchild,

Maya Aliya Gottlieb

*a precious soul created in
the image and likeness of God.*

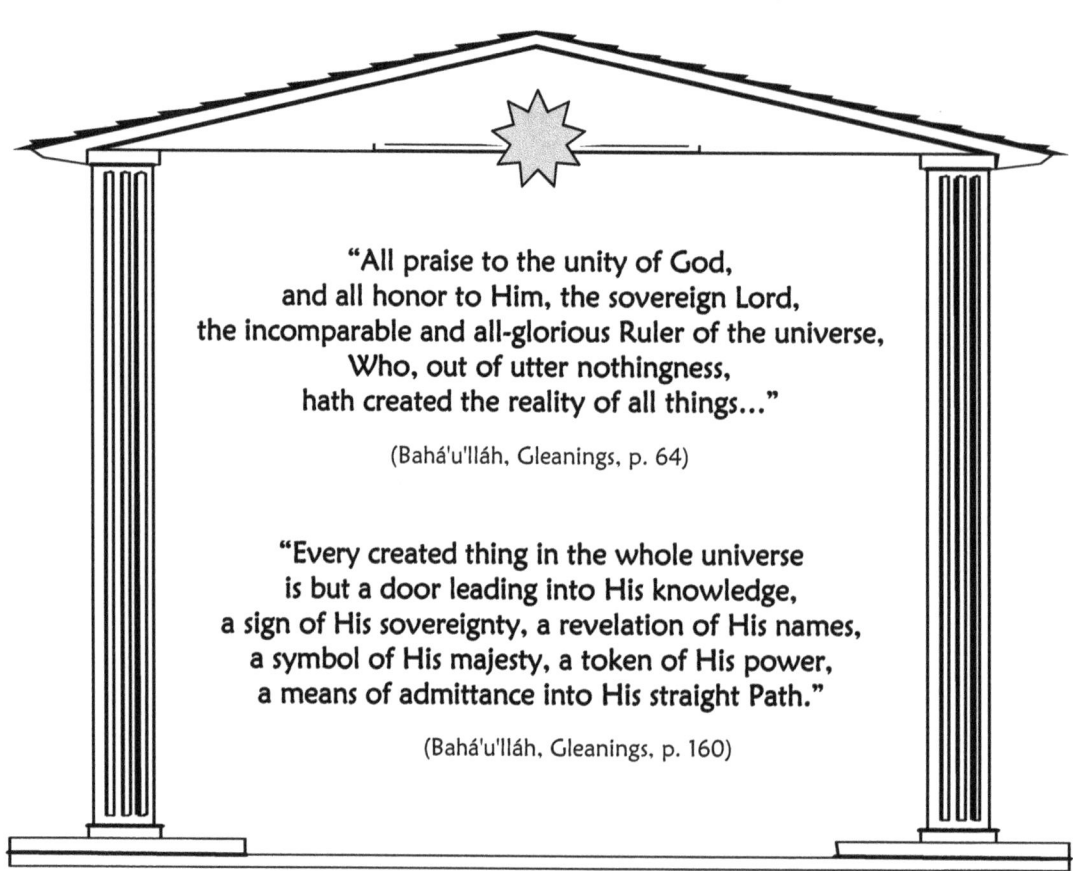

"All praise to the unity of God,
and all honor to Him, the sovereign Lord,
the incomparable and all-glorious Ruler of the universe,
Who, out of utter nothingness,
hath created the reality of all things…"

(Bahá'u'lláh, Gleanings, p. 64)

"Every created thing in the whole universe
is but a door leading into His knowledge,
a sign of His sovereignty, a revelation of His names,
a symbol of His majesty, a token of His power,
a means of admittance into His straight Path."

(Bahá'u'lláh, Gleanings, p. 160)

TABLE OF CONTENTS

Introduction 1
Overview 2
To the Organizers 4
    Teachers 4
    Special Role of Youth 4
    Schedule 5
    Handouts 5
    Sample Retreat Flyer with Registration Form 6
    Sample Retreat Schedules 7
To the Teacher 10
Opening Activities and Orientation Program 13

LESSONS

    1. The Kingdoms of Creation 17
    2. God, the Creator 45
    3. Prayer, Our Connection with God 59
    4. What is a Human Being? 97

Additional Activities 119
Children's Performance 135
Handouts 157
    Song Sheet 159
    Quotations 161
    Student Handout Packet on God and the Universe 163
Music 177
Closing Activities and Follow-up 193
References for Teachers 197
Bibliography 223
Works by the Same Author 225
List of Activities by Chapter 229
Index of Activities by Category 233

God and the Universe

INTRODUCTION

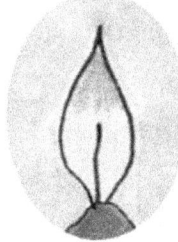

Bahá'u'lláh has prescribed unto all people, "that which will lead to the exaltation of the Word of God amongst His servants, and likewise, to the advancement of the world of being." "To this end," He states, "the greatest means is education of the child."[1]

"My highest wish and desire," proclaims 'Abdu'l-Bahá, "is that ye who are my children may be educated according to the teachings of Bahá'u'lláh…that ye may each become a lighted candle in the world of humanity."[2] He adds that we should "let them make the greatest progress in the shortest span of time."[3]

The Universal House of Justice has likewise called upon us to involve Bahá'í children in "programmes of activity that will engage their interests [and] mold their capacities for teaching and service."[4]

The International Teaching Centre has affirmed that "these young people should then be seen as a door to entry by troops and as a fruitful source of teachers…not simply as children for whom activity must be arranged…but as a living creation of God necessary at this very moment for the purposes of God…"[5]

The purpose of these classes, then, is to systematically familiarize children with the fundamental truths of the Bahá'í Revelation, and to increase their desire and capacity to teach and serve. Additional goals are to strengthen bonds of friendship, and to provide an enjoyable Bahá'í activity which children will enthusiastically look forward to and invite their friends. In the words of some of the participants and their families:

"Thank you so much for putting together the children's retreat. I loved the classes and I learned more about our connection with God…I had a much more fuller brain when I came out than when I came in." (Alonso, age 11)

"A human being cannot describe how much you guys did for me. Thank you from the bottom of my heart." (Zia, age 10)

"My grandson tells me that the children's retreat at your home this weekend was the best weekend of his life!" (Rhett Diessner)

References

1. Bahá'í Education: A Compilation, p.4
2. Selections from the Writings of 'Abdu'l-Bahá, p. 141
3. Bahá'í Education: A Compilation, p. 71
4. Riḍván 2000 Message
5. To the Boards of Counselors, 5 Dec. 1988

God and the Universe

OVERVIEW

TEACHER'S GUIDES FOR CHILDREN'S CLASSES

It is hoped that this easy-to-use teacher's guide, the first in a series for the Bahá'í education of children, will be a useful resource for Bahá'í summer and winter schools, Holy Day programs and weekend retreats. It might also be included in a parent's toolkit for home schooling, or form part of the religious curriculum for a full-time Baha'i-inspired academic school—such as the one our family established in Puerto Rico where many of these lessons were developed.

Anticipating future needs, with a few minor modifications, some of the theme books might also be appropriate for upper elementary public school classrooms. "The Manifestation of God," for example, would be well-suited for a class on comparative religion, and "The Power of Unity," could offer a valuable contribution to a unit on diversity and the oneness of humankind.

Each book is filled with fun, hands-on, kid-tested learning activities designed for ages 8-12. These activities were developed and tested in the field, in response to the needs of teachers and children, and have been used successfully in multiple settings over many years.

The lessons incorporate a variety of instructional strategies as recommended in the Bahá'í Writings on education, such as learning through play, questioning, memorization, consultation, reflection, stories, speeches, music, arts and crafts, science, independent investigation, lectures, group discussion, plays and recreational activities.

When used as part of an intensive program, such as a summer school or weekend retreat, the teacher will need to select activities to fit within the time allotted. If the lessons are part of an ongoing program such as a daily or weekly academic class, one or more activities can be selected for each session, until the entire course has been completed. Utilized in this way, there is sufficient material in each book for several months of weekly classes.

The lessons are user-friendly and ready-to-go with very little outside preparation needed by the teacher. Essentially everything is included, with the exception of craft supplies and common household items. Each book has a sample retreat schedule, detailed lesson plans, instructions and patterns for making classroom materials, copy-ready student handouts, song sheets, music, and plans for a children's performance. When optional materials are recommended (e.g., photographs or videos), the sources are given.

God and the Universe

Each teacher's guide focuses on a distinct theme, with all of the lessons, songs, crafts and other learning activities integrated around that theme. The series includes:

(1) GOD AND THE UNIVERSE
- The Kingdoms of Creation
- God, the Creator
- Prayer, Our Connection with God
- What Is a Human Being?

(2) THE MANIFESTATION
- Station of the Manifestation
- Introduction to the Prophets
- Progressive Revelation
- One Common Faith

(3) THE BÁB: GATE TO BAHÁ'U'LLÁH
- His Birth and Early Life
- Declaration of the Báb
- Martyrdom of the Báb
- The Primal Point

(4) BAHÁ'U'LLÁH: THE GLORY OF GOD
- His Birth, Early Life and Station
- Declaration of Bahá'u'lláh
- Exiles and Imprisonment
- Clouds of Glory

(5) THE POWER OF UNITY
- The Power of Unity
- Unity in Diversity
- The Colors We Are
- Overcoming Prejudice

Additional theme books are being prepared on 'Abdu'l-Bahá, Bahá'í Principles, Bahá'í Laws and Institutions, Consultation for Kids, and The Bahá'í Community.

CHILDREN'S RETREAT PLANNING GUIDE

These theme books can be used in conjunction with the *Bahá'í Children's Retreat Planning Guide,* which is available from **www.UnityWorksStore.com**. It covers the following topics:

- ❏ Scheduling
- ❏ Sponsorship
- ❏ Participants
- ❏ Teachers
- ❏ Other volunteers
- ❏ Facility
- ❏ Publicity
- ❏ Finances
- ❏ Pre-registration
- ❏ Materials
- ❏ Site preparation
- ❏ Sample schedule
- ❏ On-site registration
- ❏ Orientation
- ❏ Outdoor activities
- ❏ Children's performance
- ❏ Closing activities
- ❏ Food, forms, signs

God and the Universe

TO THE ORGANIZERS

Teachers

This teacher's guide includes four lessons on *God and the Universe*. One individual could teach all four lessons; the classes can be team-taught; or a different person might be asked to lead each class.

Special Role of Youth

Capable youth and junior youth can be invited to assist with the classes and activities. We have found that many former participants are eager to return to the children's retreats as volunteers. Inspired by this experience, a high percentage of them have gone on to complete junior youth animator training, and several have arisen to organize children's classes or junior youth groups in their own neighborhoods.

The participation of youth volunteers at the retreat is also a great help for the adults and a joy for the younger children, while offering the youth an opportunity to apply their institute training and to acquire new skills. The youth are given guided experience and hands-on teaching practice. They return home with new confidence, encouraged and motivated to support local children's classes. In addition, a wonderful community atmosphere is created with all age groups working together to educate the children.

In the words of one youth:

> *"The retreats have been an integral part of my growing up experience, and I'm so grateful for the opportunity to come and help out now as a youth. It's really special to see my brothers and cousins and their friends, and know that they'll grow up with the same wonderful friendships and learning experiences and shared memories that my generation of youth gained.*
>
> *"I learned a lot about myself and discovered how to help kids learn and grow, and ways to make their experience happy. Although I went through all the same lessons myself, it's still great to hear and see the lessons again. Us kids have so much fun every time and I am always looking forward to the next retreat."* (Brynne Haug, age 16)

Youth volunteers: Kierra, Yuri, Alonso, Layli, Alex, Brynne, Carew

Schedule

If planning a weekend retreat, the lessons can be scheduled over a two-day or a three-day period. Sample schedules for both are included below. The two-day schedule offers participants a choice of some of the crafts and activities. The three-day schedule includes more of the crafts and classroom activities, additional time for memorization practice, an evening talent show, and a group consultation on how to share with others the concepts learned at the retreat. For an ongoing class, all of the activities can be included.

Handouts

Some handouts are included with the lessons, while others have been grouped near the end of this book for convenience in photocopying. They can also be downloaded from: **www.UnityWorksStore.com** (click on Children's Classes > God and the Universe > student handouts). The handouts can be copied one at a time as needed for a particular class, or all at once as part of the handout packet for a summer school or weekend retreat.

The **Schedule, Songs** and **Quotations** should be photocopied for all participants and included in their folders during registration. If each item is copied on paper of a different color, it will be easier for the children to find. The songs and quotations should each be copied on two sides of the page to save paper and for ease of use.

The 11-page packet on **God and the Universe** (from the title sheet through "A Human Being Is") should be copied back-to-back on white paper, stapled together and included in the folders. This packet will be used in various lessons.

Each instructor should be given **To the Teacher** (pages 10-12), a copy of the appropriate lesson plan, and **References for Teachers** (found at the end of this book), along with the handouts mentioned above. Teachers should also make copies of any additional handouts needed for their specific lessons.

The coordinator of the children's performance will need copies of the entire **Children's Performance** section (pages 135-156), in addition to the schedule, song sheet, page of quotations, and the packet on **God and the Universe**.

The song leader will need **To the Music Coordinator** and sheet music for each song, found in the section on music (pages 177-191).

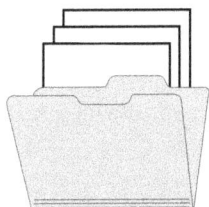

God and the Universe

— Sample Flyer —

BAHÁ'Í CHILDREN'S RETREAT #1
Sponsored by the Bahá'ís of Our Town

KIDS: AGES 8–12

Join us for a fun weekend of Bahá'í classes, prayers, singing, arts & crafts, archery, games, storytelling, tasty food & more!

THEME: God and the Universe

> **May 19-21**
> Bahá'í Center, 1919 Unity Lane
> Our Town, WA 98765 - (919) 765-4321

COST: $35 per child or $30 if paid before April 19. Additional children from same family, $20 each. Scholarships available. Make checks payable to: Bahá'ís of Our Town. Space is limited, apply now!

Participants should bring: sleeping bag, pillow, towel, toothbrush and paste, comb, any medicines with clear instructions, bathing suit, sturdy shoes, pajamas and change of clothes. Please do NOT bring: electronic games, radios, CDs, iPods, etc.

> *Starts Friday at 5:30 p.m. with registration and dinner. Ends at 2:00 p.m. on Sunday*

 ···

BAHÁ'Í CHILDREN'S RETREAT

Mail this form to: Lua Smith, 1863 Ridván Lane, Our Town, WA 98765
Email: lsmith@gmail.com - Tel: (919) 123-4567

Child's name (print): _____ Age: _____ Sex: _____

Address: _____ Phone: _____

Email: _____ Fee enclosed: $ _____ Partial scholarship requested: $_____

Emergency contact: _____ Phone: _____

Medical or dietary information: _____

The child named above has my permission to attend the Bahá'í Children's Retreat on May 19-21, 2012, at the Bahá'í Center in Our Town. I understand that s/he is participating at her/his own risk. If necessary, I hereby give the event organizers permission to administer first aid and obtain emergency medical treatment.

_____ _____ _____
Parent or Guardian (print name)   Signature   Date

God and the Universe

— Sample **2-Day** Schedule —

Bahá'í Children's Retreat [#1]

Bahá'í Center, Our Town, May 19-21, 2012

"God and the Universe"

FRIDAY
5:30 pm	Registration, decorate folders
6:00	Dinner
7:30	Prayers, singing, introductions
8:00	**Orientation program**
9:00	Volunteer briefing
9:30	Group song, prayers and bedtime
10:00	Lights out

SATURDAY
7:30 am	Morning prayers
8:00	Breakfast
8:30	Singing
8:45	**Class #1: The Kingdoms of Creation** (105 min.)
10:30	Break
10:45	**Class #2: God, The Creator** (75 min.)
12:00 pm	Lunch, quiet time
1:30	**Class #3: Prayer, Our Connection with God** (110 min.)
3:20	Snack and outdoor activities
4:30	Rehearsal for children's performance
6:00	Dinner
7:00	Prepare refreshments, practice songs
8:00	**Children's performance**
9:15	Refreshments and socializing
10:00	Group song, prayers and bedtime
10:30	Lights out

SUNDAY
8:00 am	Morning prayers
8:30	Breakfast
9:00	Singing
9:15	**Class #4: What Is a Human Being?** (90 min.)
10:45	Break
11:00	Outdoor activities
12:00 pm	Lunch
12:30	Clean-up
1:00	Closing activities, evaluation, graduation
1:30	Group photo
1:45	Dessert
2:00	Check lost-and-found; farewells

God and the Universe

– Sample **3-Day** Schedule –

Bahá'í Children's Retreat #1

Bahá'í Center, Our Town, May 19-21, 2012

"God and the Universe"

FRIDAY
5:30 pm	Registration, decorate folders
6:00	Dinner
7:30	Prayers, singing, introductions
8:00	**Orientation program**
9:00	Volunteer briefing
9:30	Group song, prayers and bedtime
10:00	Lights out

SATURDAY
7:30 am	Morning prayers
8:00	Breakfast
8:30	Singing
8:45	**Class #1: The Kingdoms of Creation** (105 min.)
10:30	Break
10:45	**Class #2: God, The Creator** (75 min.)
12:00 pm	Lunch, quiet time
1:30	Craft activities
3:00	Snack and outdoor activities
4:30	Memorization practice (alone, pairs or groups)
5:15	Group singing practice or free time
6:00	Dinner
7:30	Singing and share memorized quotes
8:15	Evening snack
8:30	Evening program (Bahá'í video, talent show, etc.)
9:30	Group song, prayers and bedtime
10:00	Lights out

SUNDAY
8:00 am	Morning prayers
8:30	Breakfast
9:00	Singing
9:15	**Class #3: Prayer, Our Connection with God** (110 min.)
11:00	Outdoor activities
12:00 pm	Lunch and quiet time
1:30	**Class #4: What Is a Human Being?** (90 min.)
3:00	Snack and outdoor activities
4:15	Rehearsal for children's performance
6:00	Dinner

God and the Universe

– Sample **3-Day** Schedule, continued –

SUNDAY
7:00 pm	Prepare refreshments, rehearse songs
8:00	**Children's performance**
9:15	Refreshments and socializing
10:00	Group song, prayers and bedtime
10:30	Lights out

MONDAY
8:30 am	Morning prayers
9:00	Breakfast
9:30	Singing
9:45	**Group consultation on how to share what we learned**
10:30	Outdoor activities
12:00 pm	Lunch
12:30	Clean-up
1:00	Closing activities, evaluation, graduation
1:30	Group photo
1:45	Dessert
2:00	Check lost-and-found; farewells

**Sean from the Nez Perce Reservation
- taking a break between classes.**

God and the Universe

TO THE TEACHER

> *"Among the greatest of all services that can possibly be rendered by man to Almighty God is the education and training of children."*
>
> 'Abdu'l-Bahá, Selections from the Writings of 'Abdu'l-Bahá, p. 133

Teacher's Guide

The teacher's guide on the following pages contains detailed lesson plans with fun, hands-on, kid-tested learning activities. It includes copy-ready student handouts and simple patterns for making instructional materials. The lessons are user-friendly and ready-to-go with little outside preparation needed by the teacher. They are organized in a sequential, step-by-step format, with each activity building on the previous one. Each lesson can also stand alone. The activities can be used for Bahá'í summer and winter schools, Holy Day programs, cluster gatherings and weekend retreats. They can also form part of the religious curriculum for an academic school.

This teacher's guide begins with an overview of the *Children's Classes and Retreats* series, sample schedules, an orientation program and lesson plans. These are followed by additional activities (dramatic movement, an outdoor kingdom hunt, prayer learning stations, a game, puzzles and more), plans for a children's performance, student handouts, a section on music (with song sheets, musical scores and instructions for group singing), and closing activities with suggestions for follow-up. A comprehensive list of the activities in each lesson, and a separate index of activities by category (music, crafts, stories, etc.), can be found at the end of the book. A compilation of selected passages on the theme of each lesson is included as a reference for teachers. A bibliography completes the manual.

Four Lessons

Each teacher's guide includes four lessons on the chosen theme. The lessons are designed to present basic Bahá'í teachings to children ages 8–12. The suggested time for each activity is in parentheses after the heading. However, if students need additional time to practice a skill, or if the class is engaged in a fruitful discussion and wishes to continue, the time can be extended, and another part of the lesson can be omitted or saved for a future class session. Be flexible.

When the lessons are used as part of an intensive program, such as a summer school or weekend retreat, you will need to select activities to fit within the time allotted. If the lessons are part of an ongoing program such as a daily or weekly academic class, one or more activities can be selected each time, until the entire course has been completed. Utilized in this way, there is sufficient material in the book for several months of weekly classes.

An ongoing class can begin with a welcome for new students, followed by singing, prayers, a review of the previous lesson (including student presentations), and the selected activities. At the beginning of each class, consider scheduling "circle time," to give children an opportunity to share news of interest to the group or to consult on pressing concerns. End the class with a review of the lesson, recitation of any memory quotes, more singing, and refreshments.

God and the Universe

Preparing to Teach

In order to present these lessons effectively, you will need to read the lesson plan and become familiar with the objectives and the concepts to be taught. For a deeper understanding of each topic, you can also study the *References for Teachers* found at the end of this book. Your presentation should be practiced until it feels smooth and comfortable.

Explanatory notes to the teacher are not meant to be read as a script, but are intended only as a guide. Key phrases and highlights from these notes can be written on the board before or during the lesson.

All instructional materials should be made or obtained well in advance. Handouts should be photocopied for students and volunteers, and either included in their folders when they arrive, or distributed during each class as needed.

Class Discussions

During class discussions, all students should be encouraged to participate, not just the ones who speak first or loudest. A child who is silent can be asked, "Maria, what do you think about this?" Have students raise their hands rather than shouting out the answer. A simple comment like, "I'm happy to see so many of you raising your hands quietly," will reinforce this rule.

If a student's answer is incorrect, rather than saying, "No, that's wrong," it is better to respond with, "Good try. You're on the right track," or "That's an interesting thought!" Then ask another question or give a small hint that will help the child succeed. Be patient and enthusiastic. Encouragement is generally more motivating than criticism. Do not allow the children to laugh at or tease each other.

With a larger group, you may find it useful to ring a bell or develop a hand signal to bring the children back to order after a discussion or other class activity. Raising your hand while standing quietly in front of the class can be very effective. As soon as one person notices the teacher, that person should stop talking and raise his/her hand. As others notice, they should join in. Teach children the signal, and practice it a few times before starting the discussion.

Volunteers

Youth and adult volunteers can be asked to assist you with learning activities and classroom management. Volunteers can be put in charge of discussion groups. They can help with craft projects, lead the singing, teach one of the classes, work one-on-one with students who need extra assistance, and remove a disruptive child if necessary. Discipline is easier to maintain if volunteers are spaced throughout the room during the lesson.

Bahá'í Children's Classes and Retreats: Theme 1, p. 11

God and the Universe

Children's Performance*

This guidebook includes instructions for a children's performance that will give students an opportunity to demonstrate and reinforce what they have learned. Friends, families, neighbors and co-workers can be invited to the show. The fact that children will be performing in front of a live audience serves as excellent motivation for them to learn the material presented in class. The presentation may include prayers, singing, recitation of Bahá'í passages, demonstrations to illustrate various concepts, an exhibition of arts and crafts, a dramatic reading and a quiz show.

The children's performance also provides an opportunity for home visits to parents before and after the show, to invite them and to talk in more depth about some of the themes presented.

A detailed agenda and plans for the performance are included in this manual. The children will need time to rehearse. If the program is part of a larger summer school or weekend retreat, the planning committee may schedule rehearsal time and appoint someone to coordinate the program. During class sessions, the teacher should make note of those children who seem to grasp the material well, and who could present it in front of an audience.

> *"It is the hope of 'Abdu'l-Bahá that those youthful souls …will be tended by one who traineth them to love."*
> 'Abdu'l-Bahá, Selections from the Writings of 'Abdu'l-Bahá, p. 134

* Note: While our student presentations have typically been scheduled for the evening, they could be held at any time. In the two-day weekend retreat format, Saturday evening is often the most convenient time for inviting neighbors and friends. This means that activities from the fourth class on Sunday morning will not be included in the presentation. If the performance follows a three-day retreat schedule or a weekly format, these activities can easily be added to the final show.

God and the Universe

OPENING ACTIVITIES

If these lessons are being used as part of an intensive program, such as a summer school or weekend retreat, it is usually a good idea to provide some self-directed activities for children during the registration period, while they are waiting for others to arrive. For example, after checking in, they can be shown to a table to decorate their folders for the class.

For more ideas, see *Additional Activities* following the lessons in this teacher's guide.

Orientation Program

The orientation program on the first day is designed to make everyone feel welcome and to help them get to know each other. Explain to the group that we will be learning about **God and the Universe**. We will focus on four main topics:

- The Kingdoms of Creation
- God, the Creator
- Prayer, Our Connection with God
- What is a Human Being?

A sample orientation program is outlined below:

1. Welcome
2. Opening music
3. Selected prayers
4. Letter from the sponsoring institution
5. Introductions [A]
6. Orientation [B]
7. Review of the schedule
8. Ice-breakers and warm-up activities (see below)
9. Group singing (see song sheet in handout section)

A. <u>Introductions</u>: Each person can be asked to introduce him or herself, sharing their name, town, and one interesting personal fact. As a variation, people can be asked to act out a hobby or favorite activity, without using any words, and the group can guess what it is.

B. <u>Orientation</u>: This should cover information about classes, supervision, the role of volunteers, any house rules, food, safety, recreation and relating to others. See the *Bahá'í Children's Retreats Planning Guide* for details.

After the orientation and review of the schedule, you can organize one or two warm-up activities (see next page) which will serve as ice-breakers and help to introduce the theme. The orientation program can be followed by a snack and a short video (e.g., *Cosmic Voyage*), which can be played for the children during the briefing for volunteers.

God and the Universe

Warm-up Activities

1. Unity Bingo (20-30 min.)

This is a fun mixer which has become a favorite activity at all our children's retreats. A sample Bingo sheet is included in the *Bahá'í Children's Retreats Planning Guide*, along with a blank form that can be downloaded and customized with your own set of questions (available from: www. UnityWorksStore.com > click on Children's Classes).

2. Thinking About God (5-10 min.)

This short warm-up activity will start everyone thinking about the main topic of the classes. Begin by distributing a small slip of paper and a pen or pencil to each child. Ask them to think for a moment, then to write down a word or phrase to explain what they think God is. They should write legibly and not include their names.

After a minute or two, collect all the slips of paper in a hat or small box, then re-distribute them. If someone receives his or her own paper, it can be returned to the box, then given out to someone else. When all the papers have been re-distributed, ask for volunteers to read the slip they have received. Tell them to speak in a strong voice so everyone can hear. (You might also repeat each phrase to acknowledge that the idea has been heard.) For a large class, it is not necessary to read every paper. A sampling of the room is sufficient.

This activity will give the teacher an idea of what the children already understand. For those who are shy or uncomfortable speaking in front of others, it allows them to share their ideas anonymously.

3. Who Am I? (10-15 min.)

In advance of the activity, prepare enough sticky labels for all participants. Each label should list a different item (mineral, plant, animal or other object) printed in large type. Choose items that the children are familiar with (water, tomato, shoe), and avoid words that may have negative connotations in the local cultures (pig, mule, etc.). Keep the labels out of sight.

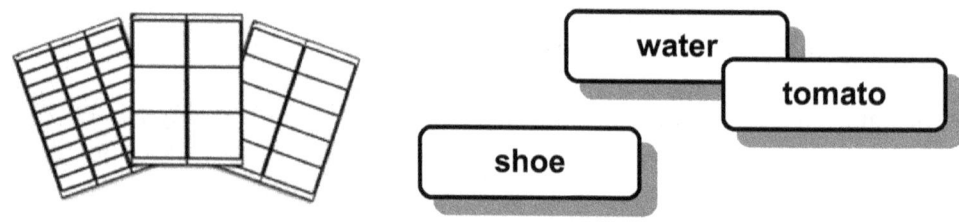

God and the Universe

At the start of the activity, explain that each person will have a label on his or her back, but won't be able to see what it is. They will work in pairs, asking each other "yes" or "no" questions, in order to figure out who or what they are. After one person's identity is discovered, it will be the other person's turn.

Have the participants pair up with someone they don't know (or don't know as well), and introduce themselves. Youth and adults can play too. While the introductions are underway, walk around the room placing a label on each person's back. If the group is a large one, an assistant or two can help speed up the labeling process.

If one pair finishes early, they may join with others and help respond to the questions. A sample dialog is shown on the right.

Child #1	Child #2
Am I an animal?	Yes.
Am I a pet?	No.
Am I a mammal?	No.
Can I fly?	No.
Do I live in the water?	No.
Do I have four legs?	No.
Two legs?	No.
Any legs?	No.
Oh! Do I make a hissing noise?	Yes.
Am I a snake?	Yes, you're a snake!

4. Video: Cosmic Voyage (36 min.)

In order to set the stage for the theme of *God and the Universe*, you may wish to show the children all or parts of a short video called **Cosmic Voyage**. Based on the traditional big-bang theory, this 1996 IMAX film combines live action with computer animation to show the relative size of humans in the physical world.

Perhaps the best part of the program is a high-speed zoom-in from star super-clusters at the edge of the known universe (the largest scale in the video) to atomic neutrons, protons and quarks (the smallest scale). Moving through space in successive orders of magnitude based on powers of 10, it gives a very effective visual picture of what big and small really are. The movie should serve as food for thought over the weekend, as children discuss the Bahá'í view of our place in the universe.

Cosmic Voyage may be available for rent from your local video store or via online streaming. New and used copies can be purchased from www.Amazon.com. Enter **Cosmic Voyage DVD** (without quotation marks) in the search box.

LESSON #1

The Kingdoms of Creation

God and the Universe – Lesson #1

The Kingdoms of Creation

Objectives: Students will be able to:
- State that God created the world.
- Explain the difference between the Creator and the creation.
- Name the four kingdoms of creation and give examples from each.
- Describe the characteristics of each kingdom, their similarities and differences.

Before class, prepare all instructional materials on the list at the end of this lesson. Arrange four chairs at the front of the room for activity #2. Orient volunteer assistants. Set up felt board and crafts. Distribute folders and pens or pencils to each participant.

1. INTRODUCTION (5 min.)

Today, we're going to learn about God and some of the things He created.

Show students photographs of people making things, and of things made by animals. Ask questions such as:

- What is this bird doing? Is the bird the same as its nest?
- Is this spider the same as its web?
- Is this shoemaker the same as the shoe?
- What is the difference? *(One is the maker or creator; the other is the thing created. One is the cause; the other is the effect.)*
- Who made this chair that I'm sitting on? *(A carpenter or woodworker.)*
- How do you know? *(The chair didn't make itself. It was built by a skilled person.)*
- Who do you think made the mountains, plants, animals, people and all the stars? *(God.)*
- Is God the same as those things? *(No. He is the Creator; what He made is the Creation.)*

2. PICTURE SORTING: Kingdoms of Creation (5-10 min.)

Place four chairs at the front of the room. Tape one label (mineral, plant, animal and human) to the top of each chair. Show the class a picture of a mineral (e.g. a rock or gemstone) and ask which chair it belongs on. Place the picture on the seat of the correct chair. Do the same for the other three chairs. Hold up the remaining pictures one at a time (about 20 pictures in random order) and ask the class to name its category while a volunteer places it on the correct chair.

Ask students:

- Who can name the four kingdoms of creation?
  (Call on several volunteers to recite.)
  (Mineral, plant, animal, human.)

- Who created all of these things?
  (That's right! God did. That's why He is called the Creator.)

- Who created God? *(No one! That is the greatest mystery of all!)*

Bahá'í Children's Classes and Retreats: Theme 1, p. 18

3. KINGDOM QUESTIONS (15-20 min.)

Distribute question cards. (See end of lesson and the list below.) Give one card to each student, going in order around the room until all of the questions have been distributed. If there are extra questions, go around again. Some children might receive more than one card. Beginning with question #1, ask each student to read the question aloud, then either answer it or call on another student to answer. As the discussion progresses, remind them to call on classmates who have not yet had a chance to speak.

Kingdom Questions – Reference List for Teachers

1. List five things that God created.
2. List five things that humans have created.
3. Where do humans get the raw materials to make things?
4. Who created people?
5. Who created God?
6. Can a rock grow? Can a tree grow?
7. What do rocks do all day? Plants? Animals? Humans?
8. Can a carrot hear? What <u>can</u> hear?
9. Can an apple seed grow into an orange tree? Why not?
10. Can a frog plan a party? Or go to school?
11. What can a horse do that a flower can't do?
12. Can a person become a bear?
13. Can a plant be generous? Honest? Loving? Can you?
14. What are some other human qualities?
15. Is a human being an animal? How are they different?
16. How are humans similar to animals? To plants? To minerals?
17. Which kingdoms can recognize God?
18. Which kingdom are you in?
19. Name the kingdoms in order from lowest to highest.
20. Are there any kingdoms higher than human?

(Yes, the Kingdom of God, and the Kingdom of Revelation which is covered in the next theme book on the Manifestation of God.)

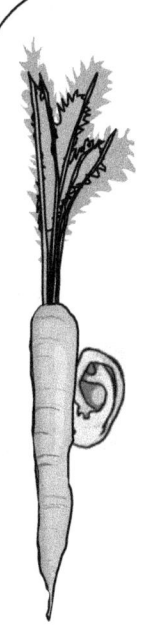

At the end of the activity, collect the question cards.

God and the Universe – Lesson #1

4. KINGDOM CATEGORIES (10 -15 min.)

Draw four columns on the board, and label each column (see illustration). Have students take a sheet of notebook paper from their folders, and do the same. Ask the class to name one item from each kingdom. Write these on the board as well.

mineral	plant	animal	human
diamond	carrot	zebra	Travis

Then ask each student to work independently, and to list five or more examples from each category. After about five minutes, call on individuals to share what they have written. An assistant can add their suggestions to the board.

5. KINGDOM COMPARISONS (10-15 min.)

Form teams of 2 or 3 students to discuss the question: **How are the kingdoms of creation alike and different?** Allow about five minutes to work, then have each group share its answers with the class. Guide the children to understand that:

All of the kingdoms have the power of cohesion - the force that holds things together and gives them structure, so they can exist. If a **mineral** didn't have cohesion, all the atoms would fly apart instead of sticking together.

The **plant** kingdom has cohesion, and it also has the power of growth. A plant might start out as a tiny seed, but it can grow larger and become more complex by adding stems and branches, leaves and flowers. It might eventually grow to become a large tree.

Animals have cohesion and growth, just like plants. Animals also have senses like sight, smell, hearing, taste and touch. They can feel heat and cold, hunger and thirst. And they have the power of movement. While plants must stay in one place to grow, animals can go looking for food.

Human beings have an animal body, and the powers of cohesion, growth, movement and the senses, just like the animal kingdom. But humans also have the power of conscious thought. Through scientific investigation, we can discover and use the laws of nature (electricity, magnetism, etc.). We have free will to choose between good and evil. And most importantly, we can learn to know and love God.

Refer students to the handout, "The Kingdoms of Creation," which is the first page in their packets. It is also included at the end of this lesson for convenience.

God and the Universe – Lesson #1

6. FELT LESSON: Kingdoms of Creation (10-15 min.)

Present the felt lesson on "The Kingdoms of Creation" (see instructions at end of lesson). Ask the children: *Who would like to try it in front of the class without any help?* You can also ask for volunteers for the children's performance.

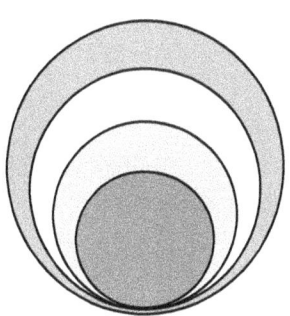

7. ADDITIONAL ACTIVITIES

If time is available and the children are interested, you may wish to plan some additional activities related to this theme. (See pages 119-134.)

8. CLOSING QUESTIONS (5 min.)

Encourage several students to answer each question. Repetition will help them to remember these concepts.

- Who can name all four kingdoms of creation in order? *(Mineral, plant, animal, human.)*

- Why are they called the kingdoms of creation? *(They were created by God.)*

- Who can describe the common characteristics of each kingdom, starting with minerals? *(Minerals have cohesion; plants add growth; animals add the senses and movement; humans have rational thought, moral behavior, and they can learn about God.)*

9. SONG: The Kingdoms of God (5 -7 min.)

Have the children take the song sheets from their folders, and lead them in singing "The Kingdoms of God." (Explain that the *plant* kingdom is sometimes called the *vegetable* kingdom.) Ask the music coordinator for help if needed.

Collect all folders and pencils.

10. CRAFT ACTIVITIES (40-60 min.)

Craft projects are designed to reinforce the material presented during class. The children will be working on a "Kingdoms of Creation" coloring page, a collage booklet, and/or a group mural. (See instructions on the following pages.) Any assistants should be oriented beforehand. Completed projects can be used by the children as teaching tools.

After the activity, dismiss the children for a short break.

✳ ✳ ✳ ✳

God and the Universe – Lesson #1

CRAFT ACTIVITIES

These activities are designed to reinforce material presented during class. For a weekend retreat, there may only be time for one or two crafts. For an ongoing class, you might choose a different craft each time. Another option is to prepare a separate table for each craft. Show the children a sample of each project and ask them to choose one to start. If their first choice is full, they can select another station. When children have completed their projects and cleaned up their work area, they may assist others who need help. Remind them to label all projects with their names. Quiet music can be played in the background if desired.

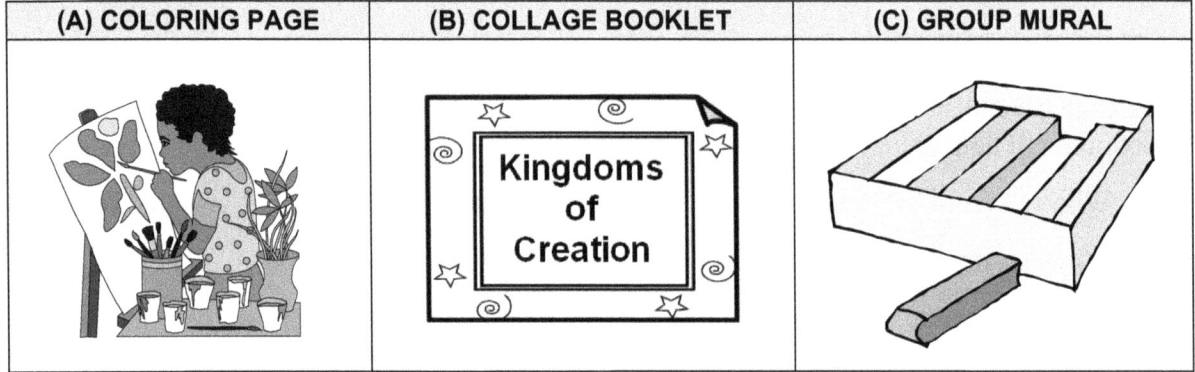

| (A) COLORING PAGE | (B) COLLAGE BOOKLET | (C) GROUP MURAL |

(A) COLORING PAGE

Materials

- ☐ Coloring page (one per child)
- ☐ White drawing paper or watercolor paper
- ☐ Pencils
- ☐ Crayons or markers
- ☐ Watercolor paints, brushes, water cups (optional)

Instructions

Photocopy the following page for children who wish to color. Provide sheets of blank white paper for those who prefer to draw their own kingdom pictures. If paint is used, be sure to protect the table with a tarp. You might also provide aprons (or large plastic garbage bags with holes cut for head and arms) to cover the children's clothes.

Bahá'í Children's Classes and Retreats: Theme 1, p. 22

God is the Creator

Dios es el Creador

God and the Universe – Lesson #1

(B) COLLAGE BOOKLET

Materials

- ☐ Plastic cloth or tarp to protect table
- ☐ Colored construction paper (5 sheets/student)
- ☐ Old magazines with photographs
- ☐ Scissors (1 for each student)
- ☐ Glue sticks
- ☐ Black felt markers
- ☐ Crayons, stickers, glitter (optional)
- ☐ Rulers
- ☐ Stapler with extra staples, or hole punch and brads

Instructions

1. Take five sheets of construction paper (one or more colors).

2. Using the felt marker, title the first page "The Kingdoms of Creation." If desired, decorate the title page using magazine cut-outs, crayons, stickers, glitter, etc.

3. Label each of the remaining pages with a different kingdom: Minerals, Plants, Animals and Humans. (Labels can be printed directly on the page, or written first on another color, then cut out and glued on. Sticky labels can also be used.)

4. Search through the magazines and neatly cut out pictures from each kingdom.

5. Arrange the appropriate pictures on each page and glue them in place.

6. Stack the pages in order and staple along the left edge to form a booklet, or use the hole punch and brads.

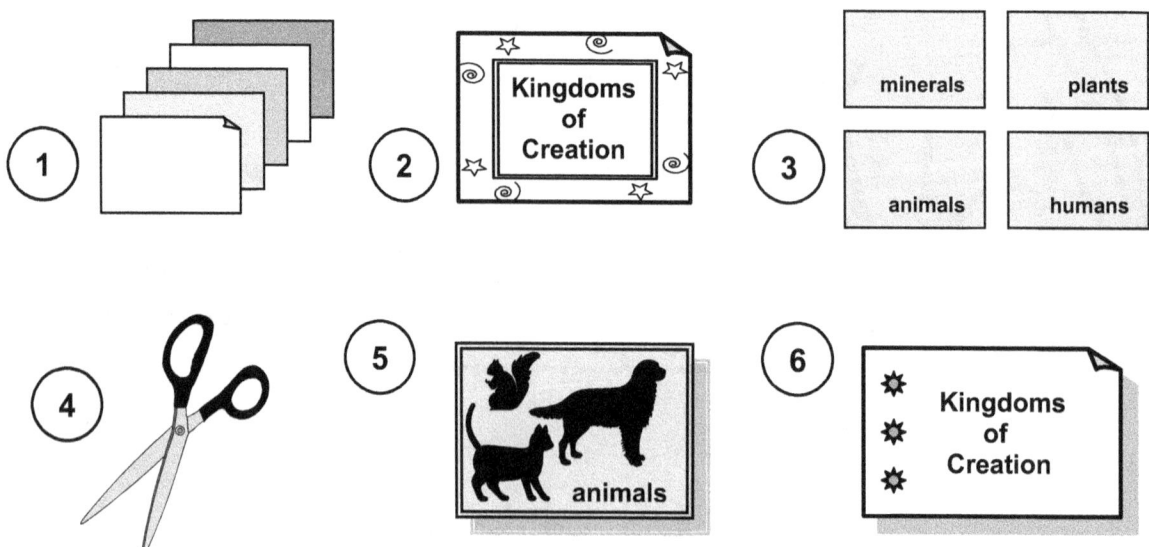

Bahá'í Children's Classes and Retreats: Theme 1, p. 24

God and the Universe – Lesson #1

(C) GROUP MURAL

Mural making can be an enjoyable cooperative project. It can be as simple as having children collaborate on a group drawing, or it might involve a complete scene, pre-sketched on canvas by a local artist. The group mural could be an option after children have finished one of the other two choices. It could also be available for them to work on during free times throughout the event.

Materials

- ☐ Large sheets of chart or butcher paper
- ☐ Masking tape
- ☐ Crayons or artists' chalk

Tip: If paint or markers are used instead of crayons or chalk, an extra backing sheet may be needed to protect the wall.

Instructions

1. Tape large sheets of paper to wall, at a height appropriate for children.

2. Write a title on the paper: *The Kingdoms of Creation.*

3. Encourage children to draw suitable objects on the paper. They can trace around themselves to make a human shape.

4. Sit back and watch the creation evolve!

God and the Universe – Lesson #1

Note to teachers: The creation of God is extremely diverse, embracing countless varieties of plant life and millions of animal species, some of which may be difficult to classify even for scientists. 'Abdu'l-Bahá has pointed out some of the common characteristics of each kingdom (see *References for Teachers*), but you should also be prepared for children's questions about some things that don't seem to fit.

For example, crystals are minerals that appear to grow, but not in the same way as living beings. A virus has some characteristics of life, but is not easily classified as a plant or animal. Coral is composed of the mineral secretions of tiny marine organisms, while living coral, despite its plant-like shape, is a colony of animals. Some plants have animal characteristics, for example, the Venus Fly Trap eats insects, and the *Mimosa pudica* is sensitive to pressure, folding up when touched. Chimpanzees have shown the ability to learn some elements of human sign language and to use rudimentary tools.

The Bahá'í Writings clearly state that humans differ from animals in that we have free will and can choose between good and evil. We have a rational mind that enables us to transcend nature, and we can know and love God.

Some definitions from the website: http://20q.net

Animal – Includes single and multi-celled organisms with the capacity for spontaneous movement and rapid motor responses. They typically lack chlorophyll and the capacity for photosynthesis.

Vegetable – Includes living things that lack locomotive movement or obvious nervous or sensory organs, and that possess cellulose cell walls.

Mineral - An inorganic substance from the earth.

For Further Information

Crystals: www.chemistry.co.nz/crystal_types.htm

Microbes: www.microbe.org/microbes/what_is.asp

Viruses: http://science.howstuffworks.com/virus-human1.htm (&) www.mrs.umn.edu/~goochv/CellBio/lectures/virus/virus.html

Coral: http://oceanworld.tamu.edu/students/coral/coral1.htm

Venus Fly Trap: www.thegardenhelper.com/flytrap.html

Mimosa pudica: www.plantoftheweek.org/week147.shtml

Chimpanzees: www.cwu.edu/~cwuchci/faq.html

God and the Universe – Lesson #1

Pictures of People and Animals Making Things – for Activity #1

God and the Universe – Lesson #1

God and the Universe – Lesson #1

God and the Universe – Lesson #1

God and the Universe – Lesson #1

Bahá'í Children's Classes and Retreats: Theme 1, p. 31

God and the Universe – Lesson #1

Bahá'í Children's Classes and Retreats: Theme 1, p. 32

God and the Universe – Lesson #1

Kingdom Labels for Activity #2
(Copy this page, cut out and laminate the cards, then post one card on each chair.)

mineral
plant
animal
human

God and the Universe – Lesson #1

Kingdom Questions - Cards for Activity #3
(Copy and laminate this page, then cut out the cards and distribute to students.)

1. List five things that God created.

2. List five things that humans created.

3. Where do humans get the raw materials to make things?

4. Who created people?

5. Who created God?

6. Can a rock grow? Can a tree grow?

7. What do rocks do all day? Plants? Animals? Humans?

8. Can a carrot hear? What *can* hear?

9. Can an apple seed grow into an orange tree? Why not?

10. Can a frog plan a party? Or go to school?

11. What can a horse do that a flower can't do?

12. Can a person become a bear?

13. Can a plant be generous? Honest? Loving? Can you?

14. What are some other human qualities?

15. Is a human being an animal? How are they different?

16. How are humans similar to animals? To plants? Minerals?

17. Which kingdoms can recognize God?

18. Which kingdom are you in?

19. Name the kingdoms in order from lowest to highest.

20. Are there any kingdoms higher than human?

Bahá'í Children's Classes and Retreats: Theme 1, p. 34

The Kingdoms of Creation

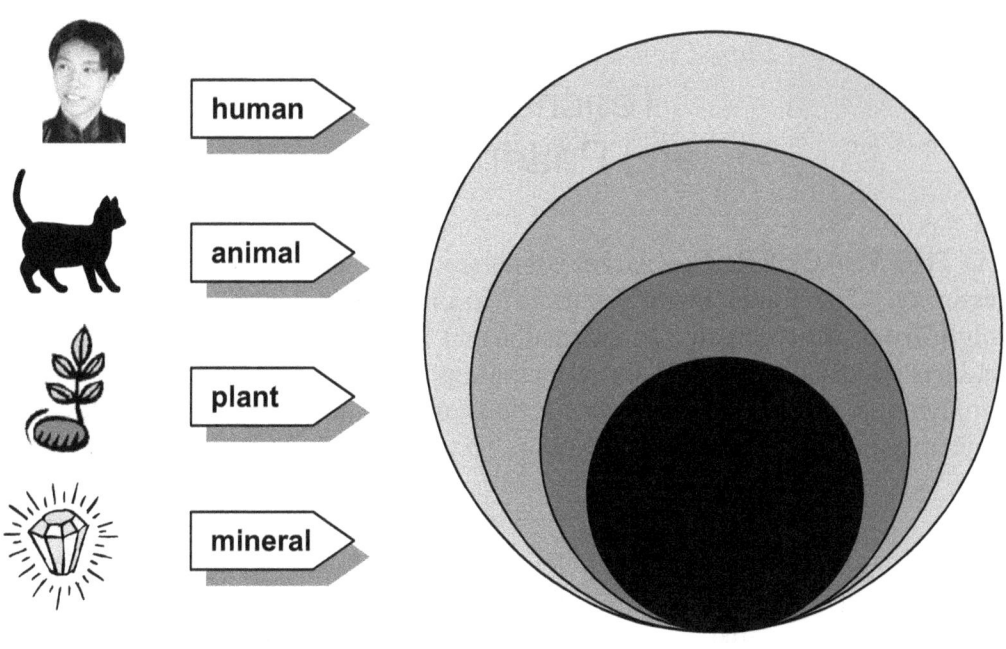

Mineral Kingdom
- cohesion or attraction[1]

Plant Kingdom
- cohesion
- growth

Animal Kingdom
- cohesion
- growth
- feelings
- senses
- locomotion[2]

Human Kingdom
- cohesion
- growth
- feelings
- senses
- locomotion
- conscious thought
- free will
- knowledge of right and wrong
- knowledge of God

---

1. The force that holds things together
2. The power to move from place to place

God and the Universe – Lesson #1

"The Kingdoms of Creation"

Teacher's Guide, Script, and Patterns for Felt Lesson

TO THE TEACHER: This packet contains a script, instructions, and patterns for making a felt lesson on "The Kingdoms of Creation." In order to present the lesson, you will need either a felt board or carpet board (see instructions on following pages). A carpet board is more durable and has a more finished look. After preparing the board and cutting out the pattern pieces, read through the script and repeat the actions until you can present the lesson smoothly. The objectives of the lesson are listed below. The children will be able to:

(1) List the basic characteristics of each kingdom.	(2) Describe some similarities and differences among the four kingdoms.	(3) Explain how lower kingdoms are contained within higher ones.

God and the Universe – Lesson #1

Script for Felt Lesson

"The Kingdoms of Creation"

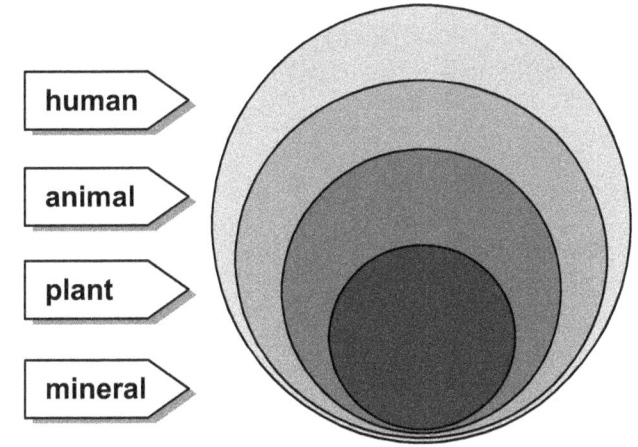

	NARRATION	ACTION
1	We're going to talk about the **Kingdoms of Creation**.	Place title on felt board.
2	This represents the **mineral** kingdom - the lowest level of the kingdoms of creation. Minerals have the power of cohesion or attraction. That's the force that holds things together.	Place smallest circle on felt board, and add the **mineral** label, as shown.
3	This represents the vegetable or **plant** kingdom. Plants have the power of cohesion, just like minerals, but they also have something new: the power of growth.	Slip next largest circle under mineral kingdom, and add the **plant** label.
4	This represents the **animal** kingdom. Like minerals, animals have cohesion, and like plants, they have the power of growth, but they add something new. Animals have feelings and the power of the senses. Animals can see and hear. They can taste and smell. They can feel heat and cold, hunger and thirst. They also have the power to move from place to place.	Add next largest circle under plant kingdom, and add the **animal** label.
5	This represents the **human** kingdom. In addition to the powers of the mineral, the plant and the animal, humans also have the power of conscious thought. Through scientific investigation, we can discover the laws of nature and the secrets of the universe. And there is something else special about humans. We have free will, to choose right or wrong, and we can learn to know and love God.	Add next largest circle under animal kingdom, and add the **human** label.

God and the Universe – Lesson #1

Instructions for Making Felt or Carpet Board

A felt board can be purchased at a teacher supply store, or one can be constructed by gluing a large piece of felt onto a stiff backing such as heavy cardboard, masonite or thin plywood. Spray glue gives the best results. A carpet board is constructed in the same way. Felt and glue are available at yardage and craft supply stores.

MATERIALS

- Sharp scissors
- Large piece of felt or indoor-outdoor carpet *
  (choose beige or other neutral color,
   approx. 24 x 36 in. or 60 x 90 cm.)
- Backing board (same size as felt or carpet)
- Spray glue or white craft glue

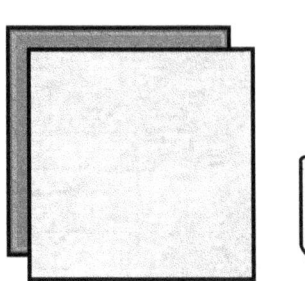

* If using carpet, test a piece of felt to be sure it sticks.
  Some types of carpeting may work better than others.

Instructions for Making Felt Pieces

1. Draw four concentric circles on different colors of felt and cut out.* Use colors that contrast with the felt board, for example, dark brown for the mineral kingdom, light green for plants, white for animals, and beige for humans.

   * The easiest method is to trace around a common object, for example, use a dinner plate for the largest circle, and a roll of masking tape for the smallest. If these objects are not available, photocopy the following pages and use them as a guide. Cut out the circle patterns, attach each pattern to the appropriate color of felt with double-stick tape, then cut out each piece.

2. Photocopy, cut out and laminate the kingdom labels and the title. Add Velcro to the back so laminated pieces stick to the felt board.

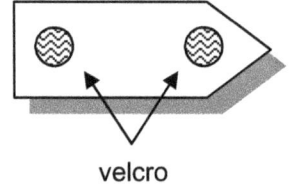
velcro

3. Store lesson and felt pieces in a zip-lock plastic bag for ease of use.

MATERIALS

- Pattern pieces (on following pages)
- Sharp scissors
- Four different colors of felt
- Double-stick tape (optional)
- Stick-on velcro (plastic loop side)

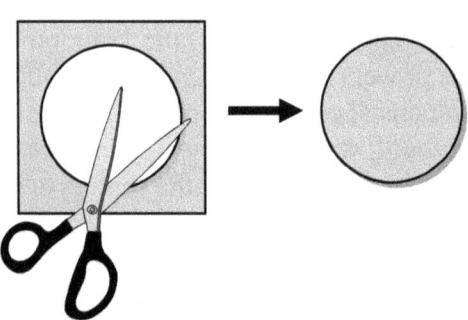

Bahá'í Children's Classes and Retreats: Theme 1, p. 38

God and the Universe – Lesson #1

Patterns for Felt Lesson on the Kingdoms of Creation

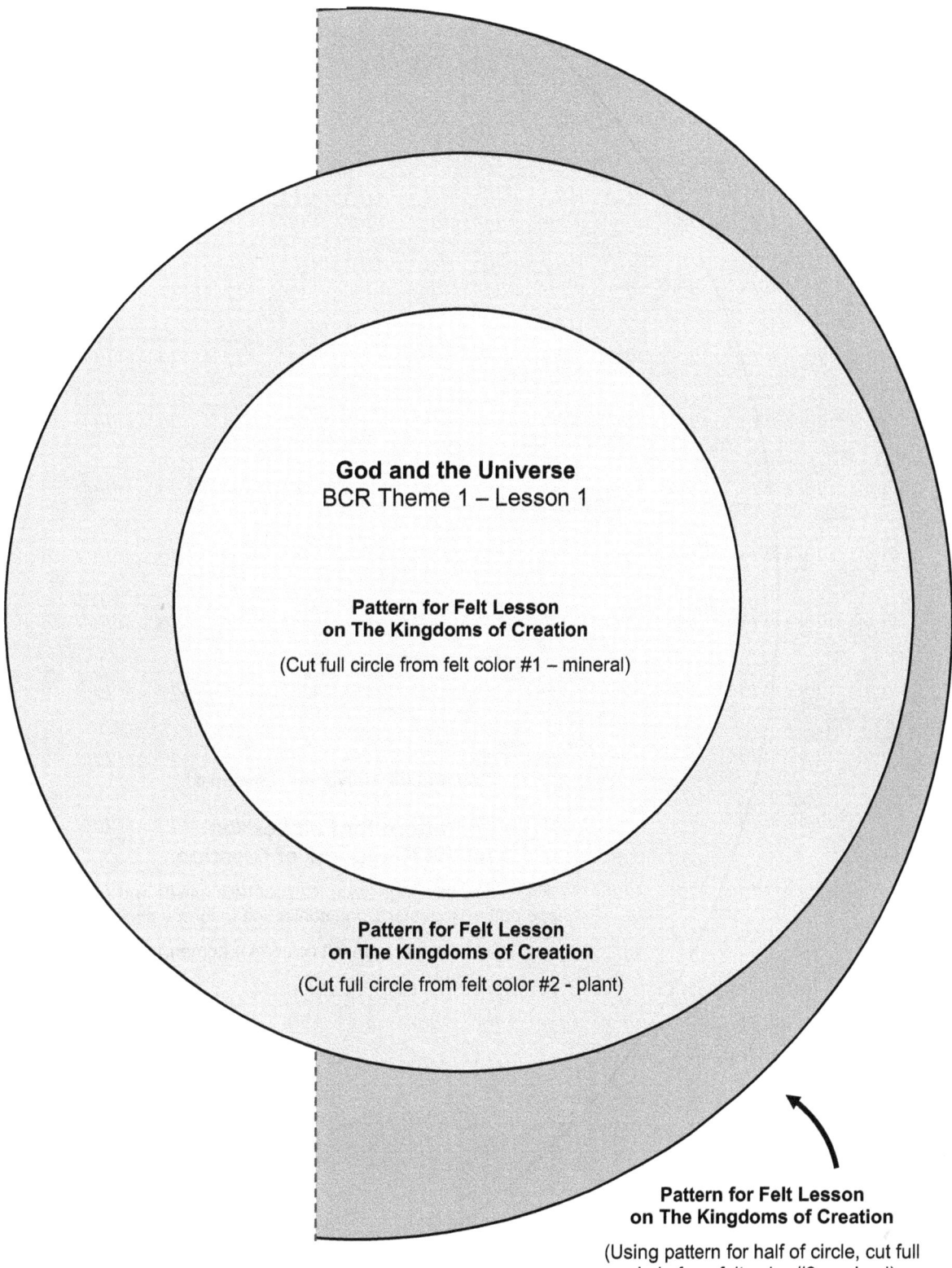

God and the Universe
BCR Theme 1 – Lesson 1

**Pattern for Felt Lesson
on The Kingdoms of Creation**

(Cut full circle from felt color #1 – mineral)

**Pattern for Felt Lesson
on The Kingdoms of Creation**

(Cut full circle from felt color #2 - plant)

**Pattern for Felt Lesson
on The Kingdoms of Creation**

(Using pattern for half of circle, cut full
circle from felt color #3 - animal)

Bahá'í Children's Classes and Retreats: Theme 1, p. 39

God and the Universe – Lesson #1

God and the Universe – Lesson #1

**Pattern for Felt Lesson
on the Kingdoms of Creation**

Photocopy this page twice. Cut out both halves and
tape pattern together along center line to form a circle.

(Cut full circle from felt color #4 – human.)

Bahá'í Children's Classes and Retreats: Theme 1, p. 40

God and the Universe – Lesson #1

Pattern for Felt Lesson on the Kingdoms of Creation
(Photocopy this page and next page. Cut out and laminate cards.
Glue small pieces of Velcro to the back of each card.)

Kingdom Labels

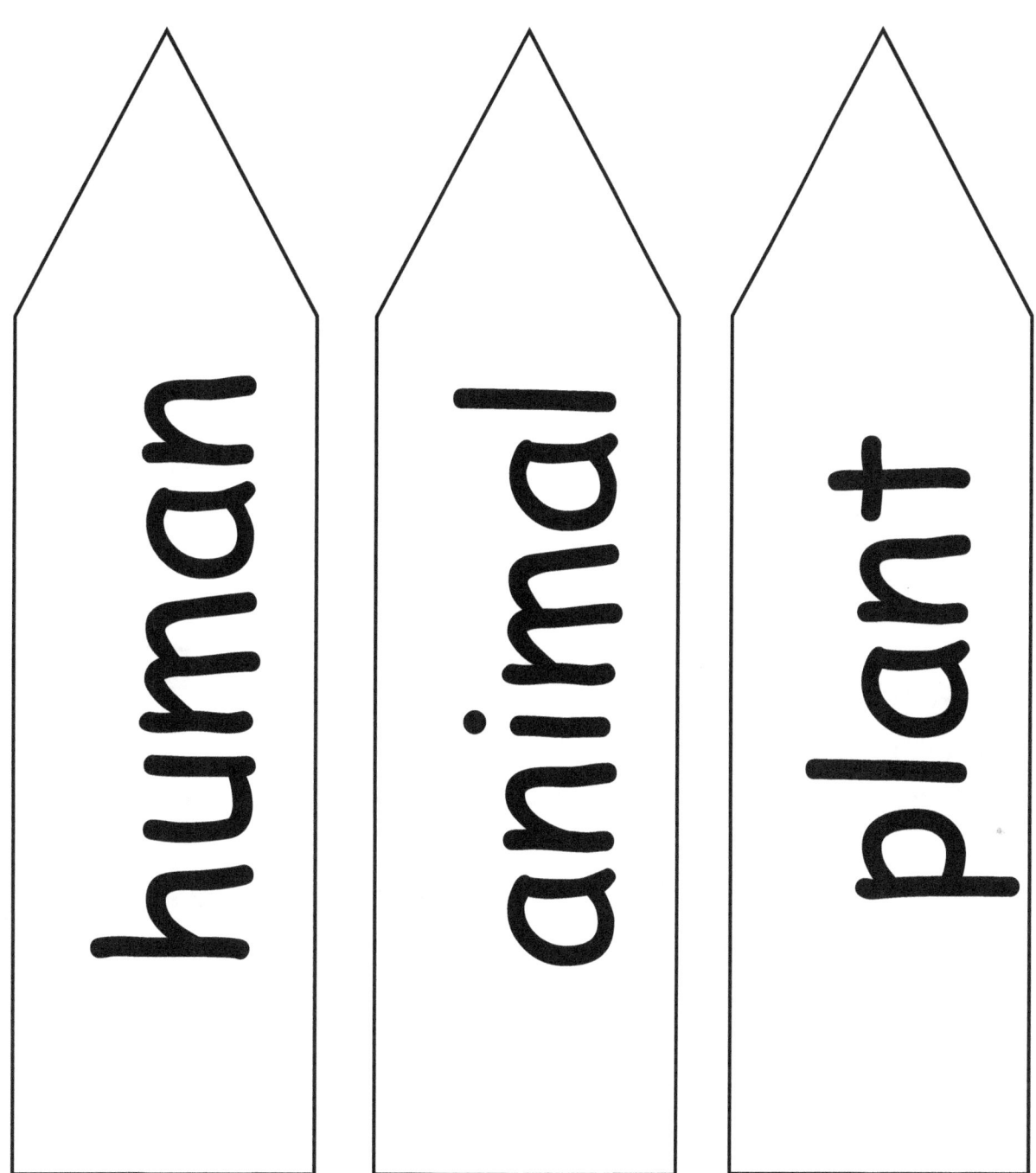

God and the Universe – Lesson #1

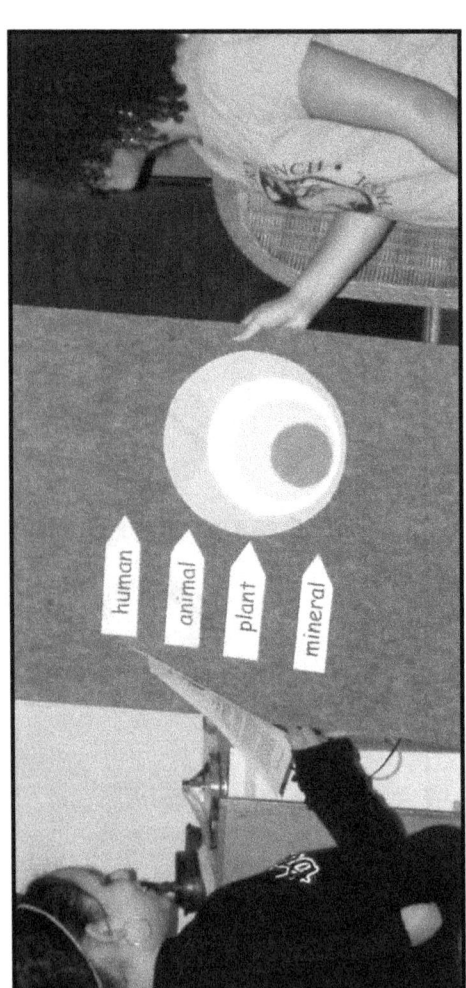

Kierra and Sanna practice the felt lesson on the Kingdoms of Creation

mineral

Kingdoms of Creation

God and the Universe – Lesson #1

MATERIALS NEEDED

- ☐ White board, easel, markers, eraser
- ☐ Folders with paper and song sheets for each student
- ☐ Pens or pencils for each student
- ☐ Dictionary
- ☐ Pictures of people making things (for activity #1) [A]
- ☐ Pictures of things made by animals (activity #1) [A]
- ☐ Four chairs (activity #2)
- ☐ Labels for mineral, plant, animal, and human kingdoms (included with this lesson)
- ☐ About 20 pictures of items from each kingdom [A]
- ☐ Laminated question cards (included)
- ☐ Handout on "The Kingdoms of Creation"
- ☐ Felt lesson on "Kingdoms of Creation" (script and patterns included)
- ☐ Felt board and easel
- ☐ Materials for craft activities (see separate list)
- ☐ Samples of each craft project and instruction sheet for any assistants
- ☐ Galaxy maps and photos (optional) [B]
- ☐ References for teachers (at the end of this lesson)

A. Things made by animals include: bird nests, spider webs, sea shells, honeycombs, termite mounds and butterfly cocoons.

A few pictures are included with this lesson as examples. These same pictures are also available in color as part of the download packet for this teacher's guide at: < www.UnityWorksStore.com >. Click on Children's Classes > God and the Universe > Student Handouts. Color images can also be found in clip art software, online, and in magazines such as National Geographic (www.nationalgeographic.com).

The pictures can be enlarged, laminated, and mounted on construction paper or inserted in a plastic sleeve for protection. They can be posted around the room and left up during the entire event.

Bahá'í Children's Classes and Retreats: Theme 1, p. 43

God and the Universe – Lesson #1

B. If desired, a map of our Milky Way Galaxy can be posted on the wall, and the children can be asked to locate our solar system and planet. An inexpensive galaxy map can be ordered from the National Geographic Map Store: **www.ngmapstore.com**. Enter "Milky Way" in the search box, click on the Milky Way Reference Map and then "more views" to zoom in to Earth's location.

Photographs of the solar system and assorted galaxies, nebulas and star clusters, many taken by the Hubble space telescope, can also be used to decorate the room and add a visual reminder of the vastness of our universe.

Some beautiful posters of space are available from **www.Zazzle.com**. Choose the "special collections" tab. Then from the drop-down menu, select "space exploration" and click on "view this collection." Choose a gallery and click on any photo of interest. Photographs and prints can be purchased for about $9.00 (U.S.) and up. The children can also view these spectacular images online for free.

Similar posters are available from:

- www.allposters.com/-sp/Orion-Nebula-Hubble-Spaceshots-posters_i390748_.htm
- www.Spaceshots.com > The Universe

As a follow-up to classes on God and the Universe, some energetic parents and teachers may wish to organize a stargazing outing. If a community member has a telescope, be sure to bring it along.

LESSON #2

God, the Creator

God and the Universe – Lesson #2

God, the Creator

Objectives: Using concrete examples, students will be able to explain:
- That everything has a creator.
- That the universe was created by God.
- That God created human beings because He loves us.
- That God is known by many names, but He is unknowable.
- That although we cannot see God, we know He exists through His Messengers, and by His signs and effects in the world.

Before class, prepare all instructional materials on the list at the end of this lesson.
Set up craft activity center. Orient assistants for discussion, demonstration, and craft activity.
Write the memory quote neatly on the board with one phrase on each line.
Distribute folders and pencils to each student.

---

1. REVIEW (2-3 min.)

- Who can name the kingdoms of creation in order? (Take several volunteers.)
- Who can describe some of the characteristics of each kingdom?

2. SONG: O God, Guide Me (2-3 min.)

Have the children take out their song sheets and lead them in singing "O God, Guide Me." Ask the music volunteer for help if needed.

3. INTRODUCTION (1-2 min.) Ask students:

- Who likes a mystery?
  (Good, because we're going to learn about the greatest mystery of all!)
- Can you guess what it is? *(That's right. God)*
- Who remembers some of the things that God created?
- Now, let's learn a little more about God.

4. READING: God the Creator (10-15 min.)

Ask students to find the page in their folders titled "God, The Creator."
A copy is included at the end of this lesson. Read the title, the quote and the first paragraph out loud, then ask the class: **Is there anything that can create itself?** *(No.)*

Ask for volunteers to read the remaining paragraphs out loud. After each one reads, that student should make up one question about the paragraph and call on other children to answer, just as you have done. Ask them to raise their hands. If necessary, encourage people to call on those who haven't had a chance. At the end, ask what they think the last quotation means: "I knew My love for thee…"

God and the Universe – Lesson #2

5. KIDS' QUESTIONS ABOUT GOD (15 -20 min.)

Tell the children they will be developing a list of questions they have about God. Then divide the class into small groups of 3-4, and assign a youth or adult volunteer to lead each group. Give each volunteer a copy of the group leader's instructions for this activity (included at the end of this lesson). The group leader's job is to take notes and encourage all the children to share their thoughts.

Groups can move to another room or outside if desired. Give them about ten minutes to work. Then call the groups back together, and have them share their questions. The questions can also be written on chart paper and posted on the walls. Keep a copy of the questions for use during the children's performance.

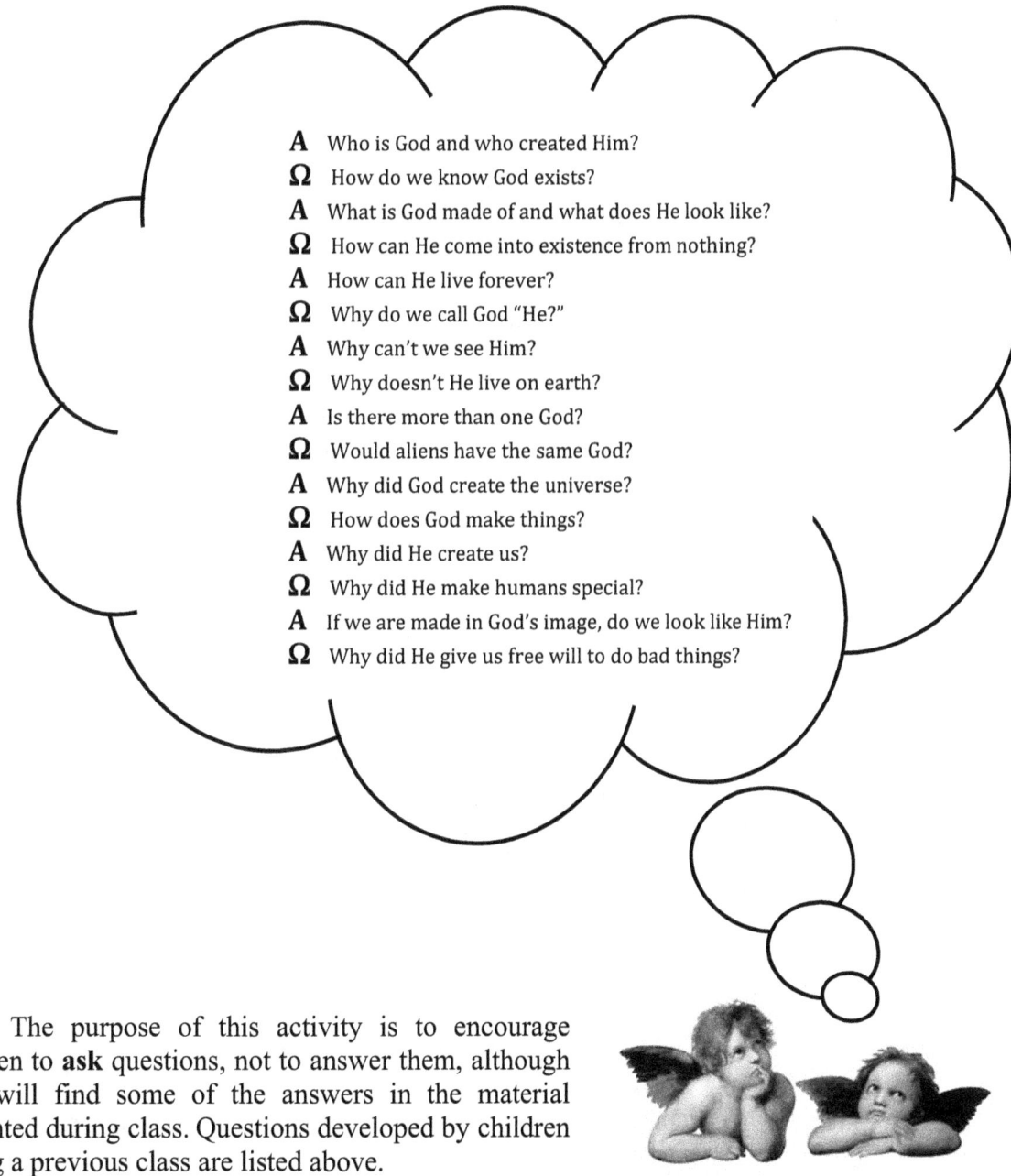

- **A** Who is God and who created Him?
- **Ω** How do we know God exists?
- **A** What is God made of and what does He look like?
- **Ω** How can He come into existence from nothing?
- **A** How can He live forever?
- **Ω** Why do we call God "He?"
- **A** Why can't we see Him?
- **Ω** Why doesn't He live on earth?
- **A** Is there more than one God?
- **Ω** Would aliens have the same God?
- **A** Why did God create the universe?
- **Ω** How does God make things?
- **A** Why did He create us?
- **Ω** Why did He make humans special?
- **A** If we are made in God's image, do we look like Him?
- **Ω** Why did He give us free will to do bad things?

Note: The purpose of this activity is to encourage children to **ask** questions, not to answer them, although they will find some of the answers in the material presented during class. Questions developed by children during a previous class are listed above.

God and the Universe – Lesson #2

6. DEMONSTRATION: The Universe (10-15 min.)

Present the demonstration on "The Universe" with two assistants. (See sample script at end of this lesson, and practice it beforehand.) Then ask for volunteers to try it in front of the class, using the script. You can also ask for three students to volunteer for the children's performance.

7. CREATION MEDITATION (20-30 min.)

This exercise provides an opportunity for children to meditate about the signs of God that have been deposited in every created thing. You may wish to meet outside for this activity.

First, explain what meditation is and why it is important (see box on following page for ideas). Then ask the children to think deeply about one of the things that God created and what spiritual lessons we can learn from it. Have them close their eyes, and play soft music in the background if desired.

> **O SON OF BOUNTY!**
>
> Out of the wastes of nothingness,
> with the clay of My command
> I made thee to appear,
> and have ordained for thy training
> every atom in existence
> and the essence of all created things.
>
> (Bahá'u'lláh, Persian Hidden Words #29)

After a few minutes of silent contemplation, have the children share their insights with a partner, and then if they wish, with the larger group. A few examples:

Flowers: Different colors add beauty to the garden. In the same way, diversity adds beauty to the human race.

Human Body: All the parts have different shapes and functions, but they all work together in harmony for the same goal—an example of unity in diversity.

Plants: They grow upward, reaching toward the sun, just as people must turn their faces toward the Sun of Truth in order to grow spiritually and receive heavenly light and life.

Breathing: We must breathe continuously in order to live. It is the same with prayer. We can't pray once a week or once a month and expect to be spiritually healthy.

Raindrops: Each raindrop by itself, has very little power, but when combined with many other drops, it can become part of a mighty river. The Bahá'í community is the same. Each person contributes a drop, but when we all work together, we can move mountains.

Bahá'í Children's Classes and Retreats: Theme 1, p. 48

Meditation

Bahá'u'lláh tells us that "every created thing in the whole universe" is a sign of the revelation of God and "a door leading into His knowledge," [1] and that "Upon the inmost reality of each and every created thing He hath shed the light of one of His names..." [2]

"Within every atom," He declares, "are enshrined the signs...of that Most Great Light," and "how vast the oceans of wisdom that surge within a drop!" [3]

How can we begin to unravel the mysteries hidden in every atom and every drop?

Throughout the Bahá'í Writings, we are instructed to "meditate on that which We have revealed unto thee, that thou mayest discover the purpose of God..." [4]

"Through the faculty of meditation man attains to eternal life; through it he receives the breath of the Holy Spirit...Meditation is the key for opening the doors of mysteries...meditation frees man from the animal nature...puts man in touch with God." [5]

To meditate, we should empty the mind of distracting thoughts, and concentrate quietly on the Word of God and the beauty of His creation. 'Abdu'l-Bahá explains:

"...The meditative faculty is akin to the mirror; if you put it before earthly objects it will reflect them." "But if you turn the mirror of your spirits heavenwards...the rays of the Sun of Reality will be reflected in your hearts..." He adds that "the sign of contemplation is silence." [5]

<u>References</u>
1. Gleanings from the Writings of Bahá'u'lláh, p. 160
2. Ibid, p. 65
3. Ibid, p.177
4. Ibid, p.152
5. 'Abdu'l-Bahá, Paris Talks, p. 174

God and the Universe – Lesson #2

8. MEMORY QUOTE (10-15 min.)

Have students take out their page of quotations and locate quote #14. They will memorize the first part only: *"O SON OF BEING! With the hands of power I made thee and with the fingers of strength I created thee."* (The quote should already be written on the board.)

> "O SON OF BEING!
> With the hands of power
> I made thee
> and with the fingers of strength
> I created thee."

A. <u>Understanding</u>: Read quote aloud slowly, then ask students:

- Who wrote these words?
  (Bahá'u'lláh, speaking with the Voice of God.)

- Who do you think Bahá'u'lláh is talking to?
  (All human beings, whether sons or daughters, male or female.)*

- What kinds of things do people create using their hands? *(Paintings, clay sculptures, baskets, etc.)*

- How do people feel after creating something special with their own hands? *(Happy, proud.)*

- Do you think God has physical hands and fingers? *(No. This is symbolic. It is a visible image used to represent an abstract idea. It's like using a flag as the symbol for a country, or a crown for a king.)*

- What is Bahá'u'lláh telling us?
  (That God created us all through His power.)

- Do you remember why God created us?
  (Because He loves us.)

B. <u>Repetition</u>: Read the quote again slowly and have students repeat after each phrase. Do it again, faster. Then read two phrases at a time as students repeat. (You can use gestures as a memory aid. For example, stretch out your arms with palms up when saying the words "hands of power." Spread your fingers wide and clasp them together for "fingers of strength.")

C. <u>Backwards Buildup</u>: Read the last phrase and have students repeat until it is memorized. Then add the previous phrase and read through to the end. Continue in this manner until you have reached the beginning and most children have the entire passage memorized.

---

* Note: Bahá'u'lláh addresses human-kind in different ways, including: O My Children, O Friends, O Servants, O My Brother, O Moving Form of Dust, O Son of Love, and O Peoples of the World.

The English translation of many Bahá'í Writings follows the conventions of 17th-century Oxford English, which uses "entirely masculine nouns and pronouns to refer both to God and people in general." [1]

The Writings also make it clear that the soul has no gender, and that women and men are equal in the sight of God:

"Know thou that the distinction between male and female is an exigency of the physical world and hath no connection with the spirit..." [2]

"The truth is that God has endowed all humankind with intelligence and perception and has confirmed all as His servants and children; therefore, in the plan and estimate of God there is no distinction between male or female." [3]

References

1. Joell Ann Vanderwagen, *Journey to the Father: New Perspectives on Gender and the Bahá'í Revelation*, Journey Pub., Toronto, 2004, p.1

2. 'Abdu'l-Bahá, quoted in *Ancient Goddess Religions*, The Universal House of Justice, 1992 Feb 23

3. Abdu'l-Bahá, *Promulgation of Universal Peace*, p. 283

God and the Universe – Lesson #2

D. <u>Disappearing Act</u>: Then, using an eraser, swipe a narrow diagonal path through the entire passage on the board. This will leave a blank space on each line. Ask for student volunteers to read the passage again. Let everyone take a turn. Then make another eraser swipe and ask for another round of volunteers. Continue until the passage has completely disappeared.

E. <u>Recitation</u>: Ask for student volunteers to recite the quote from memory. Call on the most capable ones first, as they will serve as a model for the others.

> *Tell the children they can work with a friend and use these techniques to memorize other quotes for the performance. They can memorize additional passages after returning home.*

Collect all folders and pencils.

9. CRAFT ACTIVITY: God's Eye (30-40 min.)

Craft projects are designed to reinforce the concepts presented during class. The children will be making a Mexican God's Eye or *Ojo de Dios** (see instructions at end of lesson). These attractive yarn mandalas are inexpensive, quick and easy to make. Completed God's Eyes can be given as presents, mounted on a wall, suspended from a tree or from the ceiling in a child's room.

Show the children some samples. Explain that they symbolize the loving eye of God, and remind us that He is always watching over us. God sees everything, everywhere. The crossed sticks represent the four directions (north, south, east, west), and the four basic elements (earth, air, fire and water).

For a brief history, photos, and instructions for making more complex God's Eyes, see the following websites:

> www.caron-net.com/kidfiles/kidsapr.html
>
> www.allfreecrafts.com/nature/ojo-de-dios.shtml
>
> http://ojos-de-dios.com
> (for some very elaborate examples)

* The Spanish "j" is pronounced as a light "h" sound: "**OH**-ho-day-dee-**OHS**".

✶ ✶ ✶ ✶ ✶

God and the Universe – Lesson #2

Teacher's Version – For Activity #4

God, the Creator

"God in His wisdom has created all things."
(Abdu'l-Bahá, Divine Philosophy, p. 110)

Nothing can make itself. Everything has a creator, from the tallest building to the smallest grain of sand. A wooden table is made by a carpenter. A shoe is made by a shoemaker. A nest is made by a bird.

Ask: Is there anything that can create itself? *(No.)*

There is a great power that created the entire universe: the minerals, the plants, the animals, the stars, the planets, and all the people.

Although everything has a creator, we can't always see that creator or know who it is. No matter how hard it tries, the table will never be able to recognize the carpenter. The shoe will never know the shoemaker. And the nest will never be aware of the bird. It's the same with people. It is impossible for us to understand the nature of our Creator.

We call our creator "God." He is also known as Allah, Dios, Jehovah, the Lord, the Almighty, the Great Spirit, our Heavenly Father, and by many other names.

God is a mystery. He is not a person like you or me. No one knows exactly what God is like or where He is, because we can't see or touch Him, but we do know that He is real.

We can't see the wind, but we know it exists, because we can see leaves blowing on the trees. We can't see electricity, but we know it exists because we can see its effects whenever we turn on the light. We can't see the air, but we know it is real because without air, we couldn't breathe. In the same way, we can't see thoughts, or gravity, or time, or friendship, or anger, or peace, but we know that these are real. And we can't see love, but we can feel it when someone special says "I love you."

In the same way, we can't see God, but we know He exists because we can see the world He created for us. We can learn about the great Prophets He has sent to tell us about Himself and to teach us how to live. And sometimes we can feel the love of God in our hearts when we are saying our prayers.

O SON OF MAN! ...I knew My love for thee; therefore I created thee...
(Bahá'u'lláh, Arabic Hidden Words #3)

Ask: What do you think this last quotation means?

Bahá'í Children's Classes and Retreats: Theme 1, p. 52

God and the Universe – Lesson #2

Instructions to group leaders for activity #5

Kids' Questions About God

> Gather your small group and find a quiet place to work. You will have about ten minutes. Your job is to encourage the children to **ask** questions, not to answer them. A child who is silent can be asked, "What thoughts do you have about this?" Do not allow the children to laugh at or tease each other. Take notes below, and use the back of the page if necessary. Prepare the group to share their questions with the class.

1	
2	
3	
4	
5	
6	
7	
8	
9	
10	
11	
12	
13	
14	
15	
16	

God and the Universe – Lesson #2

The Universe

(Sample script for demonstration - Activity #6)

Needed: Two narrators and one actor, small box filled with plastic letters, table covered with tablecloth, stiff placemat, tray, Lego or similar building-block construction hidden under table.

NARRATION	ACTION
(Pause between phrases while each action is performed.)	*(Start with the plastic letters spread out on the placemat inside the tray.)*
1. *(First Speaker)* Some people say there is no God, and that the universe created itself by accident. That the whole world came into being just by chance.	1. Point skyward to indicate God. Shrug shoulders at the word *accident*. Use a circular hand motion to indicate *the world*. 
2. That would be like putting a bunch of letters into a box, shaking it, dumping out the letters, and expecting them to form a beautiful poem. That just doesn't seem possible!	2. Carefully pick up the mat and pour the letters into the box. Pick up the box of letters, shake it, then dump the letters out onto the tray again.
3. Besides, **who** made the letters in the first place? **Who** put them into the box, and **who** poured them out?	3. Hold up one letter for the audience to see. 
4. *(Second Speaker)* Yeah! That would be like knocking over a box of Legos, and just by chance, they turned into this. I don't **think** so! Someone had to create a design and put the pieces together. That took a lot of planning and work!	4. Bring out hidden Lego construction, e.g. an elaborate boat or castle. 
5. *(First Speaker)* The creation of the universe is the same. This infinite universe with all its greatness and perfect order could not have come into existence all by itself – just by accident. How can there be an effect, without a cause?	5. Wait for the applause, bow, then remove the props.

God and the Universe – Lesson #2

MEXICAN GOD'S EYE

> *" With the ear of God he heareth, with the eye of God he beholdeth the mysteries of divine creation."*
> (Bahá'u'lláh, The Seven Valleys, p. 17)

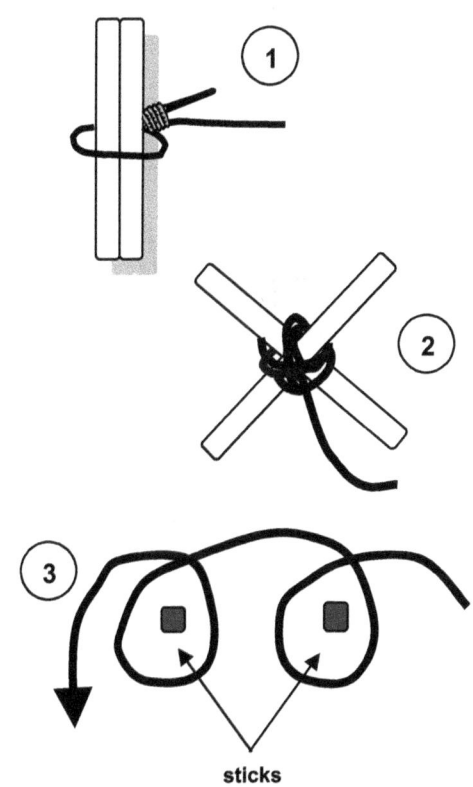

Materials

- ☐ Craft sticks, popsicle sticks, or wooden skewers
- ☐ Skeins of medium-weight yarn in different colors
- ☐ Beads, feathers, bells or other objects for decoration (optional)
- ☐ Scissors

Hints

- Multi-colored yarn makes an attractive design.
- Thicker yarn means fewer wraps, and is easier for small hands to use.
- Younger children may find it easier if you pre-tie the sticks and pre-cut the yarn.
- If a child is having difficulty, stand behind him and hold his hands while showing him how to wrap the yarn.
- Use popsicle sticks for younger children and bamboo skewers (available in the meat section of the grocery store) for older ones. If using skewers, you may wish to cut off sharp points with a scissors before giving them to children.

Instructions

1. Cut off a length of yarn (about a meter or a yard), and tie one end in a knot around the middle of two sticks. Pull tight, then wrap the yarn around the sticks a few times.

2. Spread the sticks so they form an "X", and tightly wrap yarn diagonally across the intersection a few times, first one way (top to bottom) and then the other (left to right), to anchor the sticks in place.

3. Holding the sticks where they cross, begin weaving counter-clockwise around the circle, tightly wrapping the yarn over and around each stick. In other words, wrap the yarn over and back under the top stick, over and back under the left stick, over and back under the bottom stick, and over and back under the right stick to complete one round.

Bahá'í Children's Classes and Retreats: Theme #1, p. 55

God and the Universe – Lesson #2

4. Continue with the same pattern until the length of yarn is used up. An "eye" will begin to form in the center. It is easier to work if you rotate the entire project one quarter turn each time you make a loop, so you are always working on the top. Be sure each strand lies **next** to the previous one, and **not on top** of it. Wrap tightly and keep a uniform tension on the yarn.

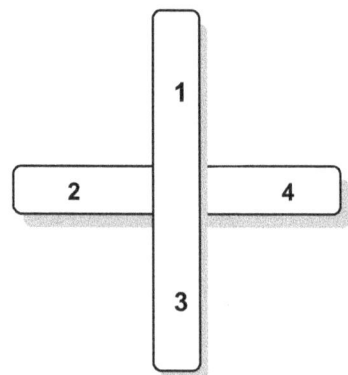

Tip: You can also mark the sticks with numbers (1,2,3,4) to help the children keep track of the order. The numbers will be covered up as they work.

5. When you reach the end of the first piece of yarn, tie it to another piece and continue wrapping. Make sure the knot is on the back side. Change colors as desired.

6. To finish the project, tie a loose knot in the end of the yarn, slip it over the last stick and pull tight. Trim off any loose ends.

7. If desired, add tassels, feathers or other objects at the end of each stick. Make tassels by wrapping about ten loops of yarn around your fingers. Remove the loops, tie a knot across the middle and cut through both ends. Use more fingers to make larger tassels.

8. Tie a loop of yarn on top for hanging the completed God's Eye.

Remind children to clean up when finished and to label all work with their names.

* * * * *

God and the Universe – Lesson #2

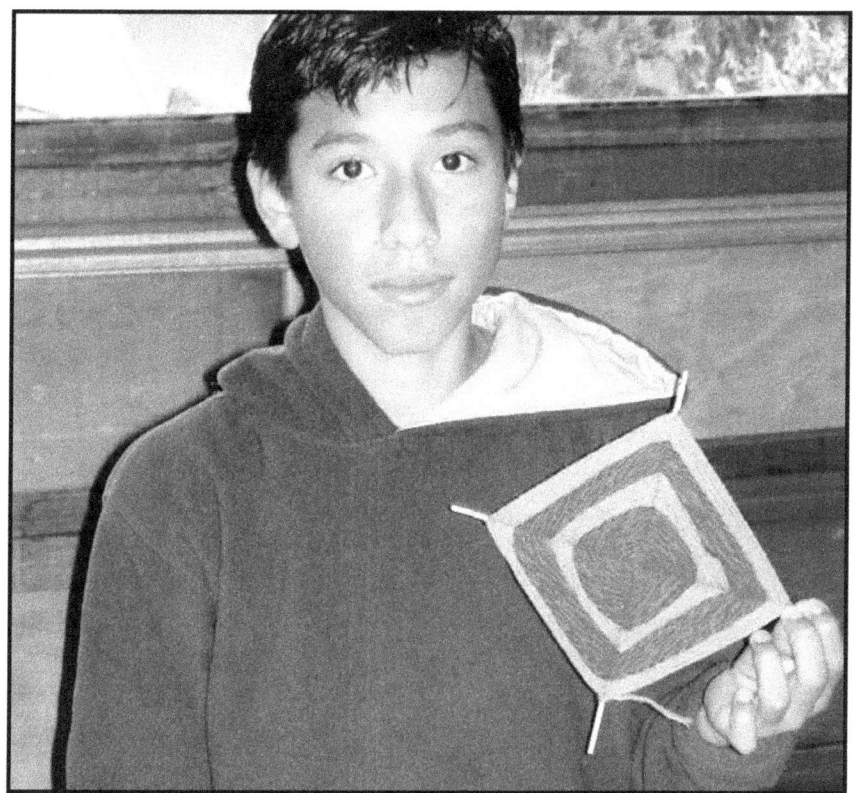

Vincent displays his handiwork.

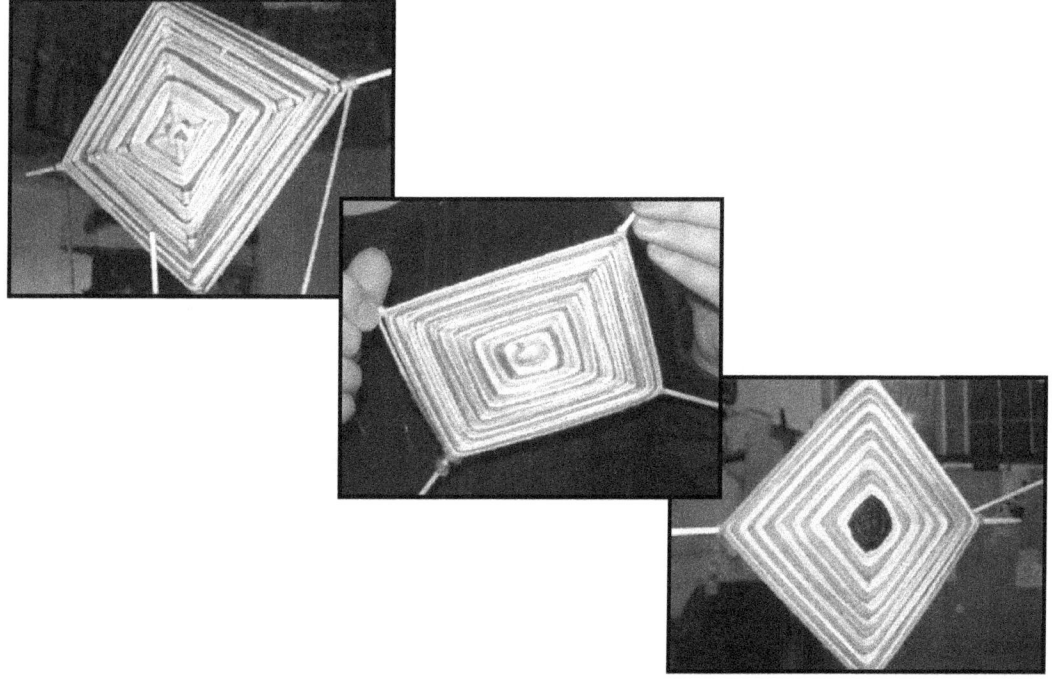

God and the Universe – Lesson #2

MATERIALS NEEDED

- White board, easel, markers, eraser
- Folders with paper and song sheets for each student
- Pens or pencils for each student
- Dictionary
- Reading on "God, The Creator" [A]
- Chart paper, tape and markers (for activity #5)
- Script and props for demonstration on "The Universe" (for activity #6) [B]
- Materials for craft activity (see separate list)
- Samples of the craft project and instruction sheet for any assistants
- References for teachers (at the end of this book)

A. Included with this lesson.

B. Make four copies of the script and place each copy in a plastic page holder for ease of use. In addition, you will need a small box filled with plastic letters (available at most toy stores and dollar stores), a table covered with a tablecloth, a tray to catch the letters, and an elaborate construction (e.g. a boat or castle) made with Legos or similar building-block toy.

* * * * *

Bahá'í Children's Classes and Retreats: Theme 1, p. 58

LESSON #3

Prayer, Our Connection with God

God and the Universe – Lesson #3

Prayer, Our Connection with God

Objectives: Students will be able to:
- Define prayer and list some of its benefits.
- Explain why it is important for us to pray every day.
- Specify different ways to pray, where to pray, and what to pray for.
- Define reverence and demonstrate postures that can help create an attitude of prayer.

Before class, prepare all instructional materials on the list at the end of this lesson. Set up lamp demo and craft area. Orient youth and adult assistants. Post the wall maps and pictures of people praying. Distribute folders and pencils to each student.

---

1. **REVIEW** (2-3 min.) Ask the class:

   a. Who created the universe and what are some of His names? *(God, Jehovah, Allah...)*
   b. Why did He create human beings? *(Because He loves us.)*
   c. Who can recite from memory the quote learned during lesson two?
      (Call on several volunteers.) *"O SON OF BEING! With the hands of power I made thee and with the fingers of strength I created thee."*

2. **SONGS** (5 min.)

   Lead the children in singing "Pray to God" and "O God, Guide Me."
   Song sheets are in their folders. Ask the music volunteer for help if needed.

3. **INTRODUCTION** (1 min.)

   Tell the students:
   - In this class, we are going to learn about prayer.
   - When we pray, we are talking with God.
   - Prayer is so important that Bahá'u'lláh says we should pray every day.
   - Prayer builds up our spiritual muscles and protects us from tests.
   - I'll bet you already know a lot about prayer.
   - I have some questions for you. Some are easy and some are hard.
   - Are you ready?

4. **PRAYER QUESTIONS** (12-15 min.)

Distribute all the questions (see end of lesson and next page) giving one card to each student. If there are extra questions, some children might receive more than one card. Beginning with question #1, ask each student to read their question aloud, and then to answer it or call on another student to answer. Other children may wish to share their thoughts as well. As the discussion progresses, remind students to raise their hands, and to call on classmates who have not yet had a chance to speak.

Bahá'í Children's Classes and Retreats: Theme 1, p. 60

God and the Universe – Lesson #3

Prayer Questions – Reference List for Teachers

1. What is prayer? *(Conversation with God.)*

2. Who should pray? *(Everyone.)*

3. When should we pray? *(God is always listening so we can talk with Him anytime. Morning, noon and evening are special times of remembrance.)*

4. Where should we pray? Do we have to be in a special building or church? *(We can pray anywhere, but special buildings such as churches, temples, mosques and houses of worship have been set aside just for this purpose.)*

5. What should we pray for? *(The Bahá'í Writings are filled with prayers for many things. Let the children share their thoughts.)*

6. Is there anything we should **not** pray for? *(For example, is it OK to pray for a new bike, or for a teammate to get hurt so you can play? Probably not, as these would be selfish requests. Encourage children to share their thoughts.)*

7. Why should we pray? *(Prayer connects us with God. It increases capacity and understanding, protects us from tests, brings divine assistance, leads to healing, strengthens our moral courage, refreshes and gladdens our spirits, purifies our hearts, etc.)*

8. Can we sing or chant while praying?
   (Yes. We are encouraged to chant melodiously.) [A]

9. Can we pray in any language? *(Yes. God hears all prayers.)*

10. Is it possible to pray without words? *(Yes.)*
    How? *(Our thoughts and actions can also be prayers.)* [B]

References

A. "Teach your children what hath been revealed through the Supreme Pen...Let them memorize the Tablets of the Merciful and chant them with melodious voices…The prayers of the Lord should be chanted in a manner to attract the hearts and souls." (Bahá'u'lláh, quoted in Bahá'í Year Book, 1925-1926, p. 59, NSA USA - Developing Distinctive Bahá'í Communities)

B. "Reveal then Thyself, O Lord, by Thy merciful utterance and the mystery of Thy divine being, that the holy ecstasy of prayer may fill our souls - a prayer that shall rise above words and letters and transcend the murmur of syllables and sounds…" ('Abdu'l-Bahá, Bahá'í Prayers, p. 69)

"When anyone occupieth himself in a craft or trade, such occupation itself is regarded in the estimation of God as an act of worship…" (Baha'u'llah, Tablets of Baha'u'llah, p. 26)

"Work done in the spirit of service is the highest form of worship...."
('Abdu'l-Bahá, Divine Philosophy, p. 78)

At the end of the activity, collect the question cards.

God and the Universe – Lesson #3

5. REVERENCE: Prayer Postures (15-20 min.)

Set out a prayer rug in front of the class.

A. Explain that we will learn about different ways to show respect for God when we pray. Show pictures of people praying in different positions and places. Ask the students:

- Where are they? Indoors? Outdoors?
- Are they alone or with other people?
- Look at their faces. How do they feel?
- Look at their bodies. Are they moving? Talking?
- What are their hands doing in each picture?
- Are their eyes open or closed?
- What are they looking at?
- What are they thinking about?
- What are the differences among these pictures?
- What are some of the things they all have in common?

Guide students to understand the concept of reverence, and write the word on the board.

B. Have the class repeat the word "reverence" several times, and ask for a few volunteers to define it in their own words. Some ideas are offered below:

> **Reverence** is a feeling of deep love and respect for God. This feeling is inside our hearts and is reflected in our actions, like bowing to a king. In some parts of the world, reverence is shown by kneeling quietly with hands together, eyes closed, and head bowed. In other places, reverence is shown by standing with eyes open and hands reaching up to our Creator. There are many ways to show reverence, but they all produce a feeling of opening our hearts and minds to be filled with the spirit of God. When we pray, our minds should concentrate and our bodies should reflect the reverence that is in our hearts.

C. Show the pictures again and have the children practice each posture. As the teacher, you should demonstrate on the prayer rug. Explain that our outer physical conditions can influence our inner thoughts and feelings. Ask how these postures make them feel.

D. Then call on several volunteers, one at a time, to demonstrate a sloppy or disrespectful posture, e.g. slouching, or feet up on a table. Ask how these postures make them feel. Which postures help create an attitude of prayer, and make them feel closer to God?

6. READING: Prayer, Our Connection with God (15-20 min.)

Have students take out their packet of readings and turn to the page titled "Prayer, Our Connection with God." Read the title and first quote.

> *"Intone, O My servants, the verses of God that have been received by thee... that the sweetness of thy melody may kindle thine own soul..."*
> (Bahá'u'lláh, Bahá'í Prayers, p. ii)

Ask the class:

- Who said these words? *(Bahá'u'lláh.)*
- What does *intone* mean? *(To chant or recite in a singing tone.)*
- What does *kindle* mean? *(Set on fire, cause to glow or light up.)*
- What do you think Bahá'u'lláh is telling us to do and why? *(Chant or recite the prayers in a beautiful voice, so that our spirits may glow with the fire of the love of God.)*

Ask for volunteers to read the remaining paragraphs out loud. After each one reads, that student should make up one or two questions about the paragraph and call on other children to answer. Have the children raise their hands. If necessary, encourage them to call on someone who hasn't yet had a chance.

> **Tip:** If desired, less fluent readers can be given an opportunity to practice their reading and prepare their questions beforehand.

7. STORY: The Prayer Lesson (10-15 min.)

Reverently place the photograph of 'Abdu'l-Bahá at the front of the room.

Tell students you are going to read them a true story about someone who learned how to really pray. Have them locate "The Prayer Lesson" in their reading packet (also at end of this lesson).

Read the story aloud in a dramatic voice as they follow along. Point to 'Abdu'l-Bahá when He is introduced in the story. When finished reading, ask students to think silently about the questions at the end:

- Who was Mr. M?
- Compare Mr. M's first attempts to pray with his last one.
- What did he do differently at the end?
- What did he learn from 'Abdu'l-Bahá?

Give students a minute to think on their own. They can take mental or written notes, and underline words if desired. Then have them pair up with the person next to them to discuss their responses. After a minute or two, call on several pairs to share their thinking with the class. This cooperative learning technique is called **"Think-Pair-Share"** (see *References for Teachers*).

God and the Universe – Lesson #3

8. LAMP DEMONSTRATION: Prayer Connection (10 min.)

Plug in a lamp in front of the room and ask the students:

- What is this? *(A lamp.)*
- What is the purpose of the lamp? *(To give light.)*

Turn lamp on and off to demonstrate.

- What happens if it's not plugged in when I turn it on? *(Nothing.)*
- Why? *(Because there's no connection to the electricity.)*

Unplug lamp to demonstrate.

> **Tip:** You can hold up an extension cord and plug the lamp into the cord for greater visibility.

- What can this demonstration teach us about prayer? *(Let children share their thoughts.)*
- What does the lamp stand for? *(A human being.)*
- What does the cord represent? *(Prayer, our connection to God.)*
- What does the electricity symbolize? *(The Spirit of God: invisible but powerful.)*
- What happens when the lamp isn't connected? *(It doesn't give light.)*
- What happens when we're not connected to God through prayer? *(Our spiritual light doesn't shine.)*

Ask for several volunteers to repeat the demonstration.

9. PERSONAL STORIES (15-20 min.)

Tell the students:

We've talked about why we pray, when and where to pray, how to pray, and what to pray for. Now let's share some personal stories about prayer. How has prayer helped you or someone you know?

> Have the children form groups of 4-5 to share their stories. Allow about three minutes each, then remind them to give the next person a turn. If there is time, each group can choose one of the stories to share with the entire class. As the teacher, you should also be ready with a story to share.

10. PRAYER MAPS (5 min. or during a break)

Set out stars near the two wall maps.

Remind the children that prayer gives us spiritual light. Invite them to place stars on the maps (like tiny points of light) in every place they have ever said a prayer. The maps can be left on the wall and stars can be added after class as well.

Bahá'í Children's Classes and Retreats: Theme 1, p. 64

11. SONG: Blessed Is the Spot (10-12 min.)

Lead the children in singing "Blessed is the Spot." (Song sheets are in their folders.) Tell them that it is a prayer set to music, so they should sing it with reverence. Ask the music volunteer for help if needed. After singing, discuss the meaning of the song:

What does "blessed" mean?
(To become holy, sacred, spiritually pure; to be near to God; set aside for or devoted to God.)

What do you think this song means?
(Any place where God is praised becomes a special place – blessed and set aside for God.)

Where can we pray to God?
(Mountains, valleys, houses, caves, islands…)

Sing the song together once again.

If this class is part of a summer school or retreat, encourage the children to memorize prayers throughout the event, and to add them to the prayer tree (see p. 125) at any time.

Collect all folders and pencils.

12. CRAFT ACTIVITIES (30-45 min.)

Craft activities are designed to reinforce material presented during class. The children will be working on a "Blessed is the Spot" coloring booklet and a hand-sewn "Prayer Pouch." (See instructions at the end of this lesson.) Any assistants should be oriented beforehand. Completed projects can be used by the children as teaching tools.

After the crafts, dismiss the children for a snack and outdoor activities.

✶ ✶ ✶ ✶ ✶

God and the Universe – Lesson #3

Prayer Question Cards

(Photocopy and laminate this page,
cut out and distribute cards to students for activity #4.)

1. What is prayer?	6. Is there anything we should <u>not</u> pray for?
2. Who should pray?	7. Why should we pray?
3. When should we pray?	8. Can we sing or chant while praying?
4. Where should we pray? Do we have to be in a special building or church?	9. Can we pray in any language?
5. What should we pray for?	10. Is it possible to pray without words? How?

God and the Universe – Lesson #3

People Praying - Composite

The following pages can be copied for activity #5. The same illustrations are available in color, and can be downloaded from: www.UnityWorksStore.com. Click on Children's Classes > God and the Universe > Student handouts.

Bahá'í Children's Classes and Retreats: Theme 1, p. 67

God and the Universe – Lesson #3

People Praying - A

God and the Universe – Lesson #3

People Praying - B

Bahá'í Children's Classes and Retreats: Theme 1, p. 69

God and the Universe – Lesson #3

People Praying - C

Bahá'í Children's Classes and Retreats: Theme 1, p. 70

God and the Universe – Lesson #3

People Praying - D

Bahá'í Children's Classes and Retreats: Theme 1, p. 71

God and the Universe – Lesson #3

People Praying - E

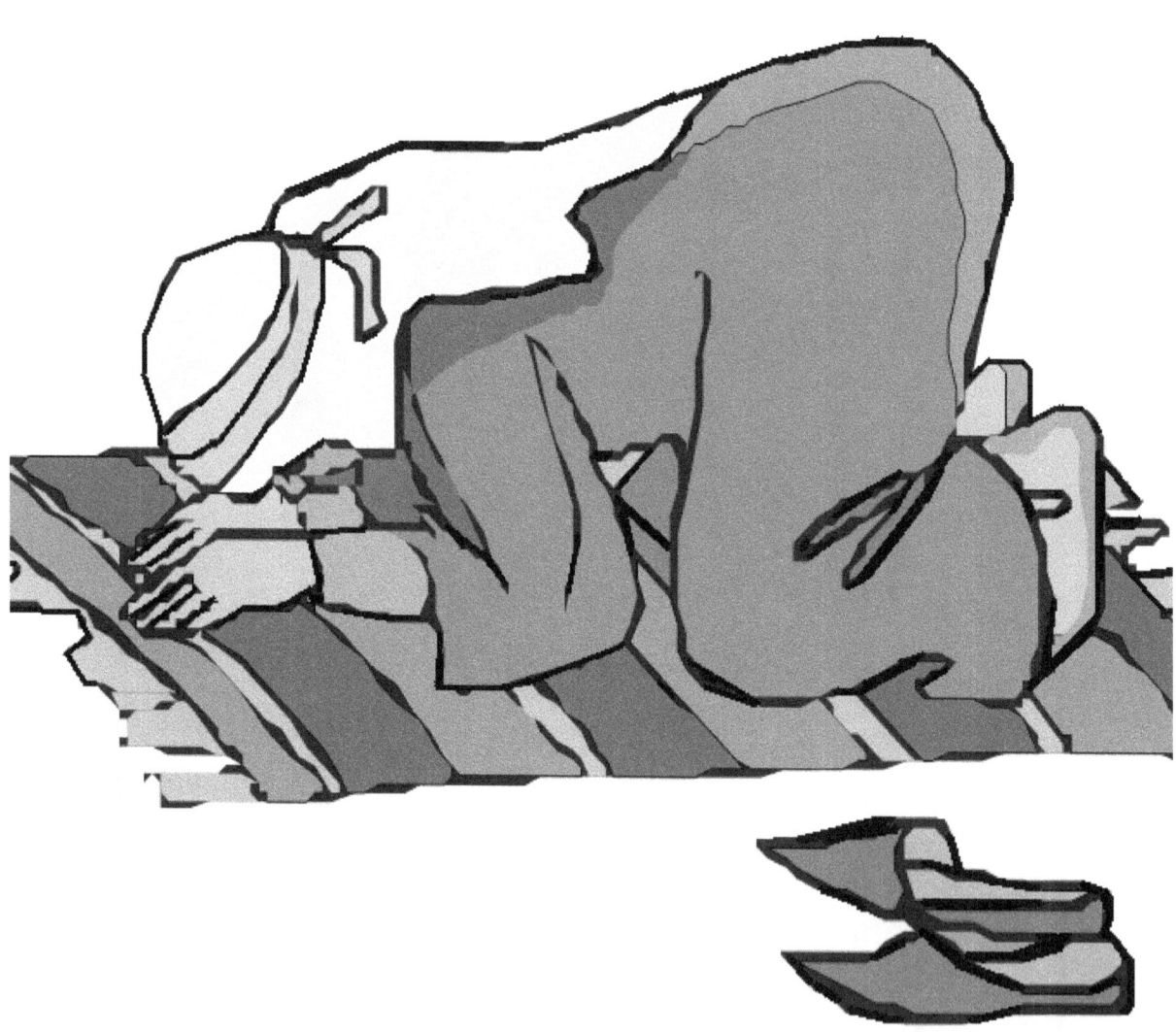

God and the Universe – Lesson #3

People Praying - F

Bahá'í Children's Classes and Retreats: Theme 1, p. 73

God and the Universe – Lesson #3

People Praying - G

God and the Universe – Lesson #3

People Praying - H

Bahá'í Children's Classes and Retreats: Theme 1, p. 75

God and the Universe – Lesson #3

People Praying - I

God and the Universe – Lesson #3

Prayer, Our Connection with God

> *"Intone, O My servants, the verses of God that have been received by thee... that the sweetness of thy melody may kindle thine own soul..."*
> (Bahá'u'lláh, Bahá'í Prayers, p. ii)

Prayer is talking with God. Through our prayers, we can thank God for creating us and for all of the things He provides.

We can ask Him to protect us, and to help us with our problems. We can pray for people who are sick or unhappy. We can ask God to grant us faith and knowledge, patience and love. We can pray for unity, peace and justice in the world.

Bahá'u'lláh says that we should pray every day. When we pray, we should show respect by focusing all of our attention on God.

We shouldn't be in a hurry or just speak the words. Rather, we should try to understand the true meaning behind the words, and our hearts must be sincere.

Bahá'u'lláh has given us many beautiful prayers to use. We should memorize some of them. That way, we will always have the Word of God with us, even when no books are available.

We can also make up our own words. And we can pray without words, straight from our hearts.

Prayer helps us to become more spiritual, even if at first we can't feel the effects.

Prayer helps us draw closer to our Creator. When we pray, God knows, and He is listening.

Intone: to chant or recite in a singing tone
Kindle: to set on fire, cause to glow or light up

God and the Universe – Lesson #3

The Prayer Lesson

Adapted from *Vignettes from the Life of 'Abdu'l-Bahá,* Honnold, p.131-32

This is a true story that took place about 100 years ago. 'Abdu'l-Bahá was in New York when He invited one of the Bahá'ís (let's call him Mr. M) to visit. 'Abdu'l-Bahá said, "If you will come to Me at dawn tomorrow, I will teach you to pray."

Mr. M was very excited! The next day, he woke up at four in the morning and went across town to where 'Abdu'l-Bahá was staying. When he entered the room, 'Abdu'l-Bahá was already praying silently, kneeling by the side of the bed.

Mr. M knelt down on the other side, directly opposite 'Abdu'l-Bahá, and also began to pray. He prayed for his family, for his friends, and for all the kings and queens of Europe. Then he said every prayer he knew by heart. He looked up, but 'Abdu'l-Bahá was still communing[1] with God, so Mr. M repeated all his prayers again. Three times!

Mr. M was becoming impatient. He rubbed his knee and thought about his aching back. He started to pray again, but was interrupted by birds singing outside his window as the sun rose. A whole hour passed. Two hours! Mr. M was growing rather numb. He looked up and noticed a large crack in the wall. By now, he was feeling annoyed, and glanced over to see if 'Abdu'l-Bahá had finished yet.

The look of ecstasy[2] on 'Abdu'l-Bahá's face astonished him. Suddenly Mr. M also wanted to pray like that! He forgot about his own selfish desires, his sorrows and problems. Even the room he was in seemed to disappear. All he knew was that he wanted to be closer to God.

Mr. M closed his eyes again and his heart filled with joyful prayer. He was cleansed and uplifted by a feeling of true peace. Immediately, 'Abdu'l-Bahá stood up and smiled directly at Mr. M. "When you pray," He said, "you must not think of your aching body, nor of the birds outside the window, nor of the cracks in the wall! When you wish to pray you must first know that you are standing in the presence of the Almighty!"

1. **communing:** communicating intimately with someone; to feel at one with someone
2. **ecstasy:** intense joy or delight; carried away with overwhelming happiness

- Who was Mr. M?
- Compare Mr. M's first attempts to pray with his last one.
- What did he do differently at the end?
- What did he learn from 'Abdu'l-Bahá?

God and the Universe – Lesson #3

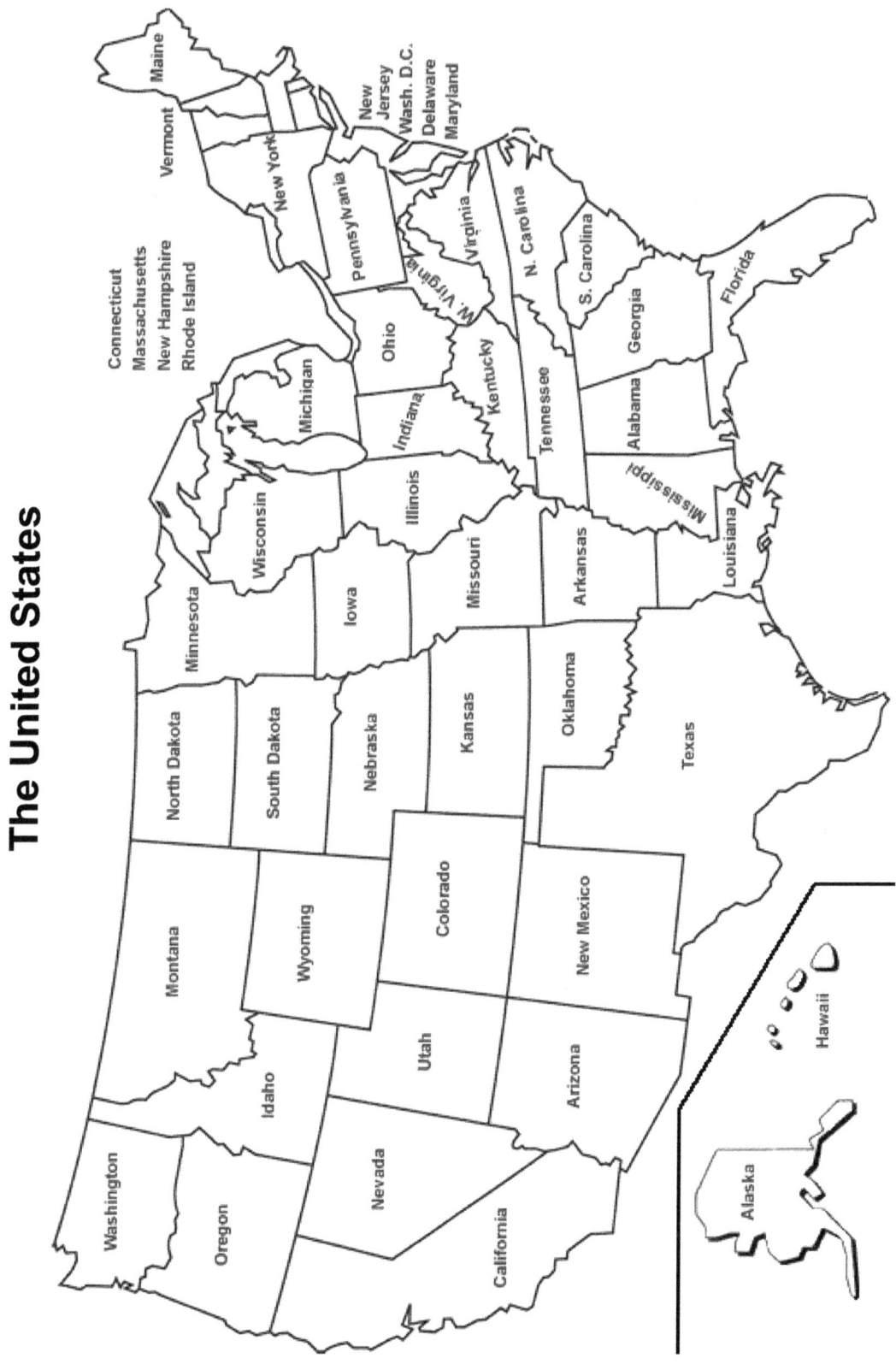

Bahá'í Children's Classes and Retreats: Theme 1, p. 79

God and the Universe – Lesson #3

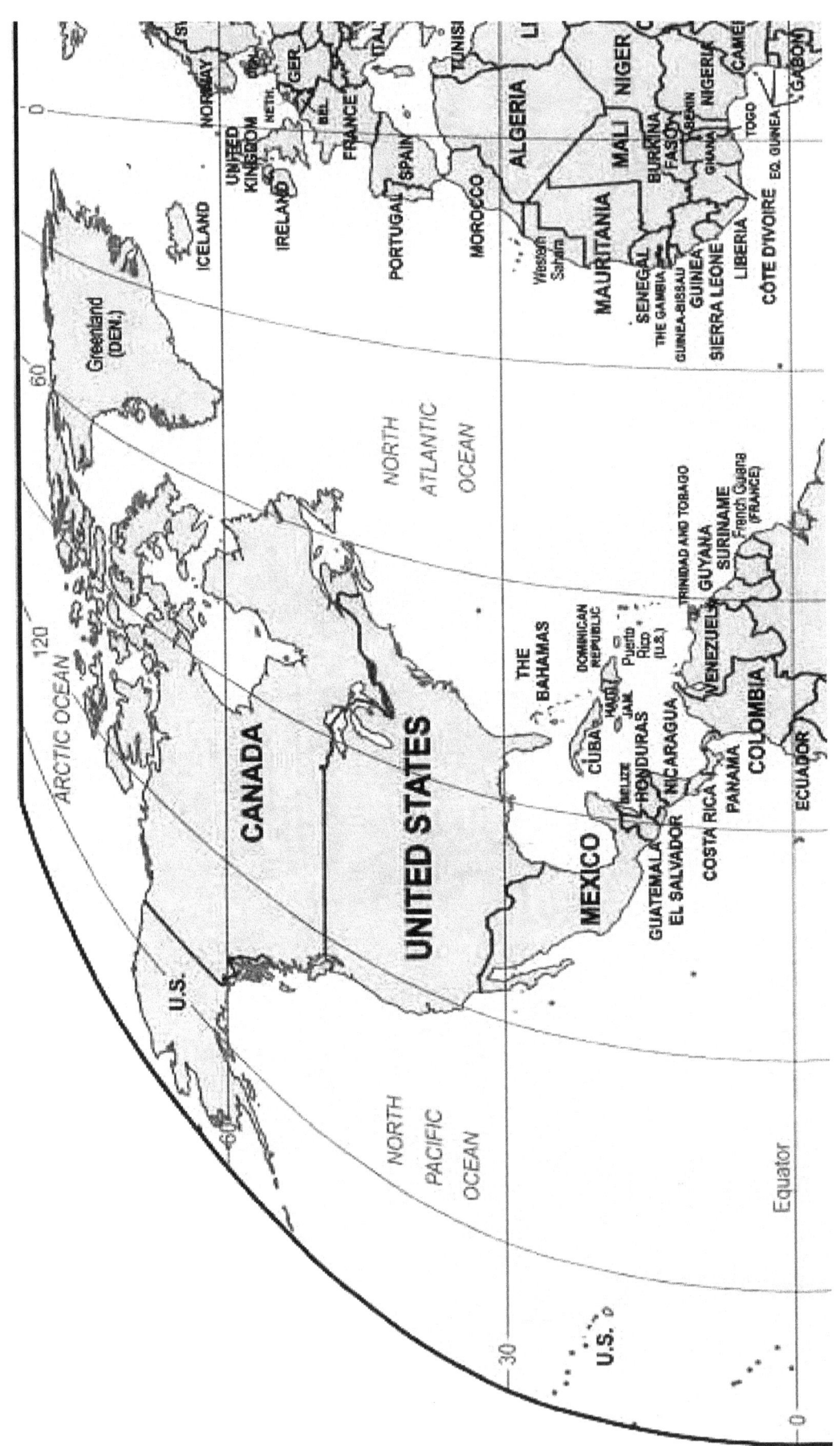

The World

Bahá'í Children's Classes and Retreats: Theme 1, p. 80

God and the Universe – Lesson #3

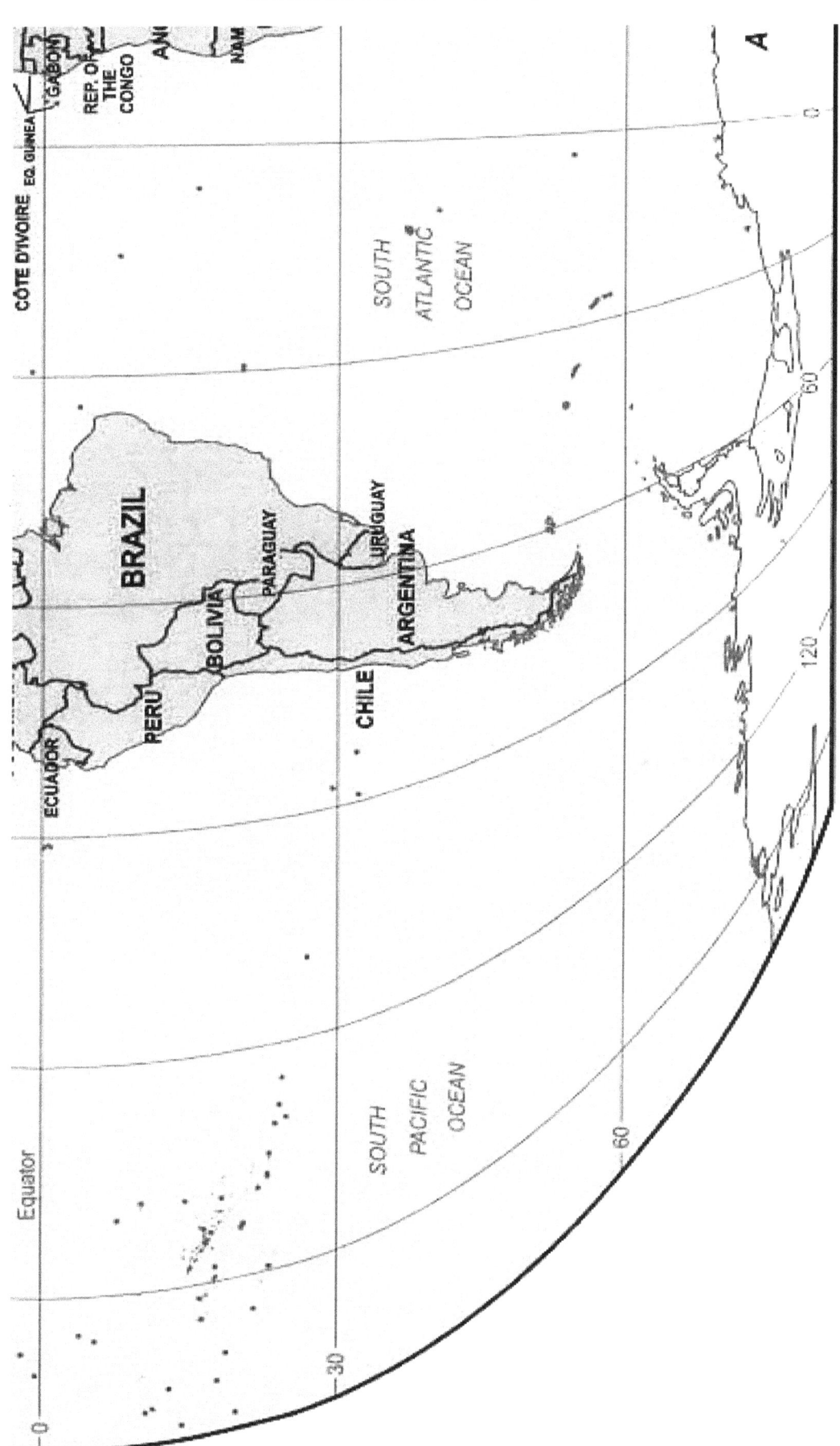

God and the Universe – Lesson #3

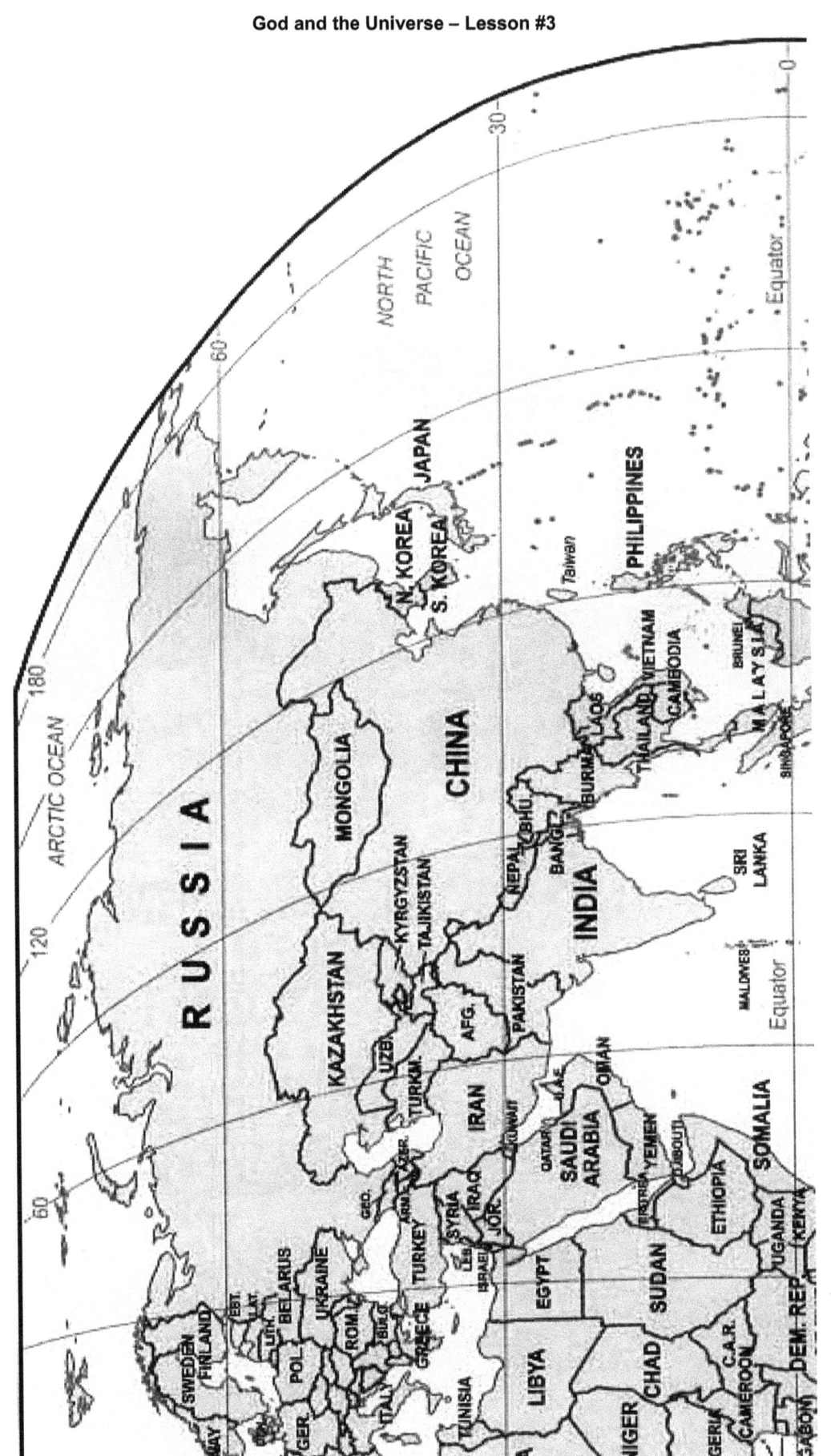

God and the Universe – Lesson #3

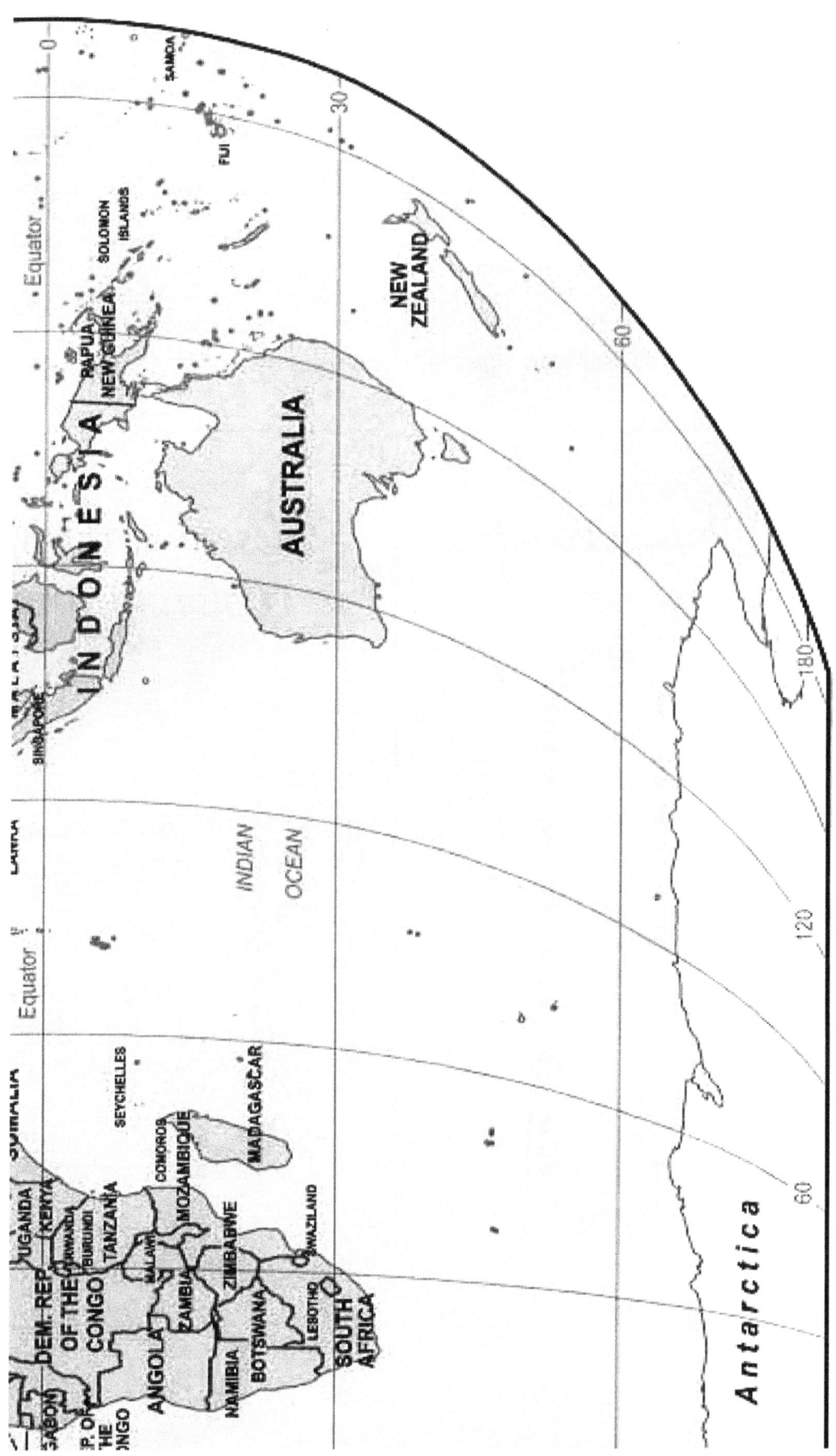

God and the Universe – Lesson #3

CRAFT ACTIVITIES

These activities are designed to reinforce material presented during class. For a weekend retreat, there may only be time for one or two crafts. For an ongoing class, you might choose a different craft each time. Another option is to prepare a separate table for each craft. Show the children a sample of each project and ask them to choose one to start. If their first choice is full, they can select another station. When children have completed their projects and cleaned up their work area, they may assist others who need help. Remind them to label all projects with their names. Quiet music can be played in the background if desired.

Prayer Pouch

Blessed-is-the-Spot Coloring Book

Bahá'í Children's Classes and Retreats: Theme 1, p. 84

God and the Universe – Lesson #3

Prayer Pouch

This hand-sewn prayer pouch is designed to hold prayers and verses that the children are memorizing. They can write down a prayer and carry it in the pouch around their necks. Once memorized, the prayer can be replaced with a new one. The pouch can also carry prayer beads or a prayer stone.[1] (Note: The skill-level of this craft makes it more appropriate for older children.)

[1] A small polished rock used as a concentration aid, as a symbol of the world that God created, and as a visual and tactile reminder to pray.

Materials

- ☐ Pre-cut strips of soft lightweight suede leather (one per child) [2]
  (approx. 3 in. wide x 6 in. long or 8 cm. x 16 cm.)
- ☐ Several pairs of sharp scissors
- ☐ Pencils or fine-tipped felt pens
- ☐ Rotary leather hole punch (one for every 5-6 children)
  (If a hole punch is not available, a snap setter tool or a hammer and large nail can also be used with careful adult supervision. Use a nail with a wide head, and a board to hammer on.)
- ☐ Yard stick or meter stick to measure the lacing
- ☐ Lacing material (approx. 1 yard or 1 meter per child if doing a weaving stitch; 1½ yards or meters if doing a loop stitch: see #7 below)

A variety of lacing materials can be used. Choose something that fits your budget and is thin enough to pass easily through the holes. Some examples:

- Suede leather lace (less expensive in spools)
- 1 mm round leather lace cord
- Vinyl or plastic craft lace
- Thin ribbon (7 mm or ¼-inch wide)

Leather items are available at craft and fabric stores, and online at:

>   www.tandyleather.com
>   http://eleathersupply.com
>   http://craft-supplies.misterart.com > craft-supplies > leather crafting

[2] Look for soft, lightweight (2-3 oz.) suede. Deerskin and pigskin are softer and more flexible than cowhide. Some craft stores offer economy packs of suede leather scraps in assorted colors. Inexpensive bulk leather can also be found on EBay (www.ebay.com) or at a local tannery or taxidermist supply. Inexpensive leather-look fabrics can also be used, but may be difficult to punch. Instead, these fabrics can be sewn using a large needle and thick thread.

God and the Universe – Lesson #3

You May Also Need

- ☐ Toothpicks and masking tape (to make lacing needles)[6]
- ☐ Small polished rocks or plastic gemstones (from aquarium, craft or dollar stores)
- ☐ Decorating materials:
   * Beads, buttons, feathers, glue
   * Ink pad and stamp (e.g. star or flower design)
   * Foam stick-on shapes (stars, hearts, flowers…)

> Protect table with tarp or cloth.

Instructions

1. Fold one strip of suede in half lengthwise to form a pouch.

2. Trim off the bottom corners so the pouch has a U-shape, being careful not to cut through the bottom of the fold.

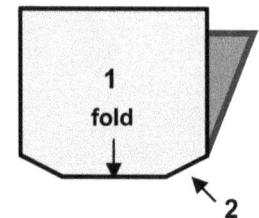

3. Using a pencil or felt pen, mark dots around the sides and bottom of the pouch, about 3/8–inch (1 cm) from the edge. Make an even number of marks (e.g. 10 or 16) and try to space them evenly. Leave the top edge unmarked.

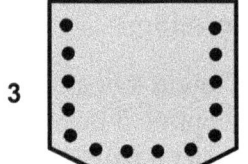

4. Using a punch tool, make holes through the marks, punching through both layers of suede at once.

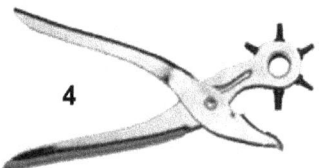

5. Cut a length of lacing material approximately 1 yard or 1 meter long, and trim both ends to a point.

6. If using a lacing material that is not stiff, e.g. ribbon or yarn, make a needle by taping one end of the lacing to a toothpick with a small piece of masking tape.

7. Starting at one corner of the pouch, sew the sides together using a weaving stitch (in and out) or a loop stitch (over the edges) to connect both sides. Adjust the stitches so that both ends of the lace are the same length.

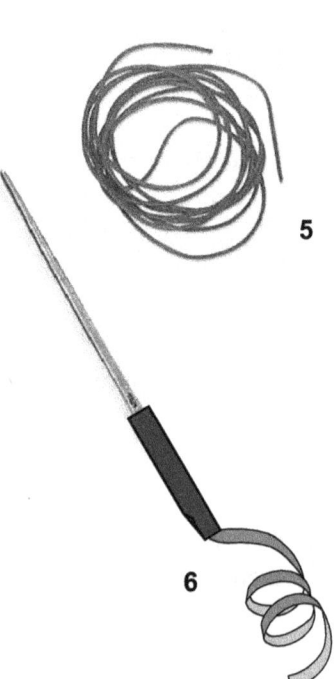

> **Tip:** To illustrate both types of stitching, the teacher can make two large samples using cardstock and a regular paper hole punch.

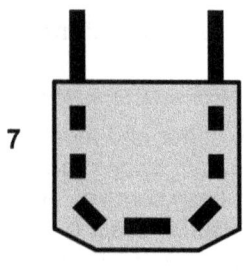
weaving stitch

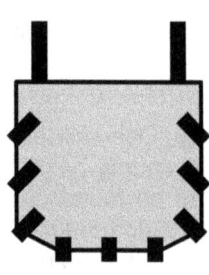
loop stitch

Bahá'í Children's Classes and Retreats: Theme 1, p. 86

God and the Universe – Lesson #3

8. Finish the ends on each side, by lacing them through the last hole again, but only through one side of the pouch. Then draw the lace up through the center of the pouch to lock it in place.

9. If desired, thread the lace through some decorative beads, and tie a knot just above the beads to hold them in place.

10. Measure the pouch around your neck to determine the correct length. Be sure you have enough room to slip it over your head. Tie the ends of the lace together in a knot, and cut off the excess.

11. Add optional decorations (ink stamp, buttons, stickers, fringe).

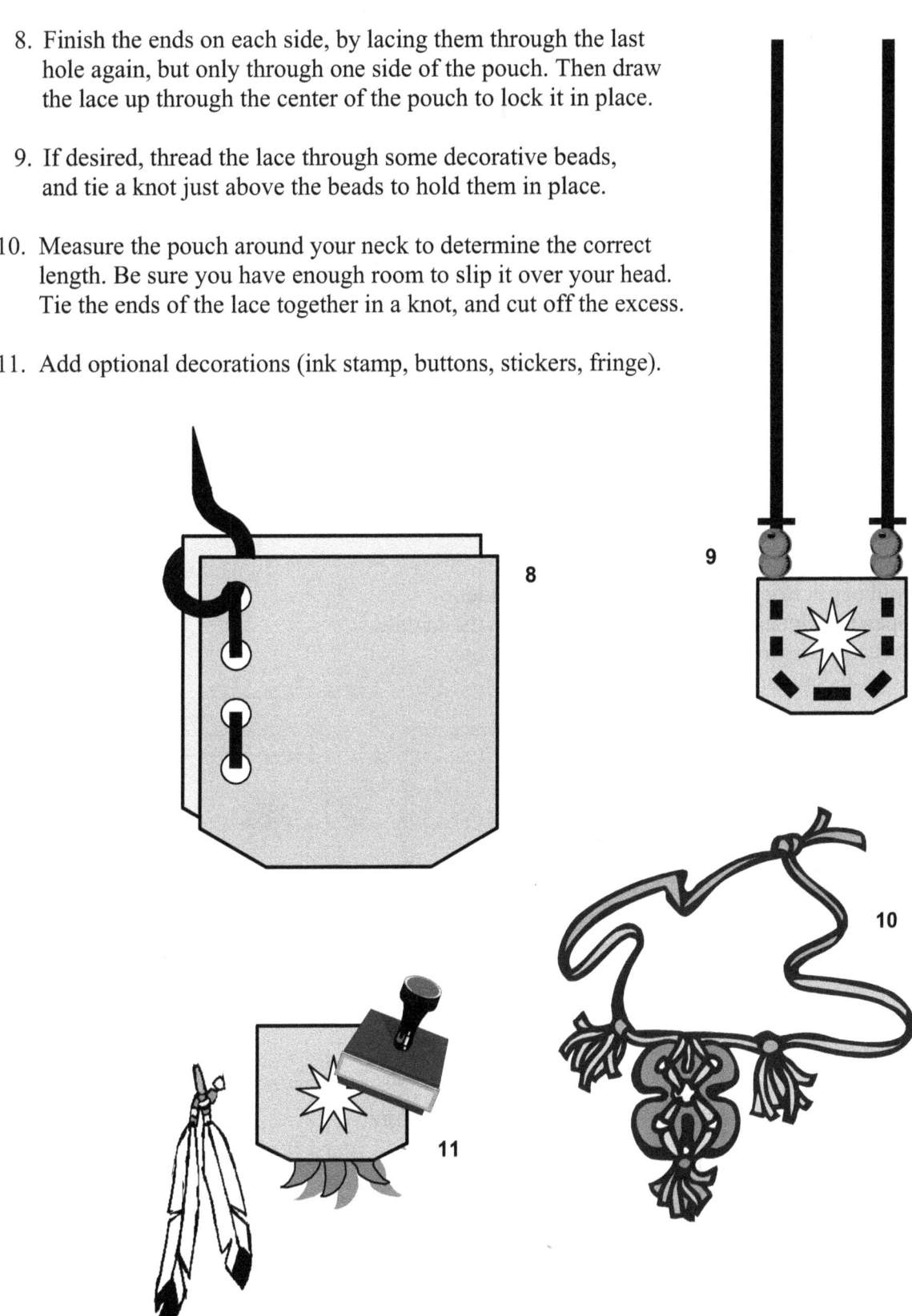

Bahá'í Children's Classes and Retreats: Theme 1, p. 87

God and the Universe – Lesson #3

Blessed-is-the-Spot Coloring Book

Materials

- ☐ Prayer poster (English and/or Spanish) to use as a reference.
- ☐ Four coloring pages – one set for each child
  (Make double-sided copies and use heavyweight paper so markers don't bleed through.)
- ☐ Blank paper for those who wish to write out the prayer and illustrate it by hand
- ☐ Scissors
- ☐ Hole punch
- ☐ Yarn
- ☐ Felt markers and colored pencils

Instructions

1. Put the two double-sided coloring pages together and fold in half from top to bottom.
2. Cut across the fold to make four half-sheets.
3. Arrange pages in order (A, B, C, D).
4. Fold pages from left to right to form a booklet.
5. Open booklet and punch two holes through the middle.
6. Thread yarn through the holes and tie in a bow.
7. Color the pictures.

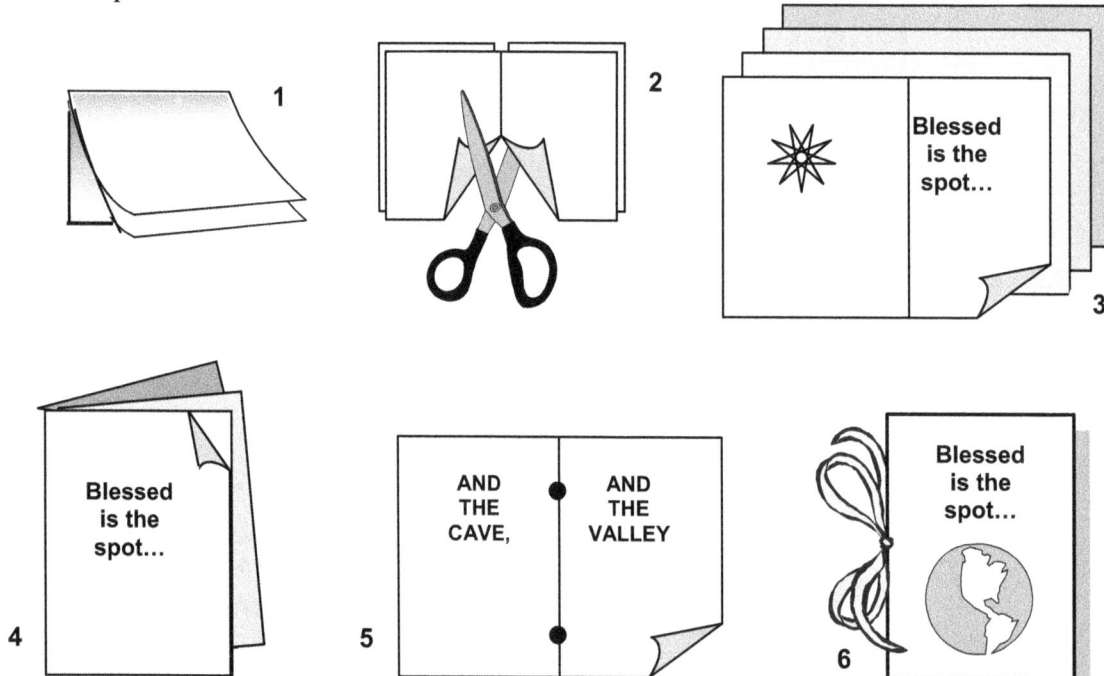

Note: English and Spanish posters and coloring pages are included here. They are also available as part of the download packet for this teacher's guide at: < www.UnityWorksStore.com >.
Click on Children's Classes > God and the Universe > Student handouts.

God and the Universe – Lesson #3

Blessed is the spot,
and the house,
and the place,
and the city,
and the heart,
and the mountain,
and the refuge,
and the cave,
and the valley,
and the land, and the sea,
and the island,
and the meadow
where mention of God
hath been made,
and His praise glorified.

~ *Bahá'u'lláh* ~

Post this page as a reference for the coloring book in activity #12

God and the Universe – Lesson #3

Bendito es el sitio,
y la casa,
y el lugar,
y la ciudad,
y el corazón,
y la montaña,
y el refugio,
y la cueva,
y el valle,
y la tierra, y el mar,
y la isla, y la pradera
donde se ha hecho
mención de Dios
y se ha glorificado
su alabanza.

~ Bahá'u'lláh ~

Post this page as a reference for the coloring book in activity #12.

*Bahá'í Children's Classes and Retreats
Theme 1: God and the Universe
Lesson 3 craft*

Words of Bahá'u'lláh

*Original drawings by Gordon Laite
(used with permission)*

BLESSED IS THE SPOT... A
Bendito es el sito…

WHERE MENTION OF GOD HATH BEEN MADE...
donde se ha hecho mención de Dios…

AND THE PLACE, B
y el lugar,

Bahá'í Children's Classes and Retreats: Theme 1, p. 91

AND THE HOUSE,
y la casa,

AND HIS PRAISE GLORIFIED.
y se ha glorificado su alabanza.
— *Bahá'u'lláh*

AND THE CITY,
y la ciudad,

AND THE MEADOW,
y la pradera,

Bahá'í Children's Classes and Retreats: Theme 1, p. 92

AND THE ISLAND,
y la isla,

AND THE HEART, C
y el corazón,

AND THE LAND,
y la tierra,

AND THE REFUGE, D
y el refugio,

Bahá'í Children's Classes and Retreats: Theme 1, p. 93

AND THE MOUNTAIN,
y la montaña,

AND THE SEA,
y el mar,

AND THE CAVE,
y la cueva,

AND THE VALLEY,
y el valle,

Bahá'í Children's Classes and Retreats: Theme 1, p. 94

God and the Universe – Lesson #3

MATERIALS NEEDED

- ❑ White board, easel, markers, eraser
- ❑ Folders with quote pages and song sheets for each student
- ❑ Pens or pencils for each student
- ❑ Dictionary
- ❑ Prayer question cards (included with this lesson)
- ❑ Small prayer rug or mat
- ❑ Pictures of people praying in different ways (for activity #5) [A]
- ❑ "Prayer, Our Connection with God" handout (included)
- ❑ Large photograph of 'Abdu'l-Bahá [B]
- ❑ "The Prayer Lesson" handout (included)
- ❑ Table lamp with extension cord
- ❑ Package of small gold or multi-colored stick-on foil stars (for map activity)
- ❑ Two large wall maps [C]
- ❑ Materials for craft activities (see separate list)
- ❑ Samples of each craft project and instruction sheets for any assistants
- ❑ Description of "Think, Pair, Share" (see description at end of *References for Teachers*)
- ❑ References for teachers (at the end of this book)

A. Large color pictures of people praying can be copied from this lesson. The same images are available in color, and can be downloaded from: **www.Unity WorksStore.com**. Click on Children's Classes > God and the Universe > Student Handouts.

Images are also available online at: www.Google.com > click on "images" and in the search box, enter various phrases such as: *international prayer, Buddhist prayer, Jewish prayer*. Most of these images are protected by copyright, but can usually be printed out by teachers for one-time classroom use. In addition, some religious bookstores carry illustrated prayer books for children.

Look for people of different ages, both genders, and from various racial and ethnic backgrounds. Include as much variety as possible, e.g. people praying silently, out loud, or singing; people standing or kneeling; alone or in groups; with eyes open or closed; hands folded or outstretched; with great fervor or with quiet serenity. The pictures can be laminated or inserted in plastic sleeves for protection, and posted around the room.

God and the Universe – Lesson #3

B. Photographs of 'Abdu'l-Bahá are available from many Bahá'í bookstores, including the U.S. Bahá'í Distribution Service, on the web at: www.BahaiBookStore.com > enter "photos" in the search box. Also see www.BahaiResources.com > click on Art Prints/ Posters > then click on Photographs.

Frame or mount the photograph and treat it with obvious respect when showing it to the children. The photo can be hung on the wall in a position of honor, or displayed on an easel or a table covered with a decorative cloth.

C. You will need a world map and a country map for your area. Tape both maps to the wall for activity #10. A black-line world map and a U.S. map are included here. To enlarge the U.S. map, first make a photocopy. Cut the copy in fourths, enlarge each fourth by 200% and tape the pieces back together, carefully matching the lines.

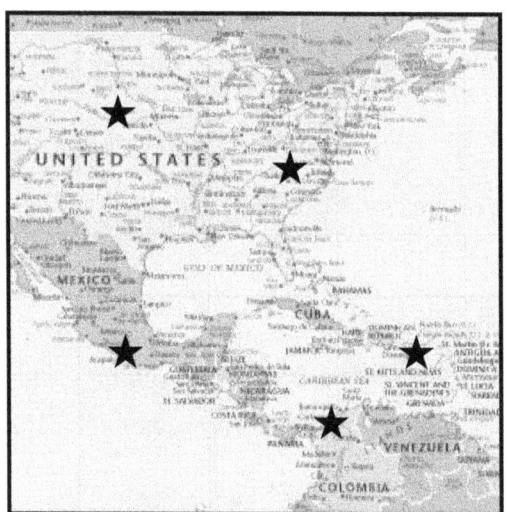

For the world map, photocopy as is or enlarge each page, then trim off the excess and tape the pages together, so the equator lines up on each section.

If desired, larger more colorful maps can be found at teacher supply stores, department stores, bookstores, some gas stations and car insurance companies (such as Triple A). Outline maps make it easier to see the stars. Also, children will have an easier time finding the correct locations for their stars if political boundaries (states, provinces, countries) are clearly labeled.

For a great online source of free maps, visit: <http://www.lib.utexas.edu/maps>.

LESSON #4

What Is a Human Being?

God and the Universe – Lesson #4

What Is a Human Being?

Objectives: Students will be able to explain:
- That human beings have two realities: physical and spiritual.
- That our true reality is spiritual and has been created in the image of God.
- That we are here in this world for a purpose.
- That when we die, our physical body returns to the earth.
- That our soul, which lives forever, returns to our Creator.

Before class, prepare all instructional materials on the list at the end of this lesson. Orient assistants. Set up felt board, felt lesson, and post photograph of a baby. Prepare craft area. Distribute folders and pens or pencils to each participant.

---

1. **REVIEW** (5-10 min.)

   For each question below, call on 2-3 students to share their answers.

   A. Who remembers the four kingdoms of creation, in order?
   (Mineral, plant, animal, human.)

   B. Who created the universe, and what are some of His names?
   (God, Allah, Jehovah, Dios, the Lord, the Almighty, the Great Spirit…)

   C. Why did God create human beings? *(Because He loves us.)*

   D. What are some of the similarities between human beings and animals?
   (Physical body, growth, movement, the senses.)

   E. What are some of the differences? *(Humans have conscious thought, rational mind, free will to choose between good and evil, moral behavior, capacity to know and love God.)*

   F. What is prayer, and why is it important to pray? *(Conversation with God. It increases our capacity and understanding, protects us from tests, brings divine assistance and healing, strengthens our moral courage, refreshes and gladdens our spirits, etc.)*

   G. Who can recite from memory the quote from lesson two? *"O SON OF BEING! With the hands of power I made thee and with the fingers of strength I created thee."*

Bahá'í Children's Classes and Retreats: Theme 1, p. 98

God and the Universe – Lesson #4

2. PAIRS DISCUSSION: What Is a Human Being? (5-10 min.)

Point to the photograph of the baby and tell the class:

Today we are going to learn about the human kingdom—who we really are.

Write the following question on the board, and ask students to think silently about the answer.

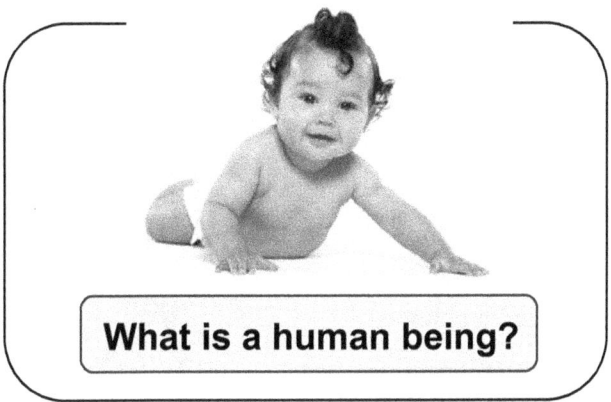

Give students a minute to think and to make mental or written notes. Then have them pair up with the person next to them to discuss their responses. After a few minutes, call on several pairs to share their thinking with the class. Their answers can be written on the board. This cooperative learning technique is called "Think-Pair-Share" (see description at end of References for Teachers).

3. SELF REFLECTION: Who Am I? (5-10 min.)

Place a large sheet of paper on the floor and invite one of the smaller children to lie down on top of it. Using a crayon, trace an outline around the child. (For older children, you may wish to trace around just the upper part of the body.) Then tape the paper to the wall where it can be easily seen. Write "Who Am I?" across the top with a felt marker.

Have the students take a sheet of notebook paper from their folders and write the heading "Who Am I?" Next, ask them to write nine or more responses to the question, beginning with their names. As the teacher, you should demonstrate on the board (see example).

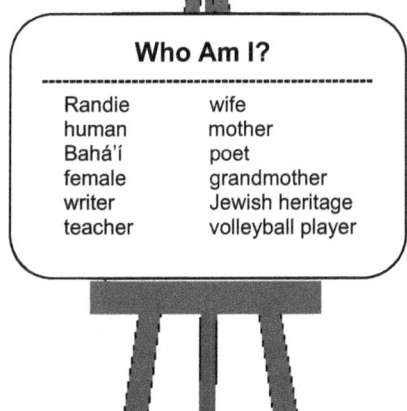

Give the class 2 to 3 minutes to work, then call on individuals to share one item from their list. Write these items on the human figure outlined on the wall.

If no one has mentioned the human soul, explain that yes, we are all of these things, and something more (see next activity).

God and the Universe – Lesson #4

4. FELT LESSON: What Is a Human Being? (10-15 min.)

Present the felt lesson "What is a Human Being" (see instructions at the end of this lesson). If there is time, ask two children if they would like to try it in front of the class on their own.

5. READING: In the Image of God (10-15 min.)

Ask students to take out their handout packets and turn to the page titled "In the Image of God." Read the two quotes in the box, then ask for volunteers to read each paragraph out loud. (Have a small mirror available to demonstrate the concept presented.) After each one reads, that student should make up one or two questions about the paragraph and call on other children to answer. Have the children raise their hands. If necessary, encourage them to call on someone who hasn't yet had a chance.

> **Tip:** If desired, less fluent readers can be given an opportunity to practice their reading and prepare their questions beforehand.

6. SMALL GROUP DISCUSSION (15-20 min.)

Write "What is the purpose of life?" on the board and ask:

> If we are spiritual beings created in the image of God, why do you think we are living here in this physical world? What is the purpose of life?

What is the purpose of life?

Explain that we will be working in small groups to answer this question. Then divide children into groups of four or five, and assign a youth or adult volunteer to lead each group. Give each volunteer a copy of the instruction sheet for "The Purpose of Life." As group facilitators, they should ask questions and encourage the children to share their thoughts. Walk around to observe the discussions. Groups can move to another room or outside if desired. Allow about 10 minutes for them to work. Bring the children back together to share their insights, making sure each group has an equal opportunity to participate. Write their ideas on the board.

A few responses from a previous class are listed on the following page: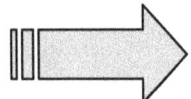

Bahá'í Children's Classes and Retreats: Theme 1, p. 100

God and the Universe – Lesson #4

> **What is the purpose of life?**
> **Why are we here in this physical world?**
>
> ❖ God wanted company.
> ❖ He wanted us to enjoy the earth that He created.
> ❖ To make the world a better place so others can enjoy it too.
> ❖ To make friends and be peaceful and help others.
> ❖ To bring up the next generation.
> ❖ To learn right from wrong.
> ❖ To learn about God.
> ❖ To grow our souls.
> ❖ So we can be happy and joyful beings.
> ❖ To be nice and keep smiling no matter what.
> ❖ Where else would He put us?

7. MEMORY QUOTES (15-20 min.)

Have students take out their handout of quotations (included at the end of this lesson for convenience) and explain that the quotes will help us to answer the questions: "What is a human being?" "Why did God create us?" and "What is the purpose of life?" Tell them to choose one quote to memorize with a partner.

You can let students choose partners, or you can assign them. For example, you might pair an older student with a younger one who needs assistance, or you might match students of equal ability so they can select a quote at the same level of difficulty.

If they choose short quotes, they may wish to memorize more than one. Review some memorization techniques with them (see end of handout). Give them about ten minutes to work together, then call on those who are ready to share.

Collect all folders and pencils.

8. SUMMARY (2-3 min.)

Ask several children to summarize the entire lesson in their own words. You can also review the concepts learned (see box below) while showing students the poster at the end of this lesson. A copy of the poster is included with their handout packets as well.

A Human Being Is . . .

- We are eternal spiritual beings, living for a time in the physical world.
- We were created because God loves us, and He wants us to know and to love Him.
- We are here to develop our spiritual qualities, to serve humanity, and to be like mirrors reflecting God's light and love to the world.

9. SONG: Song of Love (2-3 min.)

Lead the children in singing the "Song of Love." Ask the music coordinator for help if needed.

10. CRAFT ACTIVITY: Spirit Banners (30-60 min.)

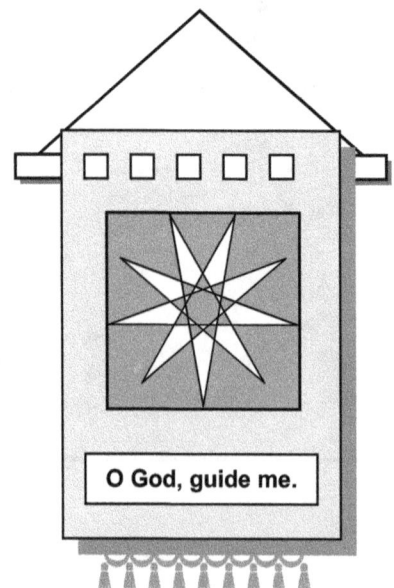

Craft projects are designed to reinforce the concepts presented during class. The children will be making felt "Spirit Banners" that can be displayed on the wall (see instructions at end of lesson). Show the children a few sample banners and encourage them to be creative in illustrating the quote they choose.

After the craft, dismiss children for a short break and outdoor activities.

God and the Universe – Lesson #4

"What Is a Human Being?"

Teacher's Guide, Script, and Patterns for Felt Lesson

TO THE TEACHER: This packet contains instructions, a script, and patterns for making a felt lesson titled "What Is a Human Being?" In order to present the lesson, you will need either a felt board or carpet board (see instructions on following pages). A carpet board is more durable and has a more finished look. After preparing the board and cutting out the pattern pieces, read through the script and repeat the actions until you can present the lesson smoothly. It may be easier if you have an assistant read the narration. You should determine the suitability of this lesson for your particular students and cultural context. The objectives of the lesson are listed below. The children will be able to state that:

| (1) People have two realities: physical and spiritual. | (2) Our true reality is spiritual. | (3) Our physical body returns to the earth when we die. | (4) Our soul lives forever, and returns to God. |

Bahá'í Children's Classes and Retreats: Theme 1, p. 103

God and the Universe – Lesson #4

Script for Felt Lesson

"What Is a Human Being?"

(Before starting, conceal star under body in center of felt board. Add red heart.)

	NARRATION	ACTION
1	What is a human being? Let's say that this is my body. What happens if I have an accident and break my leg? Am I still me? Yes, of course!	*(Fit actions to the narration)* Point to body. Tilt leg up on an angle.
2	What if I lose my arm? Or need a heart transplant? Or hurt my eyes and can't see? Am I still me?	Remove one arm. Replace red heart with pink one. Cover eyes with mask.
3	It might be harder to get around! But yes, it's still me! So if I'm not just my body, who am I really?	Point to disabled body.
4	Every human being has two natures: physical and spiritual. We have a physical body that comes from the earth. And we have a soul, an invisible spiritual reality, that comes from God. The soul has the powers of understanding, imagination and free will.	When the soul is mentioned, move body to reveal star underneath.
5	Together, the body and the soul, make up a human being.	Point to the body, then the soul as each one is mentioned.
6	When we die, our body returns to the earth, and our soul, which lives forever, returns to God.	Place body sideways near bottom of felt board, and place soul near top of board

Bahá'í Children's Classes and Retreats: Theme 1, p. 104

God and the Universe – Lesson #4

Instructions for Making Felt or Carpet Board

A felt board can be purchased at a teacher supply store, or one can be constructed by gluing a large piece of felt onto a stiff backing such as heavy cardboard, thin plywood or masonite. Spray glue gives the best results. A carpet board is constructed in the same way. Felt and glue are available at yardage and craft supply stores.

MATERIALS

- Sharp scissors
- Large piece of felt or indoor-outdoor carpet *
  (choose beige or other neutral color,
  approx. 24 x 36 in. or 60 x 90 cm.)
- Backing board (same size as felt or carpet)
- Spray glue or white craft glue

* If using carpet, test a piece of felt to be sure it sticks.
  Some types of carpeting may work better than others.

Instructions for Making Felt Pieces

1. Photocopy the two pattern pages.

2. Using the copies, cut loosely around each shape outside the line.

3. Use tape or large paper clips to attach each pattern to the correct color of felt.

4. Carefully cut out each felt piece, using the pattern as a guide.

5. Store the script and felt pieces in a zip-lock plastic bag for ease of use.

MATERIALS

- Felt pieces (light brown, bright yellow or gold, pink, red, black)
- Pattern pieces (on following pages)
- Masking tape or double-stick tape
- Sharp scissors

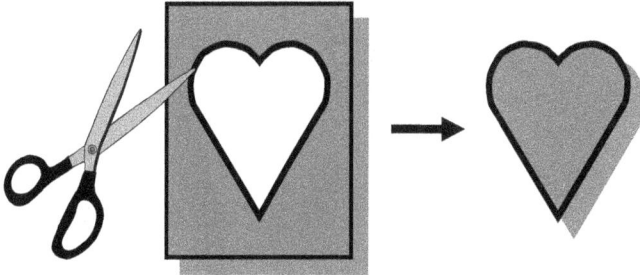

God and the Universe – Lesson #4

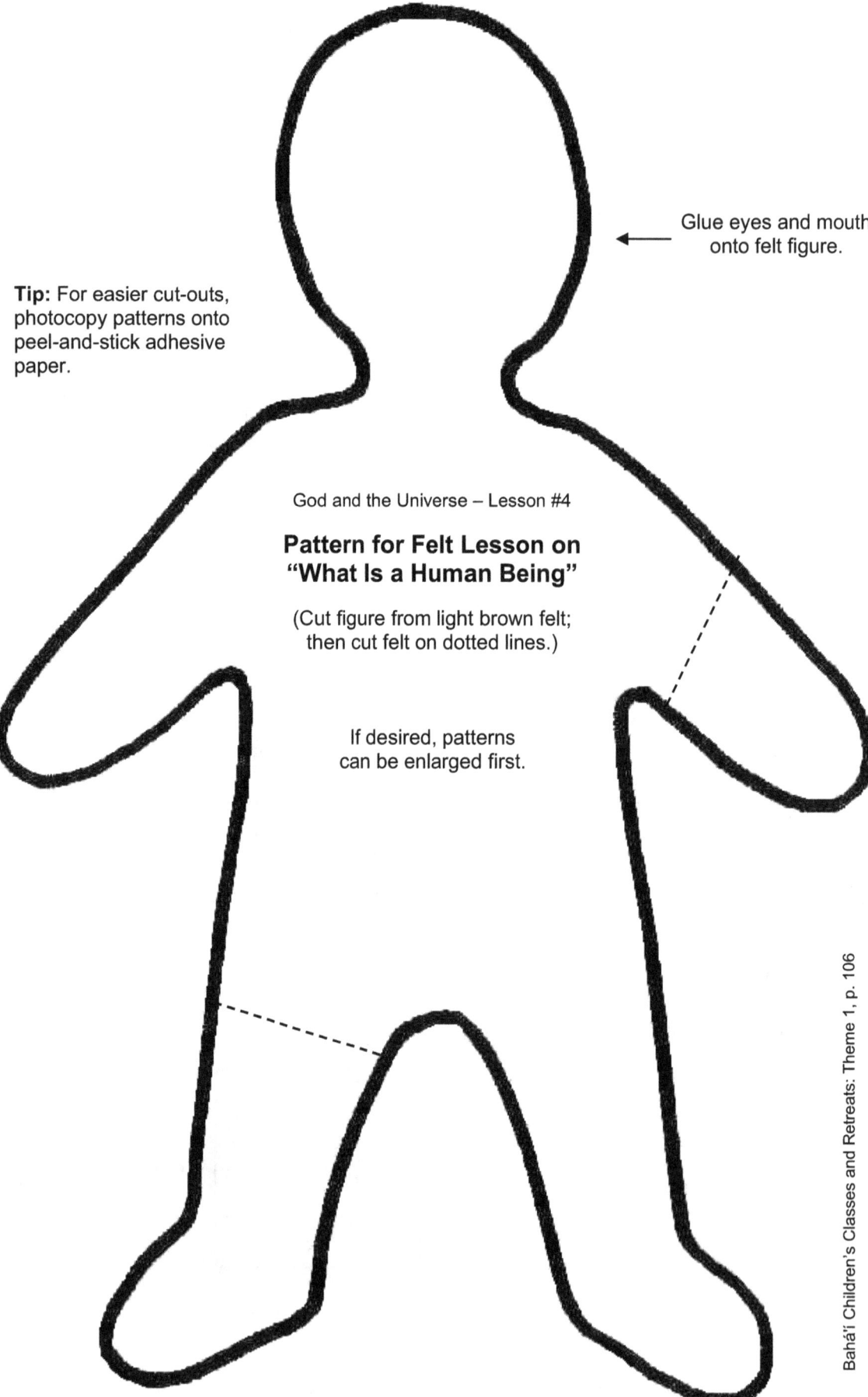

Glue eyes and mouth onto felt figure.

Tip: For easier cut-outs, photocopy patterns onto peel-and-stick adhesive paper.

God and the Universe – Lesson #4

Pattern for Felt Lesson on "What Is a Human Being"

(Cut figure from light brown felt; then cut felt on dotted lines.)

If desired, patterns can be enlarged first.

God and the Universe – Lesson #4

Patterns for Felt Lesson on "What Is a Human Being"

"It is manifest that beyond this body man is endowed with another reality…At the time of speech man says: '*I said, I saw*' Who is this 'I'? It is obvious that this 'I' is different from this body…For instance, the body of man may lose one arm, but the reality of man, which is not visible, loses nothing and is in its own normal state."

(Attributed to 'Abdu'l-Bahá, Baha'i Scriptures, p. 294-5)

God and the Universe – Lesson #4

Reading for activity #5

"In the Image of God"

> "God created man in His own image..."
> (Bible, Genesis 1:27)
>
> "O ye young Bahá'í children,
> ye seekers after true understanding and knowledge!
> A human being is distinguished from an animal in a number of ways.
> First of all, he is made in the image of God..."
> (Selections from the Writings of 'Abdu'l-Bahá, p. 140)

The Holy Writings tell us that we were created in the image of God. What does this mean? When the sun shines, it gives off heat and light. If the sun is shining on a perfect mirror, when we look at that mirror, we will see the image of the sun.

It is the same with human beings. We are like mirrors that can reflect the light of God. When we turn our faces toward the spiritual Sun, then the knowledge and love of God will shine in our hearts.

Some people think that humans were created in the physical image of God. But God is not a physical being. If God had a physical form, would He be male or female? Would He be black or white? Young or old? Tall or short? Rich or poor? And someday would He get sick and die? Is this the true reality of our Creator? No, of course not! Nor is it the true reality of a human being. God is an unknowable, invisible Spirit. Our Creator is so glorious and so far above every human attribute that we cannot even begin to understand His mystery.

So how can we reflect the spiritual image of our Creator? Just as God loves humanity, we must also love humanity. As God is truthful, we must also be truthful. As God is kind and merciful, we must be too. We should help the poor, comfort the sick, and be a friend to those who are sad or lonely. We should work for justice and peace, and strive for excellence in everything we do. And we must learn to be wise and patient.

When these attributes of God are reflected in us, just like the sun reflected in the mirror, we will be illumined with a heavenly light. Then the image of God will shine in our hearts.

References: From Bahá'u'lláh: Gleanings from the Writings of Bahá'u'lláh, p. 46, 158-9. From 'Abdu'l-Bahá: Bahá'í World Faith, p.255; Foundations of World Unity, p. 73, 79, 92; Promulgation of Universal Peace, p.70, 262, 470; Selections from the Writings of 'Abdu'l-Bahá, p. 79-80, 140; Some Answered Questions, p. 9.

God and the Universe – Lesson #4

Small group discussion for activity #6

The Purpose of Life

Instructions for group facilitator: Gather your small group and find a quiet place to work. You will have about 10 minutes. Your job is to ask the questions below, and to encourage all of the children to share their thoughts. A child who is silent can be asked, "What do you think about this?" Do not allow the children to laugh at or tease each other. Take notes below, and prepare the children to share their answers with the class.

If we are spiritual beings created in the image of God…

- Why do you think we are living here in the physical world?
- What is the purpose of life?

God and the Universe – Lesson #4   Name _____

Quotations from the Bahá'í Writings on

God and the Universe

Choose one of the quotes below. Pick something you think you can memorize in about five minutes. Identify who wrote the words. Then read the quote aloud several times and to try to understand the meaning behind the words. Work with your partner to memorize the quote.

SHORT

(1) Greater is God than every great one! *(Bahá'u'lláh, PM, p. 320)*

(2) God in His wisdom has created all things. *('Abdu'l-Bahá, DP, p. 110)*

(3) O God, my God, my Beloved, my heart's Desire *(The Báb, quoted in DB, p. 30)*

(4) Man is the sum of every previous creation, for he contains them all. *('Abdu'l-Bahá, PT, p. 23)*

MEDIUM LENGTH

(5) O God, guide me, protect me, make of me a shining lamp and a brilliant star. Thou art the Mighty and the Powerful. *('Abdu'l-Bahá, BP, p. 37)*

(6) O God! Refresh and gladden my spirit. Purify my heart. Illumine my powers. I lay all my affairs in Thy hand. *('Abdu'l-Bahá, BP, p. 150)*

(7) O Thou Compassionate God. Bestow upon me a heart which, like unto glass, may be illumined with the light of Thy love… *('Abdu'l-Bahá, BP, p. 72)*

(8) O God! …Cultivate this fresh plant in the rose garden of Thy love and aid it to grow through the showers of Thy bounty. *('Abdu'l-Bahá, BP, p. 35)*

(9) O SON OF BEING! Love Me, that I may love thee. If thou lovest Me not, My love can in no wise reach thee. Know this, O servant. *(Bahá'u'lláh: AHW #5)*

(10) O SON OF MAN! …I knew My love for thee; therefore I created thee, have engraved on thee Mine image and revealed to thee My beauty. *(Bahá'u'lláh: AHW #3)*

(11) Intone, O My servants, the verses of God that have been received by thee… that the sweetness of thy melody may kindle thine own soul…*(Bahá'u'lláh, BP, p. ii)*

(12) A human being is distinguished from an animal in a number of ways. First of all, he is made in the image of God… *('Abdu'l-Bahá, SAB, p.140)*

(13) The Perfect Man is as a polished mirror reflecting the Sun of Truth, manifesting the attributes of God. *('Abdu'l-Bahá, PT, p. 25)*

LONGER

(14) O SON OF BEING! With the hands of power I made thee and with the fingers of strength I created thee; and within thee have I placed the essence of My light. *(Bahá'u'lláh: AHW #12)*

(15) O SON OF MAN! I loved thy creation, hence I created thee. Wherefore, do thou love Me, that I may name thy name and fill thy soul with the spirit of life. *(Bahá'u'lláh: AHW #4)*

LONGEST

(16) I bear witness, O my God, that Thou hast created me to know Thee and to worship Thee. I testify, at this moment, to my powerlessness and to Thy might, to my poverty and to Thy wealth. There is none other God but Thee, the Help in Peril, the Self-Subsisting. *(Bahá'u'lláh, PM, p. 313)*

(17) Having created the world and all that liveth and moveth therein, He, through the direct operation of His unconstrained and sovereign Will, chose to confer upon man the unique distinction and capacity to know Him and to love Him… *(Bahá'u'lláh, G, p. 64)*

References

BP	Bahá'í Prayers
DB	The Dawn-Breakers
DP	Divine Philosophy
G	Gleanings from the Writings of Bahá'u'lláh
AHW	Arabic Hidden Words
PM	Prayers and Meditations
PT	Paris Talks
SAB	Selections from the Writings of 'Abdu'l-Bahá

SOME MEMORIZATION METHODS

Forward Repetition
- Repeat the first phrase out loud about ten times, or until you know it by heart.
- Sometimes it helps to write it down or say it with your eyes closed.
- Memorize the second phrase, then say both parts together.
- Continue learning each new part in the same way.

Backwards Repetition
- This is similar to forward repetition, except that you start with the last line or phrase.
- Then add the line before it and recite through to the end.
- Many people find that memorizing by backward repetition is easier.

Memory Aids
- Use hand gestures or draw small pictures to help you remember the words.
- You can also create pictures in your mind.

Disappearing Act
- Tear off a small strip of scratch paper and use it to cover up part of the quote.
- Keep adding strips of paper until the entire quote is covered and you know it by heart.

God and the Universe – Lesson #4

Copy onto cardstock and post during lesson summary - activity #8

A Human Being Is...

- ❖ We are eternal spiritual beings, living for a time in the physical world.

- ❖ We were created because God loves us, and He wants us to know and to love Him.

- ❖ We are here to develop our spiritual qualities, to serve humanity, and to be like mirrors reflecting God's light and love to the world.

Bahá'í Children's Classes and Retreats: Theme 1, p. 112

God and the Universe – Lesson #4

Spirit Banners

Craft activities are designed to reinforce material presented during class. Remind children to clean up their work area when done, and to label projects with their names. Quiet music can be played in the background if desired.

Materials

- ☐ Newspaper or tarp to protect table
- ☐ Felt rectangles in different colors, one per child (approx. 9 x 12 in. or 23 x 30 cm.)
- ☐ Felt scraps or peel-and-stick craft foam for making designs
- ☐ Pen and paper for sketching ideas
- ☐ Felt pens and rulers for drawing designs on felt
- ☐ White tailor's chalk for drawing designs on dark-colored felt
- ☐ Patterns (stars, hearts, flowers, human shapes, etc.)
- ☐ Sharp scissors for each child
- ☐ Fabric scraps (tassels, fringe, lace)
- ☐ Craft glue (not necessary if using peel-and-stick foam)
- ☐ Wooden dowel, one per child (3/16 in. wide by 1 ft. long or .5 cm. wide by 30 cm. long)
- ☐ Yarn or narrow ribbon for hanging banner for each child (approx. 3/8 in. wide by 2 ft. long, or 1 cm. wide by 60 cm long)
- ☐ Laminated quotations, one per child (see separate page)
- ☐ Velcro (pre-cut for younger children)

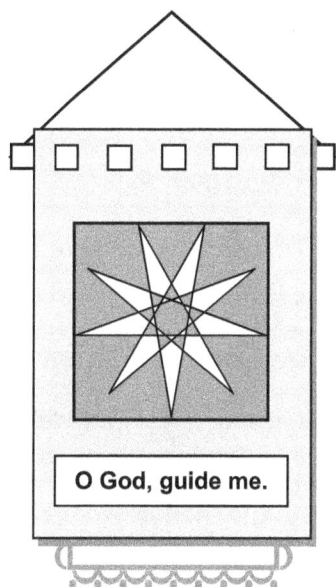

O God, guide me.

TIPS

- **Felt and Velcro** are available at craft supply and fabric stores. For attaching the quote, use the hard loop side of the velcro, not the soft fuzzy side. Peel-and-stick Velcro works best if available.

- **Patterns** can be cut from tag board or from thick solid-color vinyl placemats. Placemats are durable, easy to trace around, easy to cut, and available inexpensively at dollar and discount stores, especially during post-holiday sales.

- **Glue** can be poured into small paper cups and applied with stiff cotton swabs or wooden craft sticks. Spread glue evenly and be careful not to saturate the felt, or it will take a long time to dry.

- **Doweling** can be purchased in long rods at hardware stores, and cut to size with a hacksaw. Dowels can also be snipped with a wire cutter and any sharp edges smoothed with sandpaper.

God and the Universe – Lesson #4

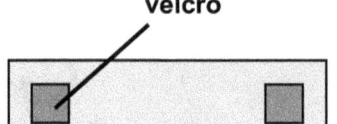

Instructions for making the banner

1. Select one of the laminated quotes to illustrate.
2. On the back of the quote, attach a small piece of velcro (the size of a thumbnail) to each side.
3. Attach the quote to the felt rectangle. The velcro will hold it in place.
4. Sketch or think up a design to illustrate the quote.
5. Using patterns or freehand, draw designs on the felt scraps, starting at the edge of the felt and working inward to avoid waste.

6. Cut out the designs and glue them in place on the felt rectangle. Leave some blank space at the top for attaching the hanger.
7. If desired, glue on tassels, fringe or other decorations.
8. Write your name or initials on the back.

Hanging the banner

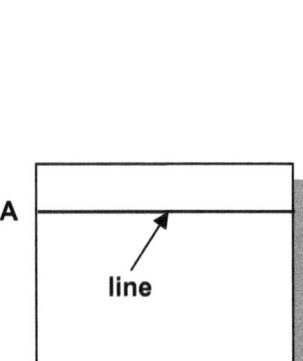

A. Using a ruler and felt pen, draw a line across the back side of the felt rectangle, ½ inch (1.5 cm.) down from the top.

B. Fold the felt along the line, and using the scissors, cut an even number of small slits approx. 1 inch apart (2.5 cm.) along the line. Be careful not to cut through to the edge of the felt. You should have 8 or 10 holes.

C. Spread the banner out flat.

D. Thread the dowel through the holes, starting from back to front.

E. Attach a length of yarn or ribbon to each end of the dowel. Add tassels if desired. Your banner is now ready to hang.

F. Let the banner dry. Place it in the sun or use a hair dryer to speed up the process.

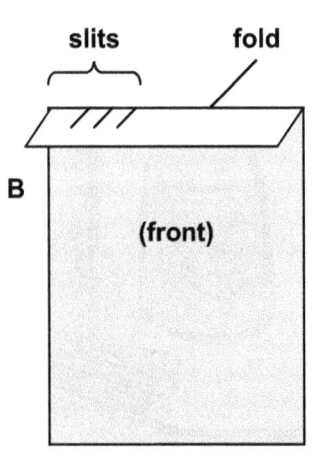 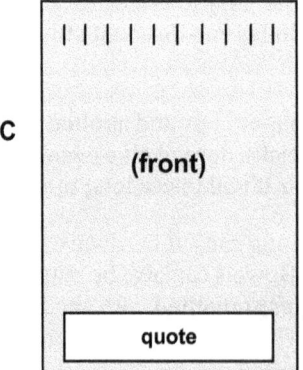 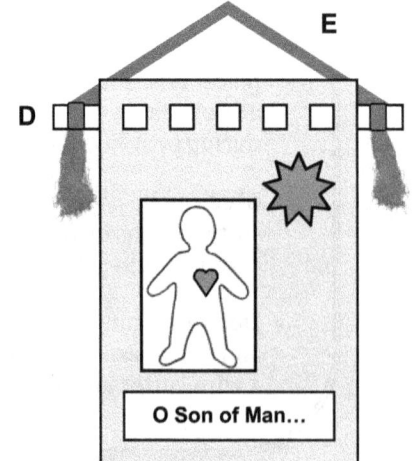

Bahá'í Children's Classes and Retreats: Theme 1, p. 114

God and the Universe – Lesson #4

Quotations for Spirit Banners

Make one copy of this page to post for reference. Make enough additional copies for each child to have one of the quotes. There are six different choices. Laminate the copies and cut along the lines, removing the numbers. Put the quotes in six numbered envelopes to make the selection process easier.

1	**O SON OF MAN!** …I knew My love for thee; therefore I created thee, have engraved on thee Mine image and revealed to thee My beauty. (Bahá'u'lláh, Arabic Hidden Words # 3)
2	I bear witness, O my God, that Thou hast created me to know Thee and to worship Thee. (Bahá'u'lláh, Prayers & Meditations, p. 313)
3	O God, guide me, protect me, make of me a shining lamp and a brilliant star. Thou art the Mighty and the Powerful. ('Abdu'l-Bahá, Bahá'í Prayers, p. 37)
4	**O God!** …Cultivate this fresh plant in the rose garden of Thy love and aid it to grow through the showers of Thy bounty. ('Abdu'l-Bahá, Baha'i Prayers, p. 35)
5	O Thou Compassionate God. Bestow upon me a heart which, like unto glass, may be illumined with the light of Thy love… ('Abdu'l-Bahá, Baha'i Prayers, p. 72)
6	O God! Refresh and gladden my spirit. Purify my heart. Illumine my powers. I lay all my affairs in Thy hand. ("Abdu'l-Bahá, Baha'i Prayers, p. 150)

Bahá'í Children's Classes and Retreats: Theme 1, p. 115

God and the Universe – Lesson #4

Patterns for Spirit Banners

(Photocopy this page and cut patterns from tag board
or stiff vinyl placemats for children to trace.)

Tip: For easier cut-outs, photocopy patterns
onto peel-and-stick adhesive paper.

God and the Universe – Lesson #4

Patterns for Spirit Banners

(Photocopy this page and post for reference.
Copy again and cut three small pattern pieces from tag board or vinyl.)

Bahá'í Children's Classes and Retreats: Theme 1, p. 117

God and the Universe – Lesson #4

MATERIALS NEEDED

- ☐ White board, easel, markers, eraser
- ☐ Folders with notebook paper, quote pages and song sheets for each student
- ☐ Pens or pencils for each student
- ☐ Dictionary
- ☐ Photograph of a baby[A]
- ☐ Large sheet of white butcher paper or chart paper[B]
- ☐ Dark crayon, masking tape or push pins, and felt marker for activity #3
- ☐ Felt lesson on "What Is a Human Being?" (script and patterns)
- ☐ Felt board and easel
- ☐ Handout titled "In the Image of God"
- ☐ Small hand mirror to accompany the above reading (optional)
- ☐ Instruction sheet for group discussion on "The Purpose of Life"
- ☐ Two-page handout of quotations on "God and the Universe"
- ☐ Poster titled "A Human Being Is…"
- ☐ Materials for Spirit Banner craft project (see separate list)
- ☐ Sample banners and instruction sheet for any assistants
- ☐ References for teachers (at the end of this book)

A. One example is available in the download packet for this teacher's guide: www.UnityWorksStore.com > Children's Classes > God and the Universe > Student Handouts.

B. Paper should be large enough for tracing around a real child. Tape two pieces together if necessary, and add a backing sheet so the marker doesn't bleed through and damage the wall. When tracing, place the paper directly on the floor or other hard surface.

* * * * *

Bahá'í Children's Classes and Retreats: Theme 1, p. 118

Additional Activities

God and the Universe

Additional Activities

If the children are interested and time is available, you may wish to plan one or more additional activities related to the theme of *God and the Universe*.

Kingdoms of Creation 121
    Dramatic Movement 121
    Twenty Questions 122
    Outdoor Kingdom Hunt 122
    Who Created It? 122
    Origami Craft 123
    Creation Boxes 124

Prayer Activities 125
    Prayer Tree 125
    Personal Prayer Book 127
    Prayer Learning Station 127

Word Puzzles 128
    Word Search 129
    Word Search with a Hidden Message 130
    Double Puzzle 131
    Letter Tiles 132
    Puzzle Solutions 133

God and the Universe – Additional Activities

Kingdoms of Creation

DRAMATIC MOVEMENT (5-10 min.)

This is a fun activity that is suitable for younger children. It can help them to internalize the different characteristics of each kingdom of creation. Begin by asking children to stand. Lead them in a few stretching exercises to loosen up, then say:

Let's pretend we're rocks!
- What do rocks do all day?
- Curl up and feel your heaviness.
- Close your eyes and listen to the silence.
- Let's see if we can be rocks for a whole minute.
- Is everyone ready? Go.

  (The children should try to remain motionless.)

Now, let's pretend we're plants!
- We're starting out as tiny seeds below the ground.
- Can you feel yourself starting to grow?
- Feel yourself pushing slowly up through the earth.
- Feel the warmth of the sun and reach towards it.
- Spread out your branches, stretching as far as you can.
- Now feel the breeze blowing gently through your leaves.

Now, let's pretend we're animals.
- Quietly think about which animal you'd like to be.
- Everybody can choose a different one.
- Think about how your animal moves.
- What sounds does it make?
- Now, walk around the room and "meet" the other animals.

  (The teacher may need to keep an eye on any carnivores!)

Now, let's be humans.
- We don't need to pretend!
- Walk around and introduce yourself to the other humans in the room.

20 QUESTIONS (5-15 min.)

This is a classic strategy game which helps to develop thinking and listening skills. One person thinks of an object and the others try to figure out what it is by asking simple questions. The first person should write the name of the object (animal, plant or mineral) on a piece of paper for the teacher to hold until the game ends. It should be something the children would know, but not a specific person, place or thing. For example, "a dog" is a good object, but "my dog Rover" is not allowed.

The questioning usually begins with: Is it animal, vegetable or mineral? After that, questions should have "yes" or "no" answers. The answer may also be "unknown" or "irrelevant." The class has twenty questions to guess the object. Make sure everyone has at least one chance to ask. If no one has guessed after twenty tries, share the answer, then give someone else a turn.

This is a great activity to fill time when the meal is late, or on a rainy day when outdoor activities are cancelled. If the children enjoy the game, they may wish to play it online as well: **http://20q.net**

OUTDOOR KINGDOM HUNT (15-20 min.)

Tell students they are going outside on a nature walk to find examples from each kingdom. They should bring paper with four labeled columns (mineral, plant, animal, human), pens or pencils, and a small notebook or clipboard to write on. Give them about ten minutes to work with adult supervision, then call them back inside to share. Rather than having each child repeat the same items when sharing (e.g. a pine tree), ask: *Who has something different for that category?*

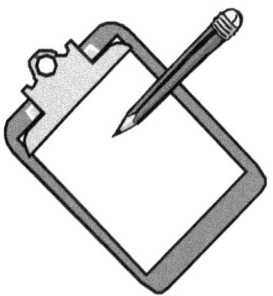

WHO CREATED IT? (15-20 min.)

CREATED BY		
People	**Animals**	**God**
house	bird's nest	people
car	gopher hole	birds
rock wall	barking noise	gophers
mirror	snail trail	rocks
shoes	baby animals*	animals

As a variation on the Kingdom Hunt activity above, have students list things by who made them. The notebook paper should be divided into three columns: *People, Animals* and *God*. Give them about ten minutes to work, then call them back inside to share. This activity can be done indoors, outdoors or both.

* If the children say that animals and humans create their own babies, you can explain that God created the very first parents, and designed them to reproduce, so there will always be more.

God and the Universe – Additional Activities

ORIGAMI (30-60 min.)

Origami is the traditional Japanese art of paper folding. It was developed hundreds of years ago, and has since evolved into a modern art form. The object is to transform a flat sheet of paper into a finished sculpture using a variety of folding techniques. If cutting and gluing are involved, the project is considered *kirigami*.

Origami is easy, inexpensive and fun to do. Children will enjoy creating a variety of plant and animal shapes to accompany their classroom activities on The Kingdoms of Creation. Origami can also help to:

- Teach children patience
- Build memory skills
- Encourage cooperation
- Improve fine motor skills
- Increase the ability to follow directions
- Reinforce math concepts such as fractions and pattern recognition
- Foster multi-cultural awareness
- Exercise the imagination

Origami comes from the Japanese words *ori* meaning "folding" and *kami* meaning "paper."

The following websites are filled with plenty of projects for beginners. They include folding instructions for hundreds of origami designs, by level of difficulty, complete with diagrams—some with video animation. The first site is especially good.

- http://en.origami-club.com
- www.origami-resource-center.com
- www.origami-instructions.com
- www.origami-fun.com

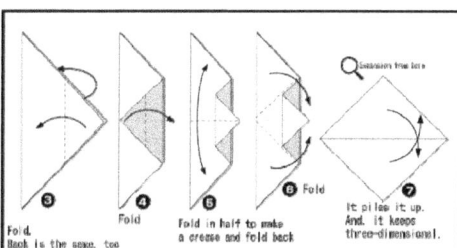

God and the Universe – Additional Activities

CREATION BOXES (15-20 min.)

This activity complements "Kingdom Categories" (Lesson #1, Activity #4). The boxes can be found inexpensively at Cash and Carry, or other food service supply stores.

Materials

- Small Chinese take-out boxes (one per child)
- Sticky labels for each kingdom (set of four for every child)
- Large basket filled with:
  - Polished rocks, minerals or plastic gemstones
  - Real or artificial leaves and flowers
  - Stickers, photographs or plastic figures of animals and people
- 3x5 cards (for mounting stickers and photographs)
- Felt markers for making labels and decorating the finished boxes
- Tape, glue or glue sticks

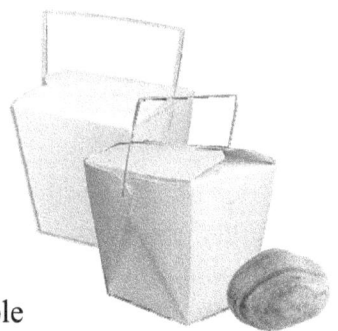

Tip: Labels can be pre-printed or children can write their own using a felt marker.

Instructions

1. Print your name on the bottom of the box.
2. Add one sticky label to each side, to represent the four kingdoms of creation.
3. Take four items from the basket, one for each kingdom, and put them in your box.
4. Attach any stickers and photographs to individual 3x5 cards.
5. Decorate the outside of your box.
6. Practice telling a classmate about the characteristics of each kingdom.
7. Bring the box home to share what you have learned.

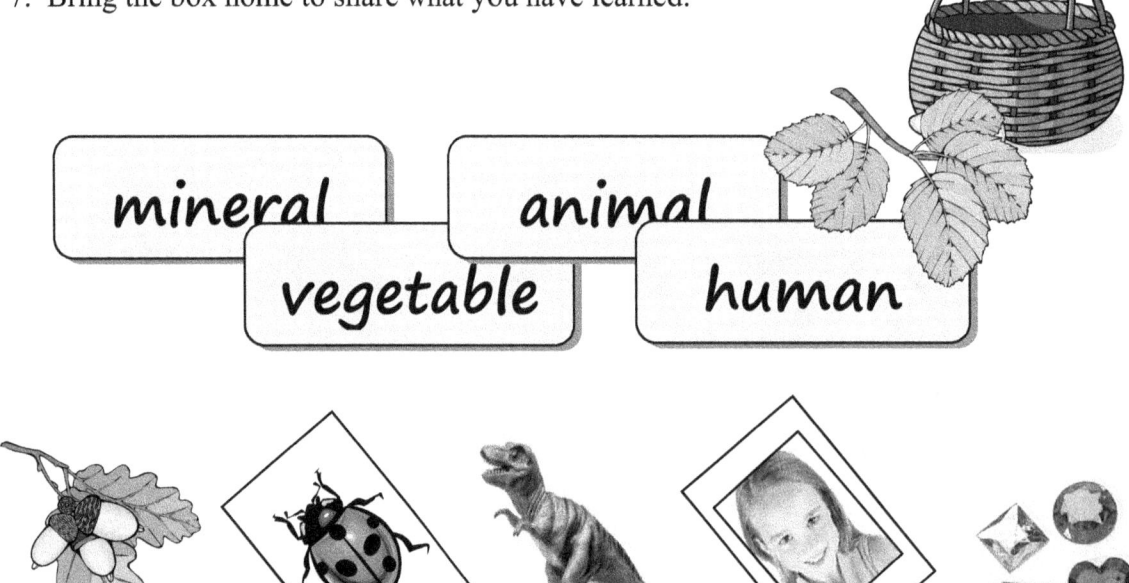

God and the Universe – Additional Activities

Prayer Activities

Prayer Tree (ongoing)

Materials

- ❑ Tree branch
- ❑ Construction paper
- ❑ Leaf patterns
- ❑ Pencils
- ❑ Scissors
- ❑ Black felt pens
- ❑ Masking tape

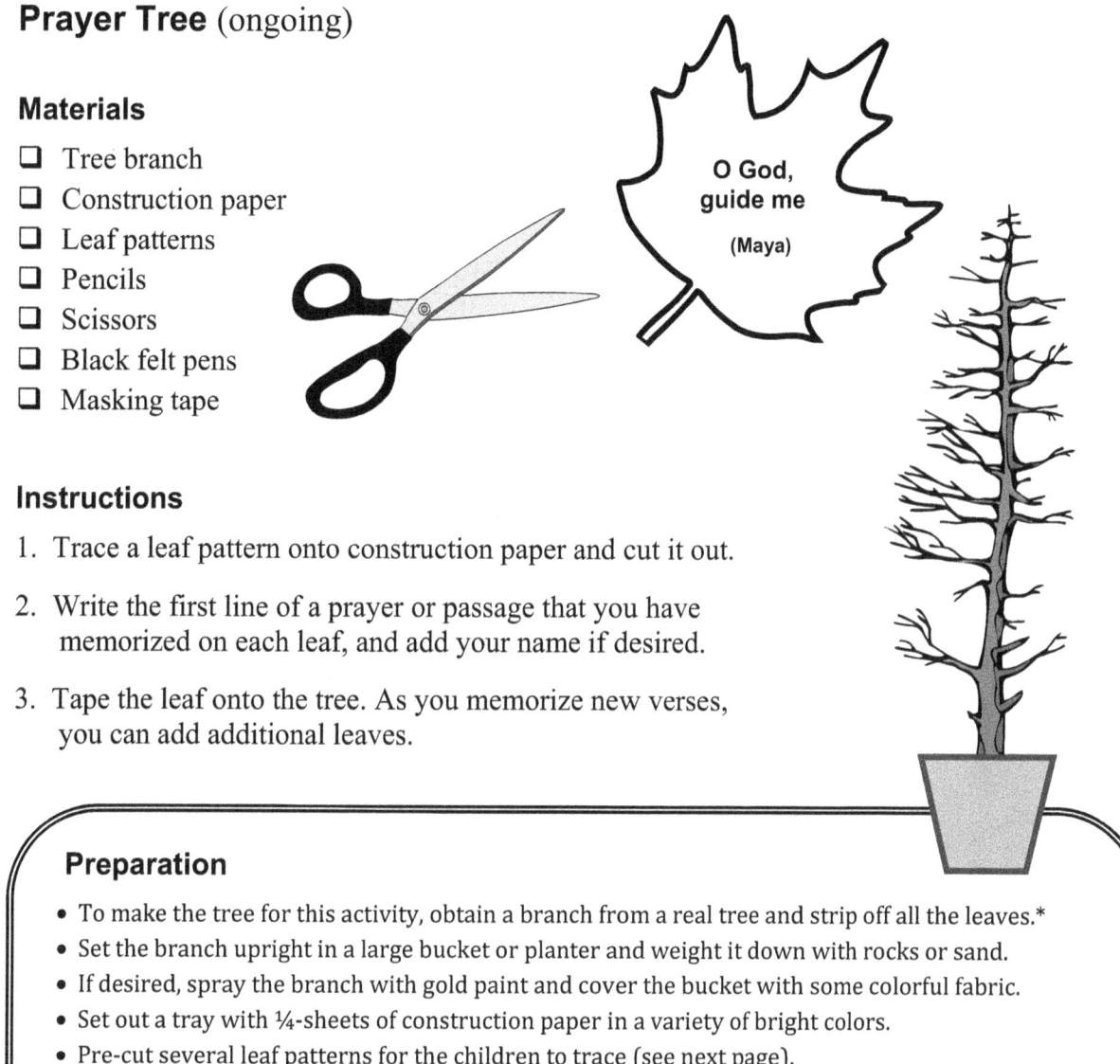

Instructions

1. Trace a leaf pattern onto construction paper and cut it out.

2. Write the first line of a prayer or passage that you have memorized on each leaf, and add your name if desired.

3. Tape the leaf onto the tree. As you memorize new verses, you can add additional leaves.

Preparation

- To make the tree for this activity, obtain a branch from a real tree and strip off all the leaves.*
- Set the branch upright in a large bucket or planter and weight it down with rocks or sand.
- If desired, spray the branch with gold paint and cover the bucket with some colorful fabric.
- Set out a tray with ¼-sheets of construction paper in a variety of bright colors.
- Pre-cut several leaf patterns for the children to trace (see next page).
- Post the quote from Bahá'u'lláh (see next page – quoted in Bahá'í Year Book, 1925-1926, p. 59, NSA USA - Developing Distinctive Bahá'í Communities).
- These materials can also be set out during the children's final performance, and audience members can be invited to add their own leaves to the tree.

---

* An easier (although less dramatic) tree can be made from brown construction paper mounted on poster board.

Note: This same tree can be used for the "Leaves of One Tree" craft for theme #5 on Unity.

God and the Universe – Additional Activities

"Let them memorize the Tablets of the Merciful..."

(Bahá'u'lláh)

> **Add your memorized verses to the prayer tree.**

Copy onto cardstock. Cut on dotted line and post sign next to tree. →

Cut leaf patterns from tag board or vinyl place mats.

God and the Universe
Additional Activities

Leaf pattern for Prayer Tree

God and the Universe
Additional Activities

Leaf pattern for Prayer Tree

Bahá'í Children's Classes and Retreats: Theme 1, p. 126

Personal Prayer Book

Materials

- Plain white paper cut into ½ sheets
- Plain manila folders cut in half across the width
- Stapler and extra staples
- Pencils, pens, felt markers

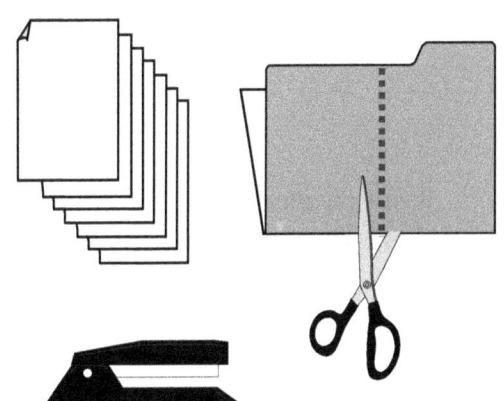

Instructions

1. Take 5 or more sheets of paper and stack together.
2. Place the paper inside the manila folder and staple through the cover.
3. Write your name on the front and decorate the cover.
4. On each page of your book, write one new prayer or passage that you want to learn. See prayer station (below) for ideas.

Prayer Learning Station

Materials

- Personal prayer books (see above)
- Page of quotations on God and the Universe (see handouts)
- Pencils, pens, markers, stickers

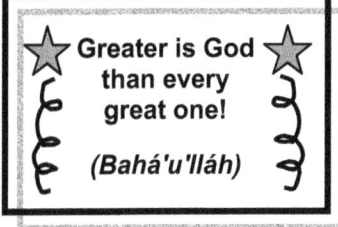

Greater is God than every great one! (Bahá'u'lláh)

Instructions

1. Locate the page of quotations titled "God and the Universe."
2. Choose one quote that you would like to learn by heart.
3. Copy it neatly on the first page of your personal prayer book.
4. Add beautiful designs around the quote to decorate it.
5. Say the words out loud many times and practice with a friend.
6. When you have the quote memorized, add a leaf to the prayer tree.

Note to Teachers: If time is available, you can set up several stations: one for copying prayers, one for decorating them, one where students work in pairs to memorize their quotes, one where they make an audio recording of the quotes, and one where they recite what they have learned. Prayers can be available in different languages as well.

God and the Universe – Additional Activities

Word Puzzles

Word puzzles are fun to do and are designed to reinforce the topics studied during class. They can be set out during free time, or offered to children who finish a task early and would like something else to do.

The puzzles on the following pages were produced using PuzzleMaker online at: < www.discoveryeducation.com/free-puzzlemaker >. Teachers and children can make their own puzzles as well. The solutions are found at the end of this section.

God and the Universe – Additional Activities

Word Search

Word search puzzles are great fun and are easy to do. Just circle the words that have been hidden in the grid. The first one has been done for you as an example. Words can be written going up, down, forward, backward or diagonally.

```
q d p l e r b p b e
u o h t a z w o r n
r a t s i m z w i i
y t h g i m p e l m
t c e t o r p r l u
e q x h j n g f i l
q d w g e r q u a l
c d i o l a o l n i
[a r t] u k x r i t m
m a k e g k b t n b
```

√ art   illumine   powerful
brilliant   lamp   protect
guide   make   star
heart   mighty   thou

The words come from a favorite prayer for children.

Word Search with a Hidden Message

Word search puzzles are great fun and are easy to do. Just circle the words that have been hidden in the grid. The first one has been done for you as an example. Words can be written going up, down, forward, backward or diagonally. Sometimes a letter can be part of two or more words.

This puzzle has a secret message. After you have circled all of the hidden words, the remaining letters will form a message that is related to the topic of our class. Solve the puzzle and write the secret message on the lines below.

```
P Y U T G O D M I E N I V I D
A T N F A S T B E S T O W E R
R H K H A E S U O R E N E G G
D G N I K S R E G D C R E A N
O I O T E S H G N T M I Y S I
N M W F O R G I V I N G F T V
E E A I R Y K O O F A L L U O
R I B R N I N F I N I T E L L
E X L W O V A N C I E N T U U
T N E T O P I N M O D R D F N
C R E A T O R S G K D Y N R S
L U F H T I A F I N R L E E E
A L M I G H T Y  V B O O I W E
L A N R E T E L E D L H R O N
E X A L T E D K R L W E F P O
```

√ ALMIGHTY	FAITHFUL	HOLY	MERCIFUL
ANCIENT	FASHIONER	INFINITE	MIGHTY
BESTOWER	FORGIVING	INVISIBLE	OMNIPOTENT
CREATOR	FRIEND	KIND	PARDONER
DIVINE	GENEROUS	KING	POWERFUL
ETERNAL	GIVER	LORD	UNKNOWABLE
EXALTED	GREAT	LOVING	UNSEEN

Secret message: __ __ __   __ __ __   __ __ __ __ __ __ __   __ __ __ __ __ __ __

__ __ __ __ __ __ __ __ __   __ __   __ __ __   __ __ __ __

God and the Universe – Additional Activities

Double Puzzle

Unscramble each of the clue words. Copy the letters in the numbered boxes into the boxes with the same number at the bottom of the page. The first one has been done for you as an example

Hint: If you get stuck, you can find many of these words in the song, "The Kingdoms of God."

Bahá'í Children's Classes and Retreats: Theme 1, p. 131

Letter Tiles

Unscramble the boxes to reveal a message.
If you get stuck, use a scissors to cut the boxes apart first.

| N G | L K I | P R A | T A | W I T | O D | I S | Y E R | H G |

***

| D | I | H E | S S E | S T | S P O | B L E | T |

***

(Spanish) Ponga las fichas en orden para revelar un mensaje.

| O | E | I T I | S | E | B E N | O | L | S | D I T |

God and the Universe – Additional Activities

Puzzle Solutions

 Word Search

Word Search with a Hidden Message
(See next page)

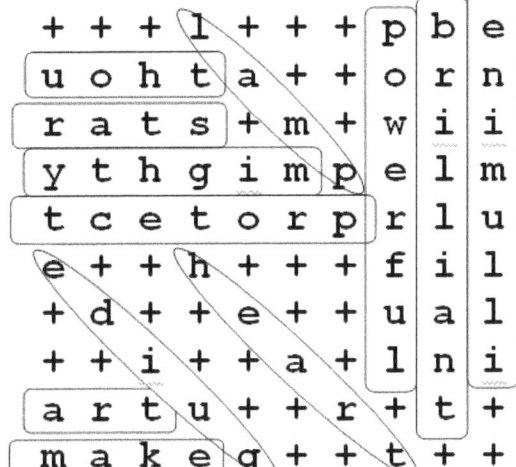

 **Letter Tiles**

PRA	YER	IS	TA
L K I	NG	WIT H	G OD

(Prayer is talking with God)

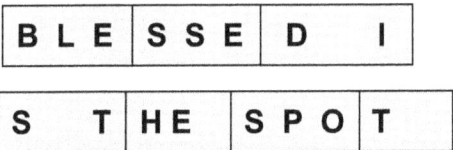

(Blessed is the spot)

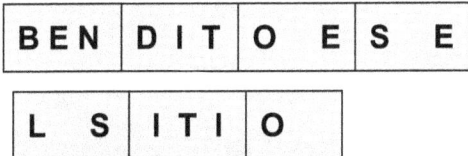

(Bendito es el sitio)

Double Puzzle

mineral	girl
plant	grow
animal	move
human	see
rock	hear
tree	taste
frog	smell
cat	think
elephant	feel
boy	know

The Kingdoms of Creation

Bahá'í Children's Classes and Retreats: Theme 1, p. 133

God and the Universe – Additional Activities

— Solution —

Word Search with a Hidden Message

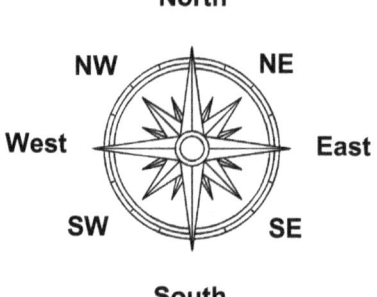

SOLUTION (column, row, direction)

ALMIGHTY (1,13,E)	FAITHFUL (8,12,W)	HOLY (12,14,N)	MERCIFUL (8,1,SE)
ANCIENT (7,9,E)	FASHIONER (4,2,SE)	INFINITE (6,8,E)	MIGHTY (2,6,N)
BESTOWER (8,2,E)	FORGIVING (4,6,E)	INVISIBLE (4,7,SE)	OMNIPOTENT (10,10,W)
CREATOR (1,11,E)	FRIEND (13,15,N)	KIND (7,7,NE)	PARDONER (1,1,S)
DIVINE (15,1,W)	GENEROUS (14,3,W)	KING (5,4,W)	POWERFUL (14,15,N)
ETERNAL (7,14,W)	GIVER (9,11,S)	LORD (11,14,N)	UNKNOWABLE (3,1,S)
EXALTED (1,15,E)	GREAT (8,5,NW)	LOVING (15,8,N)	UNSEEN (15,9,S)

Secret message: God is the greatest mystery of all.

Children's Performance

God and the Universe

CHILDREN'S PERFORMANCE*

To the Coordinator

The children's performance provides students with an opportunity to demonstrate and reinforce what they have learned. This is often the highlight for children and adults. The fact that children will be performing in front of a live audience serves as excellent motivation for them to learn the material presented in class. The program includes prayers, songs, memorized passages, short talks, demonstrations, a showing of crafts, a quiz show, humor and a dramatic reading. The following pages include a detailed agenda for the event, rehearsal instructions, scripts and other materials. Feel free to modify the program to suit the needs of the participants.

As the coordinator, it will be helpful for you to sit in on classes and take notes on which children might be best suited for which type of presentation. Some will memorize quotes easily, others may be good at explaining a concept, and still others might enjoy acting or saying a prayer. Assign parts or ask for volunteers. Be sure everyone is included.

One or two children should be asked to serve as Master or Mistress of Ceremonies (MC). Select children who are responsible, with strong voices and stage presence, who can keep the program moving forward. This places the children center stage and in charge of the presentation.

Before the rehearsal, gather any props and costumes, and remind the adult and youth volunteers that you will need their assistance. Determine their preferences for rehearsal groups. A copy of the agenda and the rehearsal groups should be given to each volunteer. Copies of the appropriate script or reading should be given to the adults and children who will be working on that part of the program.

Rehearsal for the Show

During rehearsal time, the coordinator's tasks include:

- ❑ Meet together with all the participants to explain the nature of the program.
- ❑ Talk about program order, where to sit, use of strong voices so the audience can hear, eye contact, learning the parts rather than reading them, and how to use a microphone if needed.
- ❑ Assign adults and youth to work with each rehearsal group.
- ❑ Assign parts to each child depending on interest and ability.
- ❑ Distribute costumes and props as appropriate.
- ❑ Inform groups when the rehearsal time is almost over.
- ❑ Collect all props and set them out for the show.

> * Note: While the children's performance has typically been scheduled for the evening, the program could be held at any time. During a weekend retreat, Saturday evening is often the most convenient time for inviting neighbors and friends. This means that activities from the fourth class on Sunday morning will not be included in the presentation. If using a weekly format, however, these activities can easily be added to the final program.

God and the Universe – Children's Performance

MATERIALS NEEDED

Note: Items in italics are included with this section.

- *Agenda*
- *Rehearsal groups, scripts and readings*
- Welcome sign (if desired)
- *Sample program* (for distributing to the audience)
- Background music (to be played as people are arriving)
- Microphone and sound system (if needed)
- Art exhibit (children's art can be hung from a clothesline or displayed on a table)
- Song sheets for all (including audience) and music (for song leader)
- *An American Indian Prayer*
- Memory quotes
- *The Kingdoms of Creation* (felt lesson with script and felt board)
- *True Understanding* (reading and pictures)
- *Kids' Questions About God* (as developed by the children)
- *The Universe* (demonstration with script and props)
- *Some Divine Humor*
- *The Names of God* (reading with music and candles)
- *Lamp Demonstration* (with props)
- *Prayer Postures Demonstration* (with small rug)
- *Quiz Show on Prayer* (with costumes and props if desired)
- Prayer maps
- Craft samples:
    - ___ Kingdom collage booklet
    - ___ Wall mural
    - ___ Coloring pages
    - ___ Blessed is the Spot booklet
    - ___ God's eye
    - ___ Prayer pouch
    - ___ Spirit banners
    - ___ Origami figures
- Refreshments

God and the Universe – Children's Performance

SAMPLE AGENDA FOR MC _____ (90 min.)

(1) Welcome guests to our program on **"GOD AND THE UNIVERSE"**

(2) Opening music _____

(3) Opening prayer (American Indian Prayer: "Oh, Great Spirit...") _____

(4) Intro *(don't read):* Bahá'ís believe there is only one God, creator of the universe. God is a mystery. We can't see Him, but we know He exists. God created us because He loves us, and He wants us to know and to love Him. We can speak to God through our prayers. One of the Bahá'í prayers says:

> *"I bear witness, O my God, that Thou hast created me to know Thee and to worship Thee. I testify, at this moment, to my powerlessness and to Thy might, to my poverty and to Thy wealth. There is none other God but Thee, the Help in Peril, the Self-Subsisting."*

(5) Introduce each section and each presenter, and thank them afterwards.

THE KINGDOMS OF CREATION (20 min.)

- ☐ Song: I'll Sing You a Rock (ALL)
- ☐ Felt Lesson: Kingdoms of Creation _____ _____
- ☐ Kingdom collage booklet, origami (crafts) _____ _____
- ☐ Memory quote #14 ("With the hands of power...") _____

GOD, THE CREATOR (30 min.)

- ☐ Song: O God, Guide Me (ALL)
- ☐ True Understanding (reading with photos) _____ _____
- ☐ Kids' Questions About God _____
- ☐ The Universe (demonstration) _____ _____ _____
- ☐ Some Divine Humor _____ _____ _____
- ☐ Eye of God, Blessed is the Spot booklet (crafts) _____ _____ _____ _____
- ☐ Memory quote #1 ("Greater is God...") _____
- ☐ Memory quote #2 ("God in His wisdom...") _____
- ☐ Dramatic reading: The Names of God ⟶ 1._____ 2._____ 3._____ 4._____

PRAYER, OUR CONNECTION WITH GOD (30 min.)

- ☐ Song: Pray to God (ALL)
- ☐ Memory quote #11 ("Intone, O My servants...") _____
- ☐ Lamp demo: Our Connection With God _____
- ☐ Prayer postures demo (bad and good) _____ _____
- ☐ Additional memory quotes _____ _____ _____
- ☐ Show prayer maps _____ _____
- ☐ Song: Love, Love, Love (ALL)
- ☐ Prayer pouch, spirit banner (crafts) _____ _____ _____ _____
- ☐ Quiz show on prayer ⟶ 1._____ 2._____ 3._____ 4._____
- ☐ Song: Blessed is the Spot (ALL STAND)
- ☐ *Say: "We hope you liked our program. Please join us for refreshments!"*

God and the Universe – Children's Performance

REHEARSAL GROUPS

Scripts and instructions are included on the following pages.

PROGRAM COORDINATOR: _____ MC: _____

- ❑ Select and orient 1 or 2 MCs. Provide a clipboard, pencil and copy of the agenda.
- ❑ Divide children into 4 groups and assign volunteers to each group (7-8 volunteers total).
- ❑ Make sure each child has at least one part in addition to the group songs.
- ❑ The dramatic reading can be practiced after the other small group rehearsals if necessary.
- ❑ Songs can be practiced together after the rehearsal and again after dinner.
- ❑ Invite several children to talk about their craft projects (see below).
- ❑ One or two children can be asked to perform a short musical selection to begin the program.

Rehearse each part below with the children. The order will be different during the show.

GROUP #1: Demonstrations *(1-2 adults + 3 or more children)*
- ❑ The Universe (2 narrators + 1 actor)
- ❑ Lamp demo (1 child)
- ❑ Show and talk about both prayer maps (2 children)
- ❑ Prayer postures demo (2 or 3 children)

GROUP #2: Memory Quotes, Crafts *(2 adults + 5 or more children)*
- ❑ Opening prayer
- ❑ Memory quotes (incl. #1, #2, #4, #11, #14)
- ❑ Have children show and talk about each craft made *(1 or more children for each)*
    * Collage booklet _____ _____
    * Eye of God _____ _____
    * Blessed Is the Spot booklet _____ _____
    * Prayer pouch _____ _____
    * Spirit banners _____ _____
    * Origami _____ _____

GROUP #3: Felt Lesson, Readings, Jokes, Quiz Show *(2 adults + 4 or more children)*
- ❑ Felt lesson on *The Kingdoms of Creation* (2 children)
- ❑ *True Understanding* reading with photos (2 children)
- ❑ Kids' Questions About God (2 alternating readers)
- ❑ Some Divine Humor (1 to 4 children)
- ❑ Quiz show on Prayer (4 children)

GROUP #4: Dramatic Reading *(1 adult + 4 children)*
- ❑ The Names of God

GROUP #5: Songs *(1 adult + all children)*
- ❑ Practice after dinner or as time permits.

An American Indian Prayer

*Oh, Great Spirit,
whose voice I hear in the winds
and whose breath gives life to all the world, hear me.*

*I am small and weak.
I need your strength and wisdom.
Let me walk in beauty and make my eyes
ever behold the red and purple sunset.
Make my hands respect the things you have made
and my ears sharp to hear your voice.
Make me wise so that I may understand
the things you have taught my people.
Let me learn the lessons you have hidden
in every leaf and rock.*

*I seek strength, not to be superior to my brother,
but to fight my greatest enemy - myself.
Make me always ready to come to you
with clean hands and straight eyes,
so when life fades, as the fading sunset,
my spirit will come to you
without shame.*

**Chief Yellow Lark
Lakota Nation - 1887**

God and the Universe – Children's Performance

Script for Felt Lesson

"The Kingdoms of Creation"

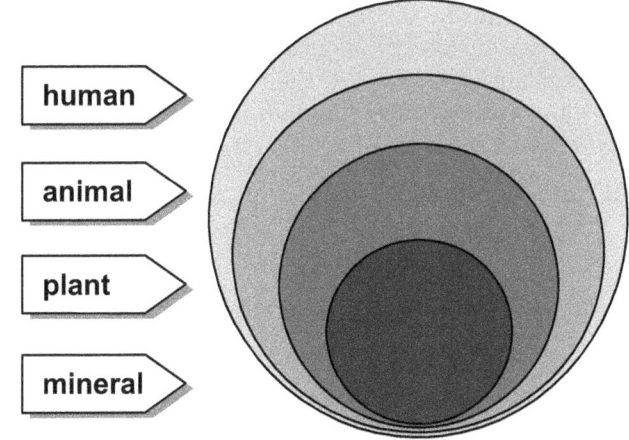

	NARRATION	ACTION
1	We're going to talk about the **Kingdoms of Creation**.	Place title on felt board.
2	This represents the **mineral** kingdom - the lowest level of the kingdoms of creation. Minerals have the power of cohesion or attraction. That's the force that holds things together.	Place smallest circle on felt board, and add the **mineral** label, as shown.
3	This represents the vegetable or **plant** kingdom. Plants have the power of cohesion, just like minerals, but they also have something new: the power of growth.	Slip next largest circle under mineral kingdom, and add the **plant** label.
4	This represents the **animal** kingdom. Like minerals, animals have cohesion, and like plants, they have the power of growth, but they add something new. Animals have feelings and the power of the senses. Animals can see and hear. They can taste and smell. They can feel heat and cold, hunger and thirst. They also have the power to move from place to place.	Add next largest circle under plant kingdom, and add the **animal** label.
5	This represents the **human** kingdom. In addition to the powers of the mineral, the plant and the animal, humans also have the power of conscious thought. Through scientific investigation, we can discover the laws of nature and the secrets of the universe. And there is something else special about humans. We have free will, to choose right or wrong, and we can learn to know and love God.	Add next largest circle under animal kingdom, and add the **human** label.

God and the Universe – Children's Performance

TRUE UNDERSTANDING

Obtain a large color picture of one item from each kingdom. The images on the following four pages can be photocopied, or downloaded in color from: www.UnityWorksStore.com. Click on Children's Classes > God and the Universe > Student Handouts. Photos can also be found in magazines, online and in clip art programs. During the performance, one child can hold up the pictures while the other speaks about each item, or the children can alternate, each presenting two of the kingdoms. The relevant section of the script can be taped to the back of each picture to help children remember their parts.

Although the mineral, vegetable,
animal and man all exist,
yet the **mineral** has no knowledge of the vegetable.
A diamond can't imagine or understand a plant.

It is the same with the **vegetable**.
Any progress it may make,
however highly it may become developed,
it will never comprehend the animal.
A plant has no ears, no sight, no understanding.

It is the same with the **animal**.
However much it may progress in its own kingdom,
however refined its feelings may become,
it will have no real understanding of the world
of man or of his special abilities of the mind.
The animal cannot understand the roundness
of the earth, or its motion in space,
or the central position of the sun.

Although the mineral, vegetable, animal
and **man himself** are actual beings,
the lower kingdoms cannot understand
the essence and nature of the higher kingdoms.
This being so, how can man comprehend God?

(Adapted from: 'Abdu'l-Bahá in London, p: 22)

God and the Universe – Children's Performance

True Understanding: Mineral

God and the Universe – Children's Performance

True Understanding: Vegetable

God and the Universe – Children's Performance

True Understanding: Animal

God and the Universe – Children's Performance

True Understanding: Human

God and the Universe – Children's Performance

Kids' Questions About God

(Alternate readers)

Reader #1: These are some of the things our class wanted to know about God.

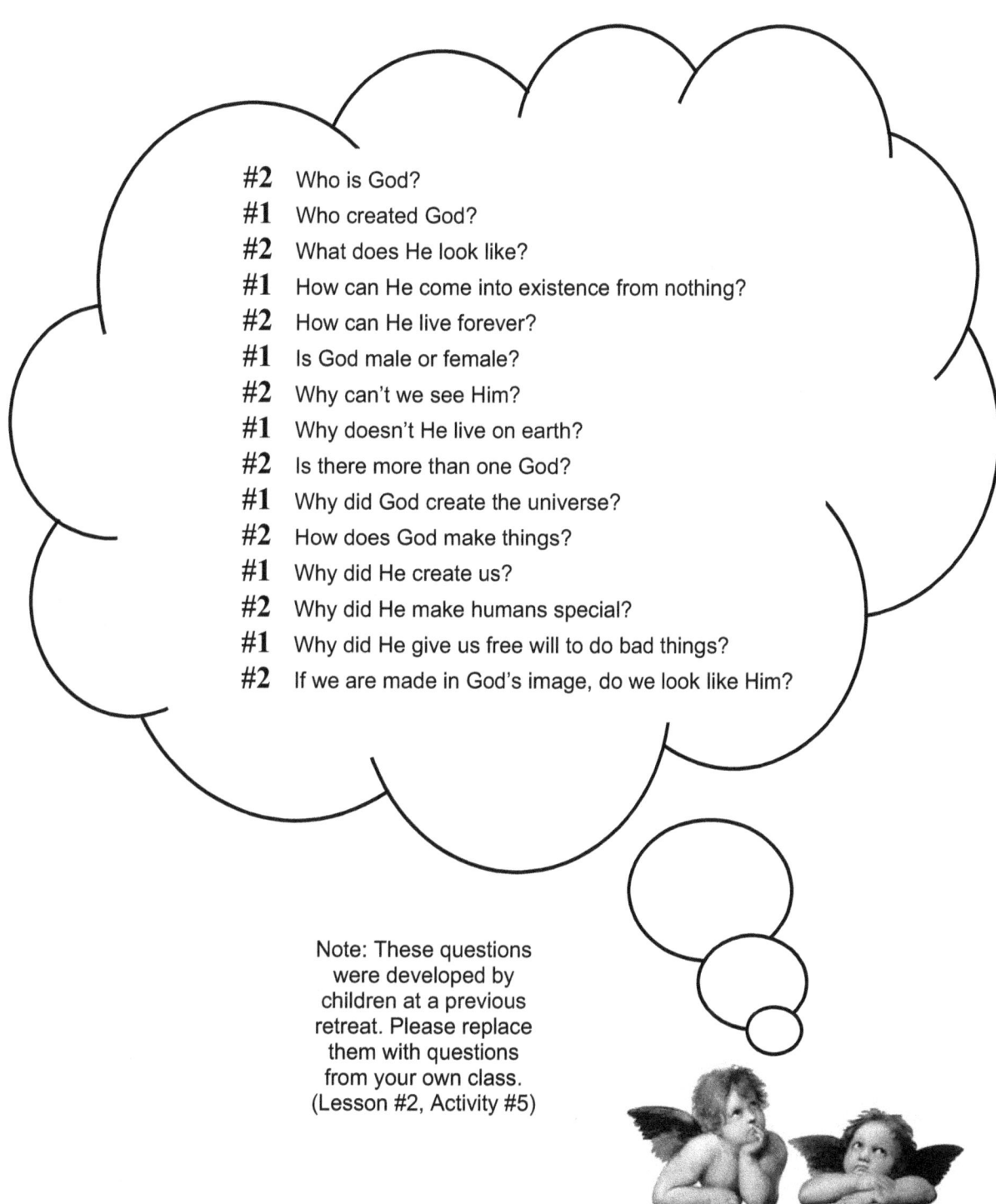

- #2 Who is God?
- #1 Who created God?
- #2 What does He look like?
- #1 How can He come into existence from nothing?
- #2 How can He live forever?
- #1 Is God male or female?
- #2 Why can't we see Him?
- #1 Why doesn't He live on earth?
- #2 Is there more than one God?
- #1 Why did God create the universe?
- #2 How does God make things?
- #1 Why did He create us?
- #2 Why did He make humans special?
- #1 Why did He give us free will to do bad things?
- #2 If we are made in God's image, do we look like Him?

Note: These questions were developed by children at a previous retreat. Please replace them with questions from your own class. (Lesson #2, Activity #5)

God and the Universe – Children's Performance

The Universe

(Sample script for demonstration – from Lesson #2, Activity #6)

Needed: Two narrators and one actor, small box filled with plastic letters, table covered with tablecloth, stiff placemat, tray, Lego or similar building-block construction hidden under table.

NARRATION	ACTION
(Pause between phrases while each action is performed.)	*(Start with the plastic letters spread out on the placemat inside the tray.)*
1. *(First Speaker)* Some people say there is no God, and that the universe created itself by accident. That the whole world came into being just by chance.	1. Point skyward to indicate God. Shrug shoulders at the word *accident*. Use a circular hand motion to indicate *the world*. 
2. That would be like putting a bunch of letters into a box, shaking it, dumping out the letters, and expecting them to form a beautiful poem. That just doesn't seem possible!	2. Carefully pick up the mat and pour the letters into the box. Pick up the box of letters, shake it, then dump the letters out onto the tray again.
3. Besides, **who** made the letters in the first place? **Who** put them into the box, and **who** poured them out?	3. Hold up one letter for the audience to see. 
4. *(Second Speaker)* Yeah! That would be like knocking over a box of Legos, and just by chance, they turned into this. I don't **think** so! Someone had to create a design and put the pieces together. That took a lot of planning and work!	4. Bring out hidden Lego construction, e.g. an elaborate boat or castle. 
5. *(First Speaker)* The creation of the universe is the same. This infinite universe with all its greatness and perfect order could not have come into existence all by itself – just by accident. How can there be an effect, without a cause?	5. Wait for the applause, bow, then remove the props. 

God and the Universe – Children's Performance

Some Divine Humor

Photocopy this page and cut along the lines. Select one or more jokes for the children to tell. They can either read the joke or tell it in their own words.

God is Watching

The children were lined up in the school cafeteria for lunch. In the middle of the table was a large pile of red apples. The teacher wrote a note and posted it on the apple tray, "Take only one. God is watching."

At the end of the table, near a large pile of chocolate chip cookies, one child whispered to another, "Take all you want. God is watching the apples."

The Image of God

A kindergarten teacher was watching her students draw pictures. She walked around to see each child's work. As she got to one little boy who was hard at work, she asked what the drawing was. "I'm drawing God," the boy replied. The teacher paused and said, "But no one knows what God looks like."

Without looking up from his drawing, the boy said, "They will in a minute."

Absent-Minded Professor

A college class was discussing the existence of God. The professor used the following logic:

"Has anyone in this class seen God?"
(No one answered.)
"Has anyone in class touched God?"
(Again, no answer.)
"Then there is no God," said the professor.

A student asked for permission to reply.

"Just because you can't see something," she said, "doesn't mean it isn't real."

"Has anyone in class seen our professor's brain?" she asked.

"Has anyone in class touched our professor's brain?"
(No one had.)

"Then, I rest my case."

Original Dirt

One day a group of scientists got together and decided that people had come a long way and no longer needed God. So they picked one scientist to go and tell Him. The scientist walked up to God and said, "We can clone animals, heal the sick, and create life, so we've decided that we no longer need You."

God listened very patiently to the scientist, then said, "Very well, how about this. Let's say we have a people-making contest?"

"OK, great!" the scientist replied. And God added, "We'll do it just like I did back in the old days with Adam and Eve."

"Sure, no problem," said the scientist, and bent down to grab a handful of dirt.

But God looked at the scientist and said, "No, no, no. You go get your own dirt!"

Bahá'í Children's Classes and Retreats: Theme 1, p. 149

God and the Universe – Children's Performance

The Names of God

This devotional activity was developed by Gary Bulkin, using terms from the Bahá'í Writings.

Select four children who read well and give each one a copy of the chart on the following page. The children should stand in the four corners of the room (A, B, C, D).

The first reader begins by reading line #1 from the first column ("Lauded be Thy name"). Then the second reader reads line #1 from the second column ("O my God…"). The third and fourth readers continue in the same manner. Then each reader reads line #2, and so forth, until the page is completed. The entire reading takes approximately 4 minutes.

When rehearsing with the children, encourage them to speak slowly and clearly, in a strong voice that can be heard on the other side of the room. They should also wait a moment before speaking, to leave a brief silence between them and the previous reader, so the words aren't all crowded together. The children may need help with the pronunciation of certain words.

If desired, a more spiritual atmosphere can be created by dimming the lights, by having each child hold a lighted candle, and by playing soft music in the background as they recite the Names of God.

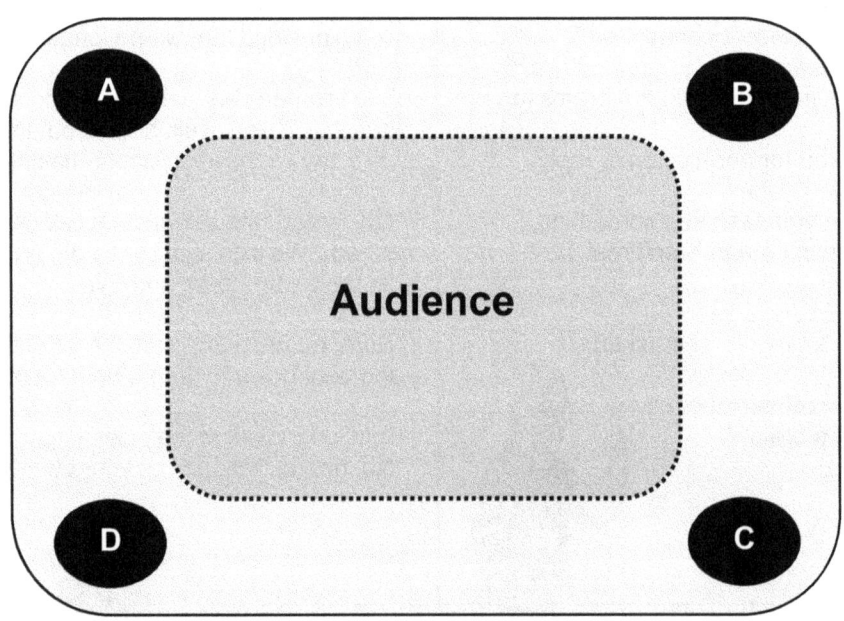

Tip: Use a highlighter pen to mark each child's part.

The Names of God

Line	Reader One	Line	Reader Two	Line	Reader Three	Line	Reader Four
1	Lauded be Thy name	1	O my God and the God of all things	1	my Glory and the Glory of all things	1	my Desire and the Desire of all things
2	my Strength and the Strength of all things	2	my King and the King of all things	2	my Possessor and the Possessor of all things	2	my Aim and the Aim of all things
3	my Mover and the Mover of all things	3	the Most Holy	3	the Most Luminous	3	the Most Mighty
4	the Most Great	4	the Most Exalted	4	the Most Glorious	4	O Lord my God
5	my Haven in my distress	5	my Shield and my Shelter in my woes	5	my Asylum and Refuge in time of need	5	in my loneliness my Companion
6	in my anguish my Solace	6	in my solitude a loving Friend	6	the Helper	6	the Healer
7	the Generous	7	the Bountiful	7	the Giver	7	the Gracious
8	Ever-Forgiving	8	Merciful	8	Compassionate	8	the Bestower
9	All-Knowing	9	All-Loving	9	Omniscient	9	the Precious
10	the Powerful	10	Omnipotent	10	the King	10	the Maker
11	the Fashioner	11	the Preserver	11	the Pardoner	11	the Kind One
12	All-Possessing	12	All-Subduing	12	All-Powerful	12	Almighty
13	Thou kind Father, God!	13	One Who overlooketh the shortcomings of all mankind	13	the Ancient	13	the Ever-Abiding
14	the Changeless	14	the Eternal	14	the One	14	the Single
15	Untrammeled	15	Exalted	15	Strong	15	Faithful
16	the Help in Peril	16	the Inaccessible	16	Unsearchable	16	Incomparable
17	the Lord of grace abounding	17	I beseech Thee, O Thou Who art the Beloved of the hearts which long for Thee	17	by the Manifestations of Thy Cause	17	and the Daysprings of Thine inspiration
18	and the Exponents of Thy majesty	18	and the Treasuries of Thy knowledge	18	not to suffer me to be deprived of Thy Holy Habitation	18	Thy Fane
19	and Thy Tabernacle	19	No God is there but Thee	19	the God of power	19	the God of glory
20	Praised be God, the Lord of the worlds!						

(Note: The final line can be read in unison by all four readers if desired.)

God and the Universe – Children's Performance

LAMP DEMONSTRATION

One child should practice the demonstration, using his or her own words. See example below.

(1) Plug in a lamp in front of the room, and tell the audience:

I'm going to demonstrate our connection with God.

(2) Ask them:

What is this? *(A lamp.)*

(3) Turn the lamp on and ask:

What is the purpose of the lamp? *(To give light.)*

(4) Unplug the lamp and turn it on and off several times.

What happens if it's not plugged in when I turn it on? *(No light.)*
Why isn't there any light? *(It's not connected to the electricity.)*

(5) Explain:

- Let's say the lamp represents a human being,
- The cord represents prayer - our connection to God.
- The electricity represents the invisible Spirit of God that gives us light.
- It's easy to see that if we're not connected to God through our prayers, then our spiritual light can't shine.

Bahá'í Children's Classes and Retreats: Theme 1, p. 152

God and the Universe – Children's Performance

prayer postures demonstration

One child should set out a prayer rug in front of the room, then either read the passage below, or explain the concept of reverence in her or his own words.

> **Reverence** is a feeling of deep love and respect for God. This feeling is inside our hearts and is reflected in our actions, like bowing to a king. In some parts of the world, reverence is shown by kneeling quietly with hands together, eyes closed, and head bowed. In other places, reverence is shown by standing with eyes open and hands reaching up to our Creator. There are many ways to show reverence, but they all produce a feeling of opening our hearts and minds to be filled with the spirit of God.
> When we pray, our minds should concentrate and our bodies should reflect the reverence that is in our hearts.

That child should then invite one or more additional children to demonstrate several sloppy or disrespectful postures, then some reverent ones.

God and the Universe – Children's Performance

Quiz Show on Prayer

- ❑ Determine which child will be the host and which three will be panelists.
- ❑ The host should explain that the quiz is about: *why, when and where we should pray.*
- ❑ Line the children up (either standing or sitting) facing the audience.
- ❑ Have the host ask the questions below, in order.
- ❑ Panelists can take turns answering, or they might ring a bell or make another sound when they wish to be called on. (Make it fun!)
- ❑ During the program, panelists can confer among themselves or ask an audience member for assistance if needed.

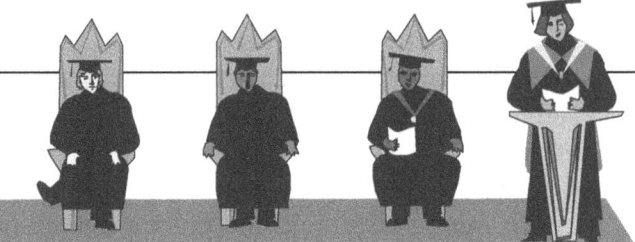

1. What is prayer? *(Conversation with God.)*

2. Who should pray? *(Everyone.)*

3. When should we pray? *(God is always listening so we can talk with Him anytime. Morning, noon and evening are special times of remembrance.)*

4. Where should we pray? Do we have to be in a special building or church? *(We can pray anywhere, but special buildings such as churches, temples, mosques and houses of worship have been set aside just for this purpose.)*

5. What should we pray for? *(The Bahá'í Writings are filled with prayers for many things. Let the panelists share their thoughts.)*

6. Is there anything we should **not** pray for? *(For example, is it OK to pray for a new bike, or for a teammate to get hurt so you can play? Probably not, as these would be selfish requests. Encourage the panelists to share their thoughts.)*

7. Why should we pray? *(Prayer connects us with God. It increases capacity and understanding, protects us from tests, brings divine assistance, leads to healing, strengthens our moral courage, refreshes and gladdens our spirits, purifies our hearts, etc.)*

8. Can we sing or chant while praying? *(Yes. We are encouraged to chant melodiously.)*

9. Can we pray in any language? *(Yes. God hears all prayers.)*

10. Is it possible to pray without words? *(Yes.)* How? *(Our thoughts and actions can also be beautiful prayers.)*

God and the Universe – Children's Performance

Sample program for the audience

Bahá'í Children's Class Performance

God and the Universe

"God in His wisdom has created all things." –'Abdu'l-Bahá

Welcome

Opening music and prayers

The Kingdoms of Creation
- I'll Sing You a Rock (song)
- Kingdoms of Creation (felt lesson)
- Kingdom collage booklet, origami (crafts)
- Memory quotes

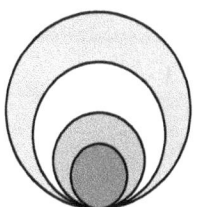

God, the Creator
- O God, Guide Me (song)
- True Understanding (presentation)
- Kids' Questions About God
- The Universe (demonstration)
- Some Divine Humor
- Eye of God, Blessed is the Spot (crafts)
- Memory quotes
- Glorious Day (song)
- The Names of God (dramatic reading)

Prayer, Our Connection with God
- Pray to God (song)
- Memory quote
- Our Connection With God (demonstration)
- Prayer Postures (demonstration)
- Additional memory quotes
- Prayer maps
- Love, Love, Love (song)
- Additional craft presentations
- Quiz Show on prayer
- Blessed is the Spot (song)

Refreshments

God and the Universe – Children's Performance

A few photos from our children's program

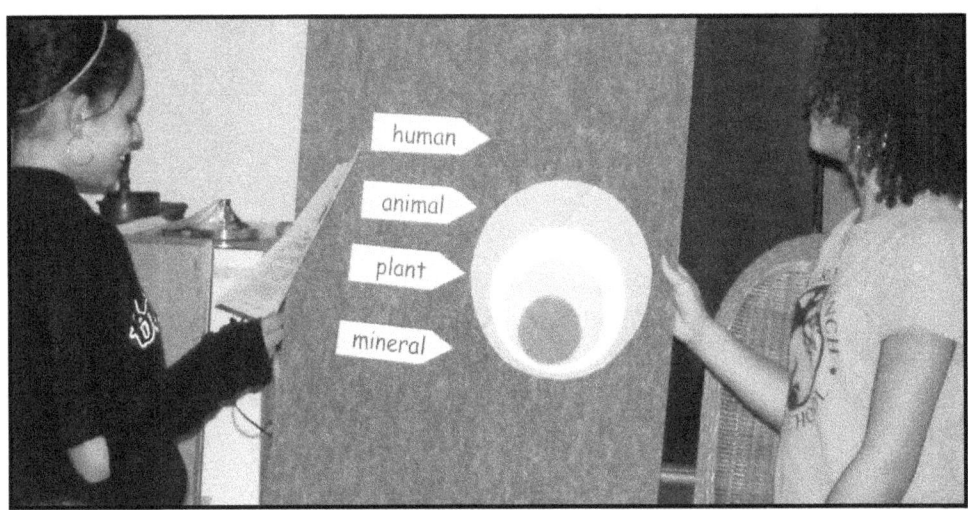
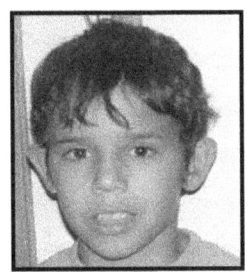

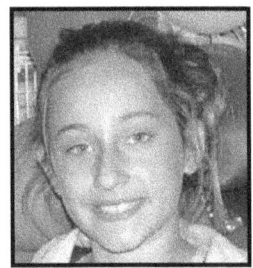
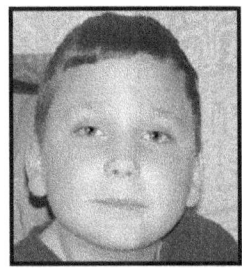

Handouts

> The student handouts from all of the lessons are included in this section for ease of photocopying. These handouts can also be downloaded from: www.UnityWorksStore.com. Click on Children's Classes > God and the Universe > student handouts.

HANDOUTS

Orientation and All Lessons

Song Sheet	159
Quotations	161
God and the Universe (student handout packet)	163

LESSON #1: The Kingdoms of Creation

The Kingdoms of Creation (chart)	164
God is the Creator (coloring page)	165

LESSON #2: God, the Creator

God, the Creator (reading)	166
Kids' Questions About God (instructions for group leaders)	53

LESSON #3: Prayer, Our Connection with God

Some Prayer Postures (pictures)	167
Prayer, Our Connection with God (reading)	168
The Prayer Lesson (reading)	169
Blessed Is the Spot (prayer and coloring poster)	170
Bendito Es el Sitio (Spanish prayer and coloring poster)	171
Questions on Prayer (for quiz show during children's performance)	172

LESSON #4: What Is a Human Being?

In the Image of God (reading)	173
The Purpose of Life (instructions for group leaders)	109
The Universe is Amazing (mazes)	174
A Human Being Is (poster)	175

God and the Universe

Name _____

SONG SHEET

Most of these songs are copyrighted and used with permission. See music section for details.

Kingdoms of God
(by Marinell Rhine)

I'll sing you a rock.
Can it grow, can it walk?
Can it do anything but be?
No, it can't grow or walk,
'Cause it's only a rock,
In the sand by the side of the sea.

**It's in the mineral kingdom,
The mineral kingdom,
The mineral kingdom of God.**
   (repeat chorus)

I'll sing you a tree. Can it talk, can it see?
Can it grow and bear fruit and be green?
Yes, it surely can grow,
But it can't move or know,
Though it be the best tree you have seen.

It's in the vegetable kingdom…

I'll sing you a frog, and a cat and a dog,
And I'll sing you an elephant, too.
They can grow, they can be,
They can walk, they can see,
But they're not quite as special as you!

They're in the animal kingdom…

I'll sing you a boy with his heart full of joy.
And I'll sing you a happy girl, too.
They can run, they can grow,
They can think, they can know.
They can learn about God just like you.

They're in the human kingdom…

I'll sing you a song that will help you along,
So you'll always remember God's love.
He wants us to know Him,
To love Him and so,
He sends Teachers of Truth from above.

They're in the heavenly kingdom…

O God Guide Me
(Words of 'Abdu'l-Bahá:
English, Spanish, French)

O God, guide me, protect me.
Illumine the lamp of my heart
And make me a brilliant star.
Thou art the Mighty and Powerful.

O Dios, guíame, protégeme,
Ilumina la lámpara de mi corazón,
Y haz de mí una estrella brillante.
Tú eres el fuerte y el poderoso.

O Dieu, guide-moi, protége-moi,
Ilumine la lampe de mon coeur,
Et fais de moi une étoile brillante.
Tu es le Fort, et le tous Puissant.

Pray to God
(Author unknown)

Pray to God in the morning,
Pray to God at noon,
Pray to God in the evening,
Keep your heart in tune.

Song of Love
(by Creadell Haley)

Love, love, love, love,
Love your fellow man.
Love, love, love is,
How the world began.
God loved creation,
So He created thee to
Love, love, love Him,
And humanity.

Bahá'í Children's Classes and Retreats: Theme 1, p. 159

God and the Universe

Blessed Is the Spot
(Words of Bahá'u'lláh;
 music by Elizabeth Habermann)

Blessed is the spot,
and the house, and the place,
and the city, and the heart,
and the mountain,
and the refuge, and the cave,
and the valley, and the land,
and the sea, and the island,
and the meadow,
where mention of God hath been made,
and His praise glorified.

God Is One
(by Margaret Jane King)

God is one, man is one,
And all the religions are one.
Land and sea, hill and valley,
Under the beautiful sun.

God is one, man is one,
And all the religions agree.
When everyone learns
  the three onenesses,
We'll have world unity.

Love Me That I May Love Thee
(Words of Bahá'u'lláh; music by Creadell Haley)

Love me that I may love thee,
If thou lovest Me not,
My love can in no wise reach thee.
Know this, O servant.
   (repeat all 3x)

Day by Day
(Traditional Episcopal hymn)

Day by day, day by day.
Oh, dear Lord, three things I pray.
To see Thee more clearly,
Love Thee more dearly,
Follow Thee more nearly,
Day by day, day by day.

Bendito Es el Sitio
(Spanish: Blessed Is the Spot)

Bendito es el sitio,
y la casa, y el lugar,
y la ciudad, y el corazón,
y la montaña,
y el refugio, y la cueva,
y el valle, y la tierra,
y el mar, y la isla,
y la pradera,
donde se ha hecho
   mención de Dios,
Y se ha glorificado su alabanza.

Dios Es Uno
(Spanish: God Is One)

Dios es uno, el hombre es uno,
Y las religiones también.
Tierra y mar, cerros y valles,
Bajo el hermoso sol.

Dios es uno, el hombre es uno,
Y las religiones concuerdan,
Cuando todos aprenden
  las tres verdades,
Habrá unidad mundial.

Glorious Day
(by Steve and Shelley Hines)

All these faces, so much love.
Isn't this what we've been dreamin' of.
All are welcome, come on in.
Join hands, let the new day begin, singin'…

**Oh, what a glorious, glorious, glorious,
Oh, what a wonderful glorious day, yeah!
God is most glorious, glorious, glorious,
Oh, what a wonderful glorious day!**

Look to the future. It shall be done.
We're finally learnin' that mankind is one.
All together, side by side.
Everybody diversified, singin'… *(chorus)*

Hand in hand, heart to heart.
Build a bond that will never part. *(chorus)*

God and the Universe

Quotations from the Bahá'í Writings on

God and the Universe

Choose one of the quotes below. Pick something you think you can memorize in about five minutes. Identify who wrote the words. Then read the quote aloud several times and to try to understand the meaning behind the words. Work with your partner to memorize the quote.

SHORT

(1) Greater is God than every great one! *(Bahá'u'lláh, PM, p. 320)*

(2) God in His wisdom has created all things. *('Abdu'l-Bahá, DP, p. 110)*

(3) O God, my God, my Beloved, my heart's Desire *(The Báb, quoted in DB, p. 30)*

(4) Man is the sum of every previous creation, for he contains them all. *('Abdu'l-Bahá, PT, p. 23)*

MEDIUM LENGTH

(5) O God, guide me, protect me, make of me a shining lamp and a brilliant star. Thou art the Mighty and the Powerful. *('Abdu'l-Bahá, BP, p. 37)*

(6) O God! Refresh and gladden my spirit. Purify my heart. Illumine my powers. I lay all my affairs in Thy hand. *('Abdu'l-Bahá, BP, p. 150)*

(7) O Thou Compassionate God. Bestow upon me a heart which, like unto glass, may be illumined with the light of Thy love... *('Abdu'l-Bahá, BP, p. 72)*

(8) O God! ...Cultivate this fresh plant in the rose garden of Thy love and aid it to grow through the showers of Thy bounty. *('Abdu'l-Bahá, BP, p. 35)*

(9) O SON OF BEING! Love Me, that I may love thee. If thou lovest Me not, My love can in no wise reach thee. Know this, O servant. *(Bahá'u'lláh: AHW #5)*

(10) O SON OF MAN! ...I knew My love for thee; therefore I created thee, have engraved on thee Mine image and revealed to thee My beauty. *(Bahá'u'lláh: AHW #3)*

(11) Intone, O My servants, the verses of God that have been received by thee... that the sweetness of thy melody may kindle thine own soul... *(Bahá'u'lláh, BP, p. ii)*

(12) A human being is distinguished from an animal in a number of ways. First of all, he is made in the image of God... *('Abdu'l-Bahá, SAB, p.140)*

(13) The Perfect Man is as a polished mirror reflecting the Sun of Truth, manifesting the attributes of God. *('Abdu'l-Bahá, PT, p. 25)*

God and the Universe

LONGER

(14) O SON OF BEING! With the hands of power I made thee and with the fingers of strength I created thee; and within thee have I placed the essence of My light. *(Bahá'u'lláh: AHW #12)*

(15) O SON OF MAN! I loved thy creation, hence I created thee. Wherefore, do thou love Me, that I may name thy name and fill thy soul with the spirit of life. *(Bahá'u'lláh: AHW #4)*

LONGEST

(16) I bear witness, O my God, that Thou hast created me to know Thee and to worship Thee. I testify, at this moment, to my powerlessness and to Thy might, to my poverty and to Thy wealth. There is none other God but Thee, the Help in Peril, the Self-Subsisting. *(Bahá'u'lláh, PM, p. 313)*

(17) Having created the world and all that liveth and moveth therein, He, through the direct operation of His unconstrained and sovereign Will, chose to confer upon man the unique distinction and capacity to know Him and to love Him… *(Bahá'u'lláh, G, p. 64)*

References
BP	Bahá'í Prayers
DB	The Dawn-Breakers
DP	Divine Philosophy
G	Gleanings from the Writings of Bahá'u'lláh
AHW	Arabic Hidden Words
PM	Prayers and Meditations
PT	Paris Talks
SAB	Selections from the Writings of 'Abdu'l-Bahá

SOME MEMORIZATION METHODS

Forward Repetition
- Repeat the first phrase out loud about ten times, or until you know it by heart.
- Sometimes it helps to write it down or say it with your eyes closed.
- Memorize the second phrase, then say both parts together.
- Continue learning each new part in the same way.

Backwards Repetition
- This is similar to forward repetition, except that you start with the last line or phrase.
- Then add the line before it and recite through to the end.
- Many people find that memorizing by backward repetition is easier.

Memory Aids
- Use hand gestures or draw small pictures to help you remember the words.
- You can also create pictures in your mind.

Disappearing Act
- Tear off a small strip of scratch paper and use it to cover up part of the quote.
- Keep adding strips of paper until the entire quote is covered and you know it by heart.

God and the Universe

Name: _____

The Kingdoms of Creation

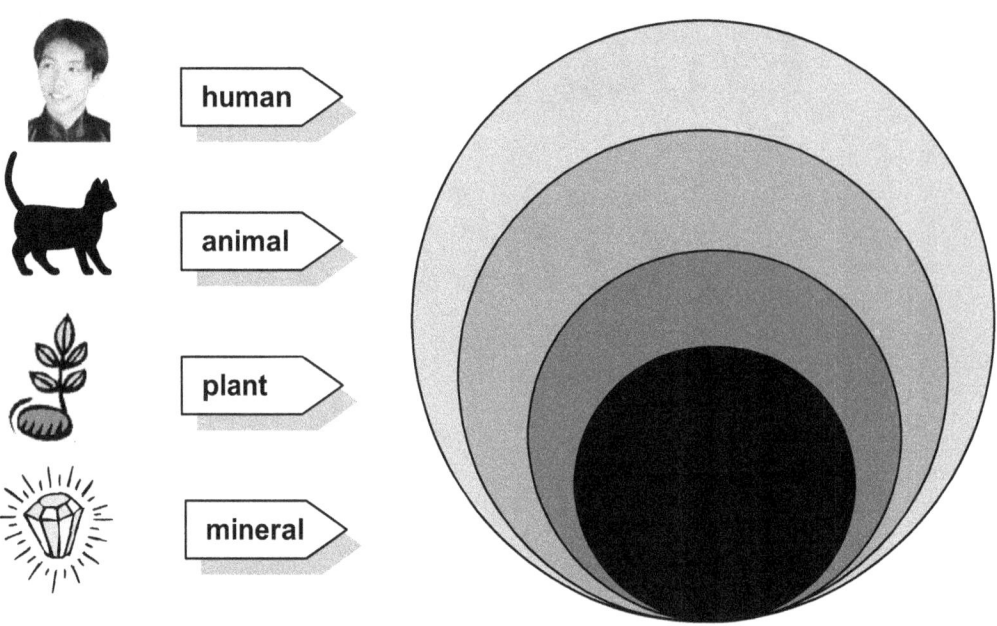

Mineral Kingdom
- cohesion or attraction [1]

Plant Kingdom
- cohesion
- growth

Animal Kingdom
- cohesion
- growth
- feelings
- senses
- locomotion [2]

Human Kingdom
- cohesion
- growth
- feelings
- senses
- locomotion
- conscious thought
- free will
- knowledge of right and wrong
- knowledge of God

---

1. The force that holds things together
2. The power to move from place to place

God and the Universe

God is the Creator

Dios es el Creador

God and the Universe

God, the Creator

"God in His wisdom has created all things."
(Abdu'l-Bahá, Divine Philosophy, p. 110)

Nothing can make itself. Everything has a creator, from the tallest building to the smallest grain of sand. A wooden table is made by a carpenter. A shoe is made by a shoemaker. A nest is made by a bird.

There is a great power that created the entire universe: the minerals, the plants, the animals, the stars, the planets, and all the people.

Although everything has a creator, we can't always see that creator or know who it is. No matter how hard it tries, the table will never be able to recognize the carpenter. The shoe will never know the shoemaker. And the nest will never be aware of the bird. It's the same with people. It is impossible for us to understand the nature of our Creator.

We call our creator "God." He is also known as Allah, Dios, Jehovah, the Lord, the Almighty, the Great Spirit, our Heavenly Father, and by many other names.

God is a mystery. He is not a person like you or me. No one knows exactly what God is like or where He is, because we can't see or touch Him, but we do know that He is real.

We can't see the wind, but we know it exists, because we can see leaves blowing on the trees. We can't see electricity, but we know it exists because we can see its effects whenever we turn on the light. We can't see the air, but we know it is real because without air, we couldn't breathe. In the same way, we can't see thoughts, or gravity, or time, or friendship, or anger, or peace, but we know that these are real. And we can't see love, but we can feel it when someone special says "I love you."

In the same way, we can't see God, but we know He exists because we can see the world He created for us. We can learn about the great Prophets He has sent to tell us about Himself and to teach us how to live. And sometimes we can feel the love of God in our hearts when we are saying our prayers.

O SON OF MAN! ...I knew My love for thee; therefore I created thee...
(Bahá'u'lláh, Arabic Hidden Words #3)

God and the Universe

Some Prayer Postures

Bahá'í Children's Classes and Retreats: Theme 1, p. 167

God and the Universe

Prayer, Our Connection with God

> *"Intone, O My servants, the verses of God that have been received by thee... that the sweetness of thy melody may kindle thine own soul..."*
> (Bahá'u'lláh, Bahá'í Prayers, p. ii)

Prayer is talking with God. Through our prayers, we can thank God for creating us and for all of the things He provides.

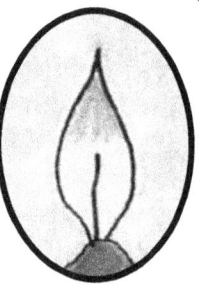

We can ask Him to protect us, and to help us with our problems. We can pray for people who are sick or unhappy. We can ask God to grant us faith and knowledge, patience and love. We can pray for unity, peace and justice in the world.

Bahá'u'lláh says that we should pray every day. When we pray, we should show respect by focusing all of our attention on God.

Intone: to chant or recite in a singing tone
Kindle: to set on fire, cause to glow or light up

We shouldn't be in a hurry or just speak the words. Rather, we should try to understand the true meaning behind the words, and our hearts must be sincere.

Bahá'u'lláh has given us many beautiful prayers to use. We should memorize some of them. That way, we will always have the Word of God with us, even when no books are available.

We can also make up our own words. And we can pray without words, straight from our hearts.

Prayer helps us to become more spiritual, even if at first we can't feel the effects.

Prayer helps us draw closer to our Creator. When we pray, God knows, and He is listening.

God and the Universe

The Prayer Lesson

Adapted from *Vignettes from the Life of 'Abdu'l-Bahá,* Honnold, p.131-32

This is a true story that took place about 100 years ago. 'Abdu'l-Bahá was in New York when He invited one of the Bahá'ís (let's call him Mr. M) to visit. 'Abdu'l-Bahá said, "If you will come to Me at dawn tomorrow, I will teach you to pray."

Mr. M was very excited! The next day, he woke up at four in the morning and went across town to where 'Abdu'l-Bahá was staying. When he entered the room, 'Abdu'l-Bahá was already praying silently, kneeling by the side of the bed.

Mr. M knelt down on the other side, directly opposite 'Abdu'l-Bahá, and also began to pray. He prayed for his family, for his friends, and for all the kings and queens of Europe. Then he said every prayer he knew by heart. He looked up, but 'Abdu'l-Bahá was still communing[1] with God, so Mr. M repeated all his prayers again. Three times!

Mr. M was becoming impatient. He rubbed his knee and thought about his aching back. He started to pray again, but was interrupted by birds singing outside his window as the sun rose. A whole hour passed. Two hours! Mr. M was growing rather numb. He looked up and noticed a large crack in the wall. By now, he was feeling annoyed, and glanced over to see if 'Abdu'l-Bahá had finished yet.

The look of ecstasy[2] on 'Abdu'l-Bahá's face astonished him. Suddenly Mr. M also wanted to pray like that! He forgot about his own selfish desires, his sorrows and problems. Even the room he was in seemed to disappear. All he knew was that he wanted to be closer to God.

Mr. M closed his eyes again and his heart filled with joyful prayer. He was cleansed and uplifted by a feeling of true peace. Immediately, 'Abdu'l-Bahá stood up and smiled directly at Mr. M. "When you pray," He said, "you must not think of your aching body, nor of the birds outside the window, nor of the cracks in the wall! When you wish to pray you must first know that you are standing in the presence of the Almighty!"

1. **communing:** communicating intimately with someone; to feel at one with someone
2. **ecstasy:** intense joy or delight; carried away with overwhelming happiness

- Who was Mr. M?
- Compare Mr. M's first attempts to pray with his last one.
- What did he do differently at the end?
- What did he learn from 'Abdu'l-Bahá?

God and the Universe

Blessed is the spot,
and the house,
and the place,
and the city,
and the heart,
and the mountain,
and the refuge,
and the cave,
and the valley,
and the land, and the sea,
and the island,
and the meadow
where mention of God
hath been made,
and His praise glorified.

~ *Bahá'u'lláh* ~

God and the Universe

Bendito es el sitio,
y la casa,
y el lugar,
y la ciudad,
y el corazón,
y la montaña,
y el refugio,
y la cueva,
y el valle,
y la tierra, y el mar,
y la isla, y la pradera
donde se ha hecho
mención de Dios
y se ha glorificado
su alabanza.

~ *Bahá'u'lláh* ~

God and the Universe

Questions on Prayer

(for quiz show during children's performance)

1. What is prayer?

2. Who should pray?

3. When should we pray?

4. Where should we pray? Do we have to be in a special building or church?

5. What should we pray for?

6. Is there anything we should <u>not</u> pray for?

7. Why should we pray?

8. Can we sing or chant while praying?

9. Can we pray in any language?

10. Is it possible to pray without words? How?

God and the Universe

"In the Image of God"

> "God created man in His own image..."
> (Bible, Genesis 1:27)
>
> "O ye young Bahá'í children,
> ye seekers after true understanding and knowledge!
> A human being is distinguished from an animal in a number of ways.
> First of all, he is made in the image of God..."
> (Selections from the Writings of 'Abdu'l-Bahá, p. 140)

The Holy Writings tell us that we were created in the image of God. What does this mean? When the sun shines, it gives off heat and light. If the sun is shining on a perfect mirror, when we look at that mirror, we will see the image of the sun.

It is the same with human beings. We are like mirrors that can reflect the light of God. When we turn our faces toward the spiritual Sun, then the knowledge and love of God will shine in our hearts.

Some people think that humans were created in the physical image of God. But God is not a physical being. If God had a physical form, would He be male or female? Would He be black or white? Young or old? Tall or short? Rich or poor? And someday would He get sick and die? Is this the true reality of our Creator? No, of course not! Nor is it the true reality of a human being. God is an unknowable, invisible Spirit. Our Creator is so glorious and so far above every human attribute that we cannot even begin to understand His mystery.

So how can we reflect the spiritual image of our Creator? Just as God loves humanity, we must also love humanity. As God is truthful, we must also be truthful. As God is kind and merciful, we must be too. We should help the poor, comfort the sick, and be a friend to those who are sad or lonely. We should work for justice and peace, and strive for excellence in everything we do. And we must learn to be wise and patient.

When these attributes of God are reflected in us, just like the sun reflected in the mirror, we will be illumined with a heavenly light. Then the image of God will shine in our hearts.

References: From Bahá'u'lláh: Gleanings from the Writings of Bahá'u'lláh, p. 46, 158-9. From 'Abdu'l-Bahá: Bahá'í World Faith, p.255; Foundations of World Unity, p. 73, 79, 92; Promulgation of Universal Peace, p.70, 262, 470; Selections from the Writings of 'Abdu'l-Bahá, p. 79-80, 140; Some Answered Questions, p. 9.

God and the Universe

The Universe is a-MAZE-ing!

Help the human to find the light.
All you need is a pencil and some patience.

A Human Being Is...

- ❖ We are eternal spiritual beings, living for a time in the physical world.

- ❖ We were created because God loves us, and He wants us to know and to love Him.

- ❖ We are here to develop our spiritual qualities, to serve humanity, and to be like mirrors reflecting God's light and love to the world.

Music

"The art of music is divine and effective. It is the food of the soul and spirit. Through the power and charm of music the spirit of man is uplifted. It has wonderful sway and effect in the hearts of children, for their hearts are pure, and melodies have great influence in them."

– 'Abdu'l-Bahá, The Promulgation of Universal Peace, p. 52

God and the Universe

Music Program

*"We, verily, have made music as a ladder for your souls,
a means whereby they may be lifted up unto the realm on high..."*

(Baha'u'llah, Kitáb-i-Aqdas, p. 38)

To the Music Coordinator

Singing brings people together for an enjoyable activity. It uplifts the souls and connects the hearts. It is also an excellent tool for memorizing information and for teaching and reinforcing new ideas.

The songs included in this teacher's guide have been selected to help children learn about God and His creation. The students should have song sheets in their folders. As the music coordinator, your job is to help them learn some of these songs.

If the children's classes are held during a weekend retreat format, a morning sing-a-long has been scheduled each day for this purpose. There are also opportunities for singing after lunch and in the evenings. Classroom teachers may ask for your assistance with music that is part of their class. In addition, the music coordinator should help with the children's performance and the rehearsal. Check with the organizers for a schedule with the exact times.

As the song leader, you should be enthusiastic, confident and encouraging. Be patient with children who are shy or who don't catch on right away. When teaching a song for the first time, you will need to sing slowly, with a lot of repetition. If you play an instrument, you can bring it with you to accompany the singing and to keep the beat.

Be sure to learn the songs and the correct meaning and pronunciation of all the words beforehand, and arrive early so your session starts on time. Bring a music stand if available.

A song sheet and musical scores are included on the following pages. Some of the selections have been simplified and shortened for group singing with children. If you know a different melody for a particular song, use the version you feel most comfortable with. Songs in other languages have been included and may be used if desired.

To start a sing-a-long session:

- Ask the children to take out their song sheets and find the first song.
- Ask them what they think the song is about, and explain if necessary.
- Pronounce and define any difficult words.
- Play the song through once, encouraging those who know it to sing with you.
- If necessary, have children repeat each line in a speaking voice before trying to sing.
- Give the starting note and play or clap out the rhythm while everyone sings.
- Practice several times before going on to the next song.

God and the Universe

Transposing a Song

> Idea from Mr. Dick Grover

If the notes of a song are too high or too low to sing comfortably, you can easily change the song to a new key – called *transposing*. On a guitar, the easiest way to change the key is by using a capo. You can also follow the steps below.

1. Start by determining the original key (usually the first chord on the sheet music). Play that chord and sing a few lines of the song. If it is too high or too low, you will need to find a more comfortable key.

2. Play a different chord and try singing the song in that key. If it feels comfortable, you have found the right key. If not, play another chord and sing a few lines until you have found a comfortable key to sing in. You will transpose the song to that key. For example, if the song is too low in the original key of D but feels just right in the key of G, you will transpose the entire song to the key of G.

3. Using the chart and moving clockwise, count the number of steps from the original chord to the transposed chord. For example, there are five steps from D to G.

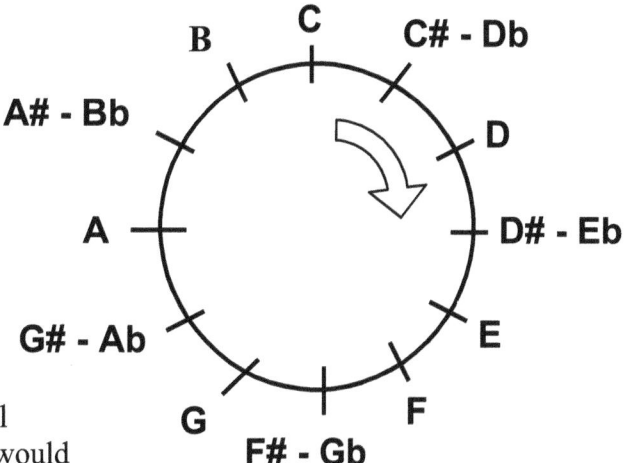

4. Then go through the entire song, changing all the chords by the same number of steps. Based on our example, you would raise all the D chords to G. All the E chords would change to A. An A7 would become a D7, etc. Write the new chord directly over the syllable you will be singing with that chord, or you will be out of rhythm when you play the song.

means "sharp" (It raises that note by a half step.)

b means "flat" (It lowers that note by a half step.)

C# and Db are the same note and count together as one step. This is also true for D# and Eb, F# and Gb, G# and Ab, A# and Bb.

Bahá'í Children's Classes and Retreats: Theme 1, p. 179

God and the Universe Name _____

🎵 SONG SHEET

Most of these songs are copyrighted and used with permission. See music section for details.

Kingdoms of God
(by Marinell Rhine)

I'll sing you a rock.
Can it grow, can it walk?
Can it do anything but be?
No, it can't grow or walk,
'Cause it's only a rock,
In the sand by the side of the sea.

**It's in the mineral kingdom,
The mineral kingdom,
The mineral kingdom of God.**
(repeat chorus)

I'll sing you a tree. Can it talk, can it see?
Can it grow and bear fruit and be green?
Yes, it surely can grow,
But it can't move or know,
Though it be the best tree you have seen.

It's in the vegetable kingdom…

I'll sing you a frog, and a cat and a dog,
And I'll sing you an elephant, too.
They can grow, they can be,
They can walk, they can see,
But they're not quite as special as you!

They're in the animal kingdom…

I'll sing you a boy with his heart full of joy.
And I'll sing you a happy girl, too.
They can run, they can grow,
They can think, they can know.
They can learn about God just like you.

They're in the human kingdom…

I'll sing you a song that will help you along,
So you'll always remember God's love.
He wants us to know Him,
To love Him and so,
He sends Teachers of Truth from above.

They're in the heavenly kingdom…

O God Guide Me
(Words of 'Abdu'l-Bahá:
English, Spanish, French)

O God, guide me, protect me.
Illumine the lamp of my heart
And make me a brilliant star.
Thou art the Mighty and Powerful.

O Dios, guíame, protégeme,
Ilumina la lámpara de mi corazón,
Y haz de mí una estrella brillante.
Tú eres el fuerte y el poderoso.

O Dieu, guide-moi, protége-moi,
Ilumine la lampe de mon coeur,
Et fais de moi une étoile brillante.
Tu es le Fort, et le tous Puissant.

Pray to God
(Author unknown)

Pray to God in the morning,
Pray to God at noon,
Pray to God in the evening,
Keep your heart in tune.

Song of Love
(by Creadell Haley)

Love, love, love, love,
Love your fellow man.
Love, love, love is,
How the world began.
God loved creation,
So He created thee to
Love, love, love Him,
And humanity.

Bahá'í Children's Classes and Retreats: Theme 1, p. 180

God and the Universe

Blessed Is the Spot
(Words of Bahá'u'lláh;
music by Elizabeth Habermann)

Blessed is the spot,
and the house, and the place,
and the city, and the heart,
and the mountain,
and the refuge, and the cave,
and the valley, and the land,
and the sea, and the island,
and the meadow,
where mention of God hath been made,
and His praise glorified.

Bendito Es el Sitio
(Spanish: Blessed Is the Spot)

Bendito es el sitio,
y la casa, y el lugar,
y la ciudad, y el corazón,
y la montaña,
y el refugio, y la cueva,
y el valle, y la tierra,
y el mar, y la isla,
y la pradera,
donde se ha hecho
   mención de Dios,
y se ha glorificado su alabanza.

God Is One
(by Margaret Jane King)

God is one, man is one,
And all the religions are one.
Land and sea, hill and valley,
Under the beautiful sun.

God is one, man is one,
And all the religions agree.
When everyone learns
   the three onenesses,
We'll have world unity.

Dios Es Uno
(Spanish: God Is One)

Dios es uno, el hombre es uno,
Y las religiones también.
Tierra y mar, cerros y valles,
Bajo el hermoso sol.

Dios es uno, el hombre es uno,
Y las religiones concuerdan,
Cuando todos aprenden
   las tres verdades,
Habrá unidad mundial.

Love Me That I May Love Thee
(Words of Bahá'u'lláh; music by Creadell Haley)

Love me that I may love thee,
If thou lovest Me not,
My love can in no wise reach thee.
Know this, O servant.
   (repeat all 3x)

Glorious Day
(by Steve and Shelley Hines)

All these faces, so much love.
Isn't this what we've been dreamin' of.
All are welcome, come on in.
Join hands, let the new day begin, singin'…

**Oh, what a glorious, glorious, glorious,
Oh, what a wonderful glorious day, yeah!
God is most glorious, glorious, glorious,
Oh, what a wonderful glorious day!**

Look to the future. It shall be done.
We're finally learnin' that mankind is one.
All together, side by side.
Everybody diversified, singin'… *(chorus)*

Day by Day
(Traditional Episcopal hymn)

Day by day, day by day.
Oh, dear Lord, three things I pray.
To see Thee more clearly,
Love Thee more dearly,
Follow Thee more nearly,
Day by day, day by day.

Hand in hand, heart to heart.
Build a bond that will never part. *(chorus)*

God and the Universe

SONGS ABOUT GOD AND HIS CREATION

1. Blessed Is the Spot / Bendito Es el Sitio …….............. 183
2. Day by Day ……………………………………………. 184
3. Glorious Day ………………………………………….. 185
4. God is One / Dios es Uno……………………………… 186
5. Kingdoms of God………………………………………. 187
6. Love Me That I May Love Thee ……………………… 188
7. O God, Guide Me …………………………………….. 189
8. Pray to God……………………………………………. 190
9. Song of Love………………………………………….. 191

Acknowledgements

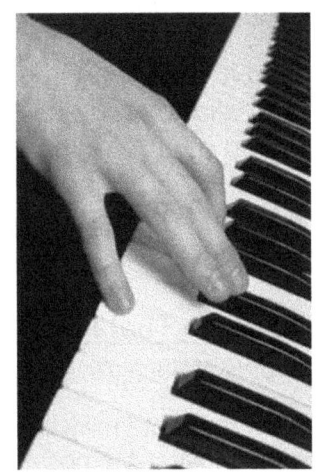

Our deepest gratitude goes to Jonathan Gottlieb for transcribing the music for these songs. Some of the songs have been simplified and shortened for the purpose of group singing with children.

Appreciation to Tony Lee for permission to use The Kingdoms of God, O God Guide Me, Love Me That I May Love Thee, and Blessed Is the Spot, songs which first appeared in: *Building Bridges: A Bahá'í Songbook,* by Peggy Caton and Dale Nomura, for the U.S. Bahá'í National Education Committee, published by Kalimát Press: Los Angeles, 1984.

The Hines' rousing song, "Glorious Day," is available for download from www.divinenotes.com. Click on "browse artists," and scroll to "Steve and Shelley Hines" and their album "A Cause to Sing."

Two songs, "Bendito Es el Sitio" and "Dios Es Uno" are Spanish translations from the English. The translators are unknown.

While most of the songs included here are used with permission, a few have passed into the realm of Bahá'í folk music and their origins have been lost. We would be pleased to hear from any artists we have been unable to locate and acknowledge.

Blessed Is the Spot
(Bendito Es el Sitio)

Words of Bahá'u'lláh
Music by Elizabeth Habermann

2. Bendito es el sitio, y la casa, y el lugar, y la ciudad,
y el corazón, y la montaña, y el refugio, y la cueva,
y el valle, y la tierra, y el mar, y la isla, y la pradera,
donde se ha hecho mención de Dios,
y se ha glorificado Su alabanza.

Day by Day

Traditional Episcopal Hymn
Adapted from music by Stephen Schwartz
Lyrics by Richard of Chichester (1197-1253)

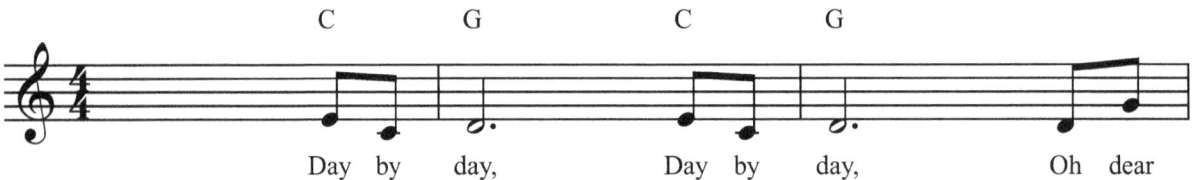
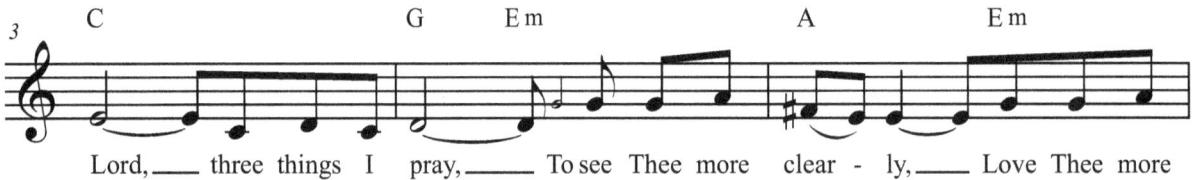

Kingdoms of God

Marinell S. Rhine
From Building Bridges songbook
Used with permisison

1. I'll sing you a rock. Can it grow, can it walk? Can it do a-ny-thing but be? No it

can't grow or walk, 'cause it's only a rock in the sand by the side of the sea. It's in the

mi-ne-ral king-dom, the mineral kingdom, the mi-ne-ral kingdom of God. It's in the

mi-ne-ral king-dom, the mi-ne-ral kingdom, the mi-ne-ral king-dom of God.

2. I'll sing you a tree. Can it talk, can it see?
   Can it grow and bear fruit and be green?
   Yes, it surely can grow,
   But it can't move or know,
   Though it be the best tree you have seen.
   It's in the vegetable kingdom…

3. I'll sing you a frog, and a cat and a dog.
   And I'll sing you an elephant, too.
   They can grow, they can be,
   They can walk, they can see,
   But they're not quite as special as you!
   They're in the animal kingdom…

4. I'll sing you a boy with his heart full of joy.
   And I'll sing you a happy girl, too.
   They can run, they can grow,
   They can think, they can know.
   They can learn about God just like you.
   They're in the human kingdom…

5. I'll sing you a song that will help you along,
   So you'll always remember God's love.
   He wants us to know Him,
   To love Him and so,
   He sends Teachers of Truth from above.
   They're in the heavenly kingdom…

Love Me That I May Love Thee

Words of Bahá'u'lláh
(Arabic Hidden Words, No. 5)
Music by Creadell Haley

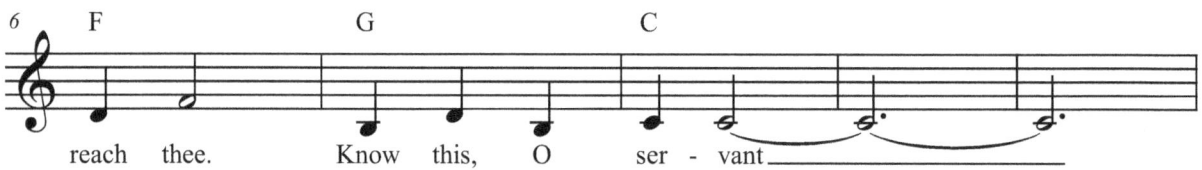

O God, Guide Me

Words of 'Abdu'l-Bahá
Music: Unknown

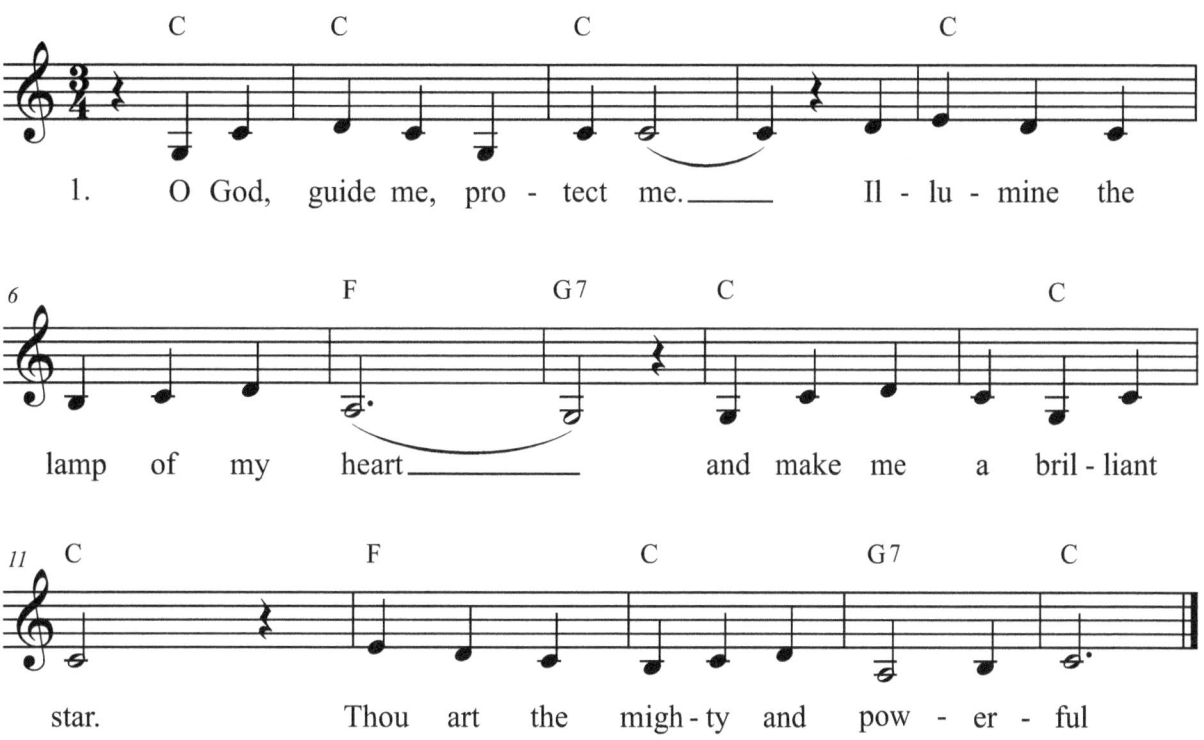

1. O God, guide me, pro-tect me. Il-lu-mine the lamp of my heart and make me a bril-liant star. Thou art the migh-ty and pow-er-ful

2. O Dios, guíame, protégeme,
   Ilumina la lámpara de mi corazón,
   Y haz de mí una estrella brillante.
   Tú eres el fuerte y el poderoso.

3. O Dieu, guide-moi, protége-moi,
   Ilumine la lampe de mon coeur,
   Et fais de moi une étoile brillante.
   Tu es le Fort, et le tous Puissant.

Pray to God

Author Unknown

Bahá'í Children's Classes and Retreats: Theme 1, p. 190

Song of Love

Words and Music by Creadell Haley

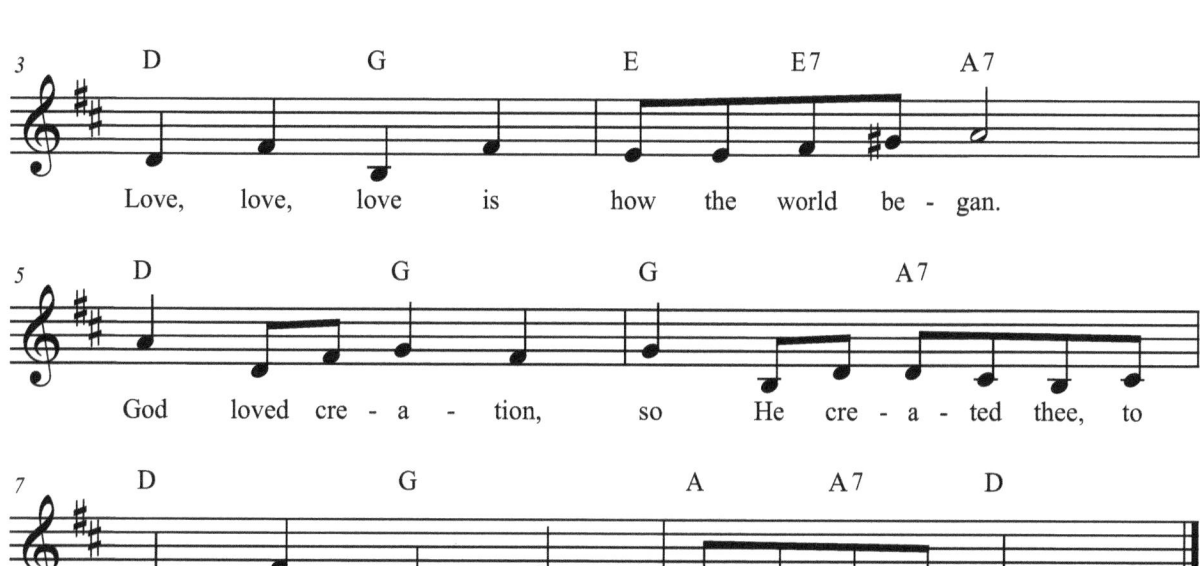

God and the Universe

CLOSING ACTIVITIES

At the end of the retreat or after the final class session on this theme, the organizers may wish to plan some closing activities for the participants. We have found the following schedule to be very effective. After the cleanup, call everyone together for a celebration of their achievements.

1. **Opening:** Begin with singing and prayers.

2. **Memory quotes:** Ask for volunteers to recite any individual memory quotes learned. Then recite the main quotes together as a group, for example:

| O SON OF BEING! With the hands of power I made thee… | Intone, O My servants, the verses of God… | Blessed is the spot, and the house, and the place… |
| Bahá'u'lláh | Bahá'u'lláh | Bahá'u'lláh |

3. **Evaluation:** Conduct a short oral evaluation of the activities. Go around the room and ask each child, youth and adult to share brief thoughts on the three items to the right, which should be written on the board. Anyone may skip his or her turn. Suggestions can be considered in planning for the next class or retreat. An adult should take notes.

   > ➢ I liked…
   > ➢ I learned…
   > ➢ I suggest…

4. **Appreciations:** The organizers can then share any closing comments regarding the importance of teachers (see sample quotes below) and present small gifts of appreciation to the teachers, youth volunteers, musicians, cooks and other helpers. Ask capable children to read the quotes. (The second quote usually gets a good laugh!)

> "Among the greatest of all services that can possibly be rendered by man to Almighty God is the education and training of children…It is, however, very difficult to undertake this service, even harder to succeed in it." (Selections from the Writings of 'Abdu'l-Bahá, p. 133)
>
> "If, in this momentous task, a mighty effort be exerted, the world of humanity will shine out with other adornings…The very demons will change to angels…the wild-dog pack to gazelles…and ravening beasts to peaceful herds…" (Selections from the Writings of 'Abdu'l-Bahá, p. 130)
>
> "It followeth that whatever soul shall offer his aid to bring this about will assuredly be accepted at the heavenly Threshold, and extolled by the Company on high." (Selections from the Writings of 'Abdu'l-Bahá, p. 134)
>
> "If one should, in the right way, teach and train the children, he will be performing a service than which none is greater at the Sacred Threshold." ('Abdu'l-Bahá, Bahá'í Education, p. 32)

God and the Universe

5. **Follow-up:** Any follow-up suggestions and messages from the sponsoring Institution can be shared at this time (see next page for ideas).

6. **Graduation:** A simple ceremony (see Retreat Manual) can be held to recognize children who will be "graduating" to the Junior Youth Spiritual Empowerment Program.

7. **Announcements:** Share logistical information (lost-and-found items, rides home, etc.).

8. **Song:** Close with a sing-along, for example, "The Kingdoms of God."

9. **Group photo:** Be sure everyone is included!

10. **Dessert:** We have a well-loved tradition of serve-yourself ice cream sundaes.

Ideas for Thank-you Gifts

As part of the closing activities, you may wish to present small thank-you gifts to the volunteers. A few ideas are offered below.

- *An American Indian Prayer* (see end of this section) makes a nice gift when photocopied onto parchment or rainbow print paper. The prayer was translated into English by Chief Yellow Lark of the Lakota Sioux, and is in the public domain (www.worldprayers.org).

- *Blessed Is the Spot* posters from the end of Lesson #3 (in English and Spanish) are available in color as part of the download packet for this teacher's guide: **www.UnityWorksStore.com**. Click on Children's Classes > God and the Universe > Student Handouts.

- A variety of Bahá'í prayer booklets and post cards are available from Special Ideas, including an Interfaith Prayer Book, The Hidden Words, and A Children's Prayers Postcard Booklet. Visit **www.bahairesources. com**.

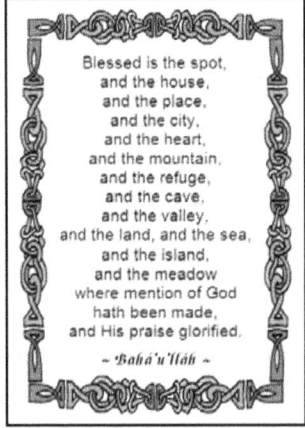

God and the Universe

FOLLOW-UP ACTIVITIES

Teachers and sponsoring institutions can help children apply their new knowledge and skills by providing a variety of opportunities for practice. Some examples are listed below:

- Ask the children to share during Feast what they have learned.

- Encourage them to recite memorized passages during a devotional meeting.

- Invite them to visit a class for younger children and to share some of the songs, felt lessons, stories or other activities from the theme of God and the Universe.

- Ask them to talk about the importance of prayer during a home visit.

- Encourage them to teach their friends and invite them to children's classes.

- Organize a children's fireside on "God and the Universe" including songs, *Kids' Questions About God, The Universe* demonstration and the *Quiz Show*. Have children invite their families, friends and neighbors.

- Finished craft projects can be used as teaching tools.

- Skits, demonstrations and songs from the lessons can be performed during Holy Days, Unit Convention or cluster reflection meetings.

- Teachers can write a brief report on the children's class activities and submit this with photos to the local paper.

Bahá'í Children's Classes and Retreats: Theme 1, p. 195

God and the Universe

An American Indian Prayer

*Oh, Great Spirit,
whose voice I hear in the winds
and whose breath gives life to all the world, hear me.*

*I am small and weak.
I need your strength and wisdom.
Let me walk in beauty and make my eyes
ever behold the red and purple sunset.
Make my hands respect the things you have made
and my ears sharp to hear your voice.
Make me wise so that I may understand
the things you have taught my people.
Let me learn the lessons you have hidden
in every leaf and rock.*

*I seek strength, not to be superior to my brother,
but to fight my greatest enemy - myself.
Make me always ready to come to you
with clean hands and straight eyes,
so when life fades, as the fading sunset,
my spirit will come to you
without shame.*

**Chief Yellow Lark
Lakota Nation – 1887**

God and the Universe

References
for Teachers

God and the Universe

References for Teachers

LESSON #1: The Kingdoms of Creation 199
    God Created All Things, Each with a Special Destiny 199
    Four Kingdoms 199
    Every Atom Journeys Through All Kingdoms 200
    Every Created Thing a Door to the Knowledge of God 200
    The Universe Is a Theatre 201

LESSON #2: God, the Creator 202
    God, the Creator 202
    God, the Unknowable Essence 202
    One God, Everlasting, Exalted Above All 203
    God Is Eternal 203
    God Is All-Knowing 204
    The Love of God 204
    Creation Without Beginning or End 205
    Man Did Not Create Himself; A Proof of the Existence of God 206
    The Manifestation Reflects the Reality of God 206
    Knowledge of the Manifestation Is Knowledge of God 206
    The Worlds of God; the Phenomenon of Dreams 207

LESSON #3: Prayer, Our Connection with God 208
    Created to Know and Worship God 208
    The Wisdom of Prayer 208
    Strive that Your Actions May Be Beautiful Prayers 209
    When To Pray 209
    Obligatory Prayer 209

LESSON #4: What is a Human Being? 211
    Mankind Created by God for a Purpose 211
    Man Contains the Lower Kingdoms 211
    Unique Distinction and Capacity to Know and Love God 212
    Human Capacities Latent; Obscured by Worldly Desires 212
    Qualities Manifested As a Result of Own Volition 212
    Human Beings Created in the Image of God 213
    All Things Captives of Nature Except Man 214
    Power of Understanding, God's Greatest Gift to Man 215
    The Inner Reality of Man 216
    Nature of the Soul 217
    Life After Death 217

ADDITIONAL REFERENCES 218
    Meditation 218
    Creation and Evolution 219
    Think-Pair-Share (educational strategy) 221

LESSON #1

The Kingdoms of Creation

Teachers may wish to study the following references in order to gain a deeper understanding of the material presented in each lesson.

God Created All Things, Each with a Special Destiny

God in his wisdom has created all things. Nothing has been created without a special destiny, for every creature has an innate station of attainment. This flower has been created to mirror forth a harmonious ensemble of color and perfume. Each kingdom of nature holds potentialities and each must be cultivated in order to reach its fulfillment…The flower needs light that it may achieve its fruitage; man needs the light of the Holy Spirit, and the measure of illumination throughout creation is proportionate to the different kingdoms.

('Abdu'l-Bahá, *Divine Philosophy*, p. 110)

Four Kingdoms

In the differentiation of life in the world of existence, there are four degrees or kingdoms, -- the mineral, vegetable, animal, and human. The mineral kingdom is possessed of a certain virtue which we term cohesion. The vegetable kingdom possesses cohesive properties plus the power of growth or power augmentative. The animal kingdom is possessed of the virtues of the mineral and vegetable plus the powers of the senses. But the animal although gifted with sensibilities is utterly bereft of consciousness, absolutely out of touch with the world of consciousness and spirit. The animal possesses no powers by which it can make discoveries which lie beyond the realm of the senses. It has no power of intellectual origination. For example, an animal located in Europe is not capable of discovering the continent of America. It understands only phenomena which come within the range of its senses and instinct. It cannot abstractly reason out anything. The animal cannot conceive of the earth being spherical or revolving upon its axis. It cannot apprehend that the little stars in the heavens are tremendous worlds vastly greater than the earth. The animal cannot abstractly conceive of intellect. Of these powers it is bereft. Therefore these powers are peculiar to man and it is made evident that in the human kingdom there is a reality of which the animal is minus. What is that reality? It is the spirit of man. By it man is distinguished above all the other phenomenal kingdoms. Although he possesses all the virtues of the lower kingdoms he is further endowed with the spiritual faculty, the heavenly gift of consciousness.

('Abdu'l-Bahá, *Foundations of World Unity*, p. 90-91)

Every Atom Journeys Through All Kingdoms

Every single atom has its coursings throughout all the kingdoms of life. For instance, that which has gone into the composition of a human being was at one time in the mineral kingdom. Along the degrees of the mineral kingdom it journeyed, appearing in various forms and reflecting various images, manifesting a peculiar virtue in each. In the vegetable kingdom, it again partook of many experiences and through each experience became adorned with an added attribute. Having perfected its journeyings here, it entered the animal kingdom and was incarnated throughout multitudes of animal forms and finally, in the human kingdom it traversed endless forms of humanity, in each form of composition showing forth a particular aspect of the one power....

All phenomena are involved in all phenomena. Consider what a transcendent unity exists, that, from this standpoint, every monad is the expression of all creation; this is the law and order in the world of existence. What wondrous symmetry! What stupendous organization! What divine completeness! What elysian co-ordination! What celestial union!

('Abdu'l-Bahá, *Divine Philosophy*, p. 168)

Thus this flower once upon a time was of the soil. The animal eats the flower or its fruit, and it thereby ascends to the animal kingdom. Man eats the meat of the animal, and there you have its ascent into the human kingdom, because all phenomena are divided into that which eats and that which is eaten. Therefore, every primordial atom of these atoms, singly and indivisible, has had its coursings throughout all the sentient creation.

...Let us again take the example of this flower. The flower is indestructible. The only thing that we can see, this outer form, is indeed destroyed, but the elements, the indivisible elements which have gone into the composition of this flower are eternal and changeless.

('Abdu'l-Bahá, *Foundations of World Unity*, p. 51)

Every Created Thing a Door to the Knowledge of God

Every created thing in the whole universe is but a door leading into His knowledge, a sign of His sovereignty, a revelation of His names, a symbol of His majesty, a token of His power, a means of admittance into His straight Path.

(Bahá'u'lláh, *Gleanings from the Writings of Bahá'u'lláh*, p. 160)

Know thou that every created thing is a sign of the revelation of God. Each, according to its capacity, is, and will ever remain, a token of the Almighty. Inasmuch as He, the sovereign Lord of all, hath willed to reveal His sovereignty in the kingdom of names and attributes, each and every created thing hath, through the act of the Divine Will, been made a sign of His glory. So pervasive and general is this revelation that nothing whatsoever in the whole universe can be discovered that doth not reflect His splendor...Were the Hand of Divine power to divest of this high endowment all created things, the entire universe would become desolate and void.

(Bahá'u'lláh, *Gleanings from the Writings of Bahá'u'lláh*, p. 184)

Whatever is in the heavens and whatever is on the earth is a direct evidence of the revelation within it of the attributes and names of God, inasmuch as within every atom are enshrined the signs that bear eloquent testimony to the revelation of that Most Great Light. Methinks, but for the potency of that revelation, no being could ever exist. How resplendent the luminaries of knowledge that shine in an atom, and how vast the oceans of wisdom that surge within a drop!

(Bahá'u'lláh, *Gleanings from the Writings of Bahá'u'lláh,* p. 177)

The Universe Is a Theatre

The sea of materialism is at flood tide and all the nations of the world are immersed in it. It is my hope that the fish will rise to the surface, so that they may behold other wondrous aspects of creation; for the people are like unto the fish swimming in the deep - ignorant of the rest of the universe. May they be transformed into birds of the air and soar in the nether atmosphere! May they break all bonds of limitation, so that they can observe from the height the lordly processions of infinite creatures; they will see the blue heavens studded with luminous stars, rivers flowing with salubrious water, gardens bedecked with fragrant flowers, trees adorned with blossoms and fruits, birds singing songs of light, humanity ever striving forward, every atom of existence breathing life and force - the universe of God a wonderful theatre upon the stage of which every created thing plays its part.

('Abdu'l-Bahá, *Divine Philosophy,* p. 139)

LESSON #2

God, the Creator

Teachers may wish to study the following references in order to gain a deeper understanding of the material presented in each lesson.

God, the Creator

All praise to the unity of God, and all honor to Him, the sovereign Lord, the incomparable and all-glorious Ruler of the universe, Who, out of utter nothingness, hath created the reality of all things, Who, from naught, hath brought into being the most refined and subtle elements of His creation, and Who, rescuing His creatures from the abasement of remoteness and the perils of ultimate extinction, hath received them into His kingdom of incorruptible glory. Nothing short of His all-encompassing grace, His all-pervading mercy, could have possibly achieved it. How could it, otherwise, have been possible for sheer nothingness to have acquired by itself the worthiness and capacity to emerge from its state of non-existence into the realm of being?

(Bahá'u'lláh, *Gleanings from the Writings of Bahá'u'lláh*, p. 64-65)

Magnified be Thy Name, O God. Thine in truth are the Kingdoms of Creation and Revelation, and verily in our Lord have we placed our whole trust. All praise be unto Thee, O God; Thou art the Maker of the heavens and the earth and that which is between them, and Thou in truth art the supreme Ruler, the Fashioner, the All-Wise.

(The Báb, *Selections from the Writings of the Báb*, p. 175)

God, the Unknowable Essence

Glorified, immeasurably glorified art Thou, O Lord! Every man of insight is far astray in his attempt to recognize Thee, and every man of consummate learning is sore perplexed in his search after Thee. Every evidence falleth short of Thine unknowable Essence and every light retreateth and sinketh below the horizon when confronted with but a glimmer of the dazzling splendour of Thy might.

(The Báb, *Selections from the Writings of the Báb*, p. 208)

All these sacred words show us that man is made in God's image: yet the Essence of God is incomprehensible to the human mind, for the finite understanding cannot be applied to this infinite Mystery. God contains all: He cannot be contained. That which contains is superior to that which is contained. The whole is greater than its parts.

Things which are understood by men cannot be outside their capacity for understanding, so that it is impossible for the heart of man to comprehend the nature of the Majesty of God. Our imagination can only picture that which it is able to create.

The power of the understanding differs in degree in the various kingdoms of creation. The mineral, vegetable, and animal realms are each incapable of understanding any creation beyond their own. The mineral cannot imagine the growing power of the plant. The tree cannot understand the power of movement in the animal, neither can it comprehend what it would mean to possess sight, hearing or the sense of smell. These all belong to the physical creation.

Man also shares in this creation; but it is not possible for either of the lower kingdoms to understand that which takes place in the mind of man. The animal cannot realize the intelligence of a human being, he only knows that which is perceived by his animal senses, he cannot imagine anything in the abstract. An animal could not learn that the world is round, that the earth revolves round the sun, or the construction of the electric telegraph. These things are only possible to man. Man is the highest work of creation, the nearest to God of all creatures.

All superior kingdoms are incomprehensible to the inferior; how therefore could it be possible that the creature, man, should understand the almighty Creator of all?

That which we imagine, is not the Reality of God; He, the Unknowable, the Unthinkable, is far beyond the highest conception of man.

('Abdu'l-Bahá, *Paris Talks,* p. 23-26)

One God, Everlasting, Exalted Above All

Regard thou the one true God as One Who is apart from, and immeasurably exalted above, all created things. The whole universe reflecteth His glory, while He is Himself independent of, and transcendeth His creatures. This is the true meaning of Divine unity. He Who is the Eternal Truth is the one Power Who exerciseth undisputed sovereignty over the world of being, Whose image is reflected in the mirror of the entire creation. All existence is dependent upon Him, and from Him is derived the source of the sustenance of all things.

(Bahá'u'lláh, *Gleanings from the Writings of Bahá'u'lláh,* p. 166)

He, verily, is from everlasting. No peer or partner has been, or can ever be, joined with Him. No name can be compared with His Name. No pen can portray His nature, neither can any tongue depict His glory. He will, for ever, remain immeasurably exalted above any one except Himself.

(Bahá'u'lláh, *Gleanings from the Writings of Bahá'u'lláh,* p. 149-151)

God Is Eternal

God is eternal and ancient; not a new God. His sovereignty is of old, not recent; not merely existent these five or six thousand years… Therefore as God is creator, eternal and ancient, there were always creatures and subjects existing and provided for…If we conceive of a time when there were no creatures, no servants, no subjects of divine lordship we dethrone God and predicate a time when God was not. It would be as if He had been recently appointed and man had given these names to Him. The divine sovereignty is ancient, eternal.

('Abdu'l-Bahá: *Foundations of World Unity,* p. 102)

God Is All-Knowing

He knoweth the secrets both of the heavens and of the earth. His knowledge embraceth all things.

(Bahá'u'lláh, *Gleanings from the Writings of Bahá'u'lláh*, p.128-129)

O Heedless Ones! Think not the secrets of hearts are hidden, nay, know ye of a certainty that in clear characters they are engraved and are openly manifest in the holy Presence.

(Bahá'u'lláh, *Persian Hidden Words*, No. 59)

Verily, God will bring everything to light, though it were but the weight of a grain of mustard-seed, and hidden in a rock or in the heavens or in the earth; for God is Subtile, informed of all. This Day the deceitful of eye, and all that men's breasts conceal, are made known and laid bare before the throne of His Revelation. Nothing whatsoever can escape His knowledge. He heareth and seeth, and He, in truth, is the All-Hearing, the All-Seeing.

(Bahá'u'lláh, *Epistle to the Son of the Wolf*, p. 107)

…Every act ye meditate is as clear to Him as is that act when already accomplished. There is none other God besides Him. His is all creation and its empire. All stands revealed before Him; all is recorded in His holy and hidden Tablets. This fore-knowledge of God, however, should not be regarded as having caused the actions of men, just as your own previous knowledge that a certain event is to occur, or your desire that it should happen, is not and can never be the reason for its occurrence.

(Bahá'u'lláh, *Gleanings from the Writings of Bahá'u'lláh*, p. 149-150)

GLORY be unto Thee, O Lord my God! Nothing whatsoever escapeth Thy knowledge… whether in the heavens or on the earth, of the past or of the future.

(The Báb, *Selections from the Writings of the Báb*, p. 178)

The Love of God

For God is love, and all phenomena find source and emanation in that divine current of creation. The love of God haloes all created things. Were it not for the love of God, no animate being would exist.

('Abdu'l-Bahá, *The Promulgation of Universal Peace*, p. 315)

Were it not for the love of God the hearts would not be illumined. Were it not for the love of God the pathway of the Kingdom would not be opened. Were it not for the love of God the holy books would not have been revealed. Were it not for the love of God the divine prophets would not have been sent to the world. The foundation of all these bestowals is the love of God. Therefore in the human world there is no greater power than the love of God.

('Abdu'l-Bahá, *Foundations of World Unity*, p. 90)

God has created His servants in order that they may love and associate with each other. He has revealed the glorious splendor of His sun of love in the world of humanity. The cause of the creation of the phenomenal world is love.

('Abdu'l-Bahá, *The Promulgation of Universal Peace*, p. 297)

God and the Universe – References

Creation Without Beginning or End

As to thy question concerning the origin of creation. Know assuredly that God's creation hath existed from eternity, and will continue to exist forever. Its beginning hath had no beginning, and its end knoweth no end. His name, the Creator, presupposeth a creation, even as His title, the Lord of Men, must involve the existence of a servant.

As to those sayings, attributed to the Prophets of old, such as, "In the beginning was God; there was no creature to know Him," and "The Lord was alone; with no one to adore Him," the meaning of these and similar sayings is clear and evident, and should at no time be misapprehended. To this same truth bear witness these words which He hath revealed: "God was alone; there was none else besides Him. He will always remain what He hath ever been." Every discerning eye will readily perceive that the Lord is now manifest, yet there is none to recognize His glory. By this is meant that the habitation wherein the Divine Being dwelleth is far above the reach and ken of any one besides Him.

(Bahá'u'lláh, *Gleanings from the Writings of Bahá'u'lláh*, p. 150-151)

The sun is the sun because of its rays, because of its heat. Were we to conceive of a time when there was a sun without heat and light, it would imply that there had been no sun at all and that it became the sun afterward. So likewise if we say there was a time when God had no creation or created beings, a time when there were no recipients of His bounties and that His names and attributes had not been manifested, this would be equivalent to a complete denial of divinity, for it would mean that divinity is accidental. To explain it still more clearly, if we think that fifty thousand years ago or one hundred thousand years ago there was no creation, that there were then no worlds, no human beings, no animals, this thought of ours would mean that previous to that period there was no divinity. If we should say that there was a time when there was a king but there were no subjects, no army, no country for him to rule over, it would really be asserting that there was a time when no king existed and that the king is accidental. It is therefore evident that inasmuch as the reality of divinity is without a beginning, creation is also without a beginning. This is as clear as the sun. When we contemplate this vast machinery of omnipresent power, perceive this illimitable space and its innumerable worlds it will become evident to us that the lifetime of this infinite creation is more than six thousand years; nay, it is very, very ancient.

Notwithstanding this, we read in Genesis in the Old Testament that the lifetime of creation is but six thousand years. This has an inner meaning and significance; it is not to be taken literally. For instance it is said in the Old Testament that certain things were created in the first day. The narrative shows that at that time the sun was not yet created. How could we conceive of a day if no sun existed in the heavens; for the day depends upon the light of the sun? Inasmuch as the sun had not been made, how could the first day be realized? Therefore these statements have significances other than literal.

…One thousand years ago, two hundred thousand years ago, one million years ago the bounty of God was flowing, the radiance of God was shining, the dominion of God was existing.

('Abdu'l-Bahá, *Foundations of World Unity*, p. 108)

God and the Universe – References

Man Did Not Create Himself; A Proof of the Existence of God

One of the proofs and demonstrations of the existence of God is the fact that man did not create himself: nay, his creator and designer is another than himself.

It is certain and indisputable that the creator of man is not like man because a powerless creature cannot create another being. The maker, the creator, has to possess all perfections in order that he may create.

Can the creation be perfect and the creator imperfect? Can a picture be a masterpiece and the painter imperfect in his art? For it is his art and his creation. Moreover, the picture cannot be like the painter; otherwise, the painting would have created itself. However perfect the picture may be, in comparison with the painter it is in the utmost degree of imperfection...

It is certain that the whole contingent world is subjected to a law and rule which it can never disobey; even man is forced to submit to death, to sleep and to other conditions -- that is to say, man in certain particulars is governed, and necessarily this state of being governed implies the existence of a governor...

Throughout the world of existence it is the same; the smallest created thing proves that there is a creator. For instance, this piece of bread proves that it has a maker.

Praise be to God! the least change produced in the form of the smallest thing proves the existence of a creator: then can this great universe, which is endless, be self-created and come into existence from the action of matter and the elements? How self-evidently wrong is such a supposition!

('Abdu'l-Bahá, *Some Answered Questions,* p. 5)

The Manifestation Reflects the Reality of God

The Reality of Divinity may be compared to the sun, which from the height of its magnificence shines upon all the horizons and each horizon, and each soul, receives a share of its radiance. If this light and these rays did not exist, beings would not exist; all beings express something, and partake of some ray and portion of this light. The splendors of the perfections, bounties, and attributes of God shine forth and radiate from the reality of the Perfect Man, that is to say, the Unique One, the universal Manifestation of God. Other beings receive only one ray, but the universal Manifestation is the mirror for this Sun, which appears and becomes manifest in it, with all its perfections, attributes, signs, and wonders.

('Abdu'l-Bahá, *Bahá'í World Faith,* p. 322-323)

Knowledge of the Manifestation Is Knowledge of God

The knowledge of the Reality of the Divinity is impossible and unattainable, but the knowledge of the Manifestations of God is the knowledge of God, for the bounties, splendors, and divine attributes are apparent in them. Therefore if man attains to the knowledge of the Manifestations of God, he will attain to the knowledge of God; and if he be neglectful of the knowledge of the Holy Manifestation, he will be bereft of the knowledge of God.

('Abdu'l-Bahá, *Bahá'í World Faith,* p. 323)

The Worlds of God; the Phenomenon of Dreams

As to thy question concerning the worlds of God. Know thou of a truth that the worlds of God are countless in their number, and infinite in their range. None can reckon or comprehend them except God, the All-Knowing, the All-Wise. Consider thy state when asleep. Verily, I say, this phenomenon is the most mysterious of the signs of God amongst men, were they to ponder it in their hearts. Behold how the thing which thou hast seen in thy dream is, after a considerable lapse of time, fully realized. Had the world in which thou didst find thyself in thy dream been identical with the world in which thou livest, it would have been necessary for the event occurring in that dream to have transpired in this world at the very moment of its occurrence. Were it so, you yourself would have borne witness unto it. This being not the case, however, it must necessarily follow that the world in which thou livest is different and apart from that which thou hast experienced in thy dream. This latter world hath neither beginning nor end. It would be true if thou wert to contend that this same world is, as decreed by the All-Glorious and Almighty God, within thy proper self and is wrapped up within thee. It would equally be true to maintain that thy spirit, having transcended the limitations of sleep and having stripped itself of all earthly attachment, hath, by the act of God, been made to traverse a realm which lieth hidden in the innermost reality of this world. Verily I say, the creation of God embraceth worlds besides this world, and creatures apart from these creatures. In each of these worlds He hath ordained things which none can search except Himself, the All-Searching, the All-Wise. Do thou meditate on that which We have revealed unto thee, that thou mayest discover the purpose of God, thy Lord, and the Lord of all worlds.

(Bahá'u'lláh, *Gleanings from the Writings of Bahá'u'lláh,* p. 151-153)

LESSON #3

Prayer, Our Connection with God

Teachers may wish to study the following references in order to gain a deeper understanding of the material presented in each lesson.

Created to Know and Worship God

I bear witness, O my God, that Thou hast created me to know Thee and to worship Thee. I testify, at this moment, to my powerlessness and to Thy might, to my poverty and to Thy wealth. There is none other God but Thee, the Help in Peril, the Self-Subsisting.

(Bahá'u'lláh, *Prayers and Meditations*, p. 313)

I testify, O my God, and my King, that Thou hast created me to remember Thee, to glorify Thee, and to aid Thy Cause.

(Bahá'u'lláh, *Epistle to the Son of the Wolf*, p. 3)

The Wisdom of Prayer

O thou spiritual friend! Thou hast asked the wisdom of prayer. Know thou that prayer is indispensable and obligatory, and man under no pretext whatsoever is excused from performing the prayer unless he be mentally unsound, or an insurmountable obstacle prevent him. The wisdom of prayer is this: That it causeth a connection between the servant and the True One, because in that state man with all heart and soul turneth his face towards His Highness the Almighty, seeking His association and desiring His love and compassion. The greatest happiness for a lover is to converse with his beloved, and the greatest gift for a seeker is to become familiar with the object of his longing; that is why with every soul who is attracted to the Kingdom of God, his greatest hope is to find an opportunity to entreat and supplicate before his Beloved, appeal for His mercy and grace and be immersed in the ocean of His utterance, goodness and generosity.

Besides all this, prayer and fasting is the cause of awakening and mindfulness and conducive to protection and preservation from tests.

('Abdu'l-Bahá, *Bahá'í World Faith*, p. 368)

Supplication to God at morn and eve is conducive to the joy of hearts, and prayer causes spirituality and fragrance.

('Abdu'l-Bahá, *Tablets of 'Abdu'l-Bahá*, v1, p. 185)

Strive that Your Actions May Be Beautiful Prayers

Therefore strive that your actions day by day may be beautiful prayers. Turn towards God, and seek always to do that which is right and noble. Enrich the poor, raise the fallen, comfort the sorrowful, bring healing to the sick, reassure the fearful, rescue the oppressed, bring hope to the hopeless, shelter the destitute!

('Abdu'l-Bahá, *Paris Talks,* p. 80)

When To Pray

Glorified art Thou, O Lord, Thou forgivest at all times the sins of such among Thy servants as implore Thy pardon. Wash away my sins and the sins of those who seek Thy forgiveness at dawn, who pray to Thee in the daytime and in the night season, who yearn after naught save God, who offer up whatsoever God hath graciously bestowed upon them, who celebrate Thy praise at morn and eventide, and who are not remiss in their duties.

(The Báb, *Bahá'í Prayers,* p. 81)

Day and night devote thyself to prayer, supplication and entreaty, especially at the prescribed times.

('Abdu'l-Bahá, *Compilation on the Importance of Obligatory Prayer*, Section 2)

Obligatory Prayer

IX. The Obligatory Prayers have been set down by the Pen of the Most High...They are clearly binding, and without a doubt everyone must perform one of these three prayers.

XI. Obligatory prayer causeth the heart to become attentive to the Divine kingdom. One is alone with God, converseth with Him, and acquireth bounties. Likewise, if one performeth the Obligatory Prayer with his heart in a state of utmost purity, he will obtain the confirmations of the Holy Spirit, and this will entirely obliterate love of self.

XIII. Obligatory prayer and supplication cause man to reach the kingdom of mystery, and the worship of the Supreme One. They bestow nearness unto His threshold. There is a pleasure in offering prayers that transcendeth all other pleasures, and there is a sweetness in chanting and singing the verses of God which is the greatest desire of all the believers, men and women alike. While reciting the Obligatory Prayer, one converseth intimately and shareth secrets with the true Beloved. No pleasure is greater than this, if one proceedeth with a detached soul, with tears overflowing, with a trusting heart and an eager spirit. Every joy is earthly save this one, the sweetness of which is divine.

XIV. Obligatory prayer is the very foundation of the Cause of God. Through it joy and vitality infuse the heart. Even if every grief should surround Me, as soon as I engage in conversing with God in obligatory prayer, all My sorrows disappear and I attain joy and gladness.

XVI. Persevere in the use of the Obligatory Prayer and early morning supplications, so that day by day thine awareness may increase, and, through the power of the knowledge of God, thou mayest rend asunder the veil of error of the people of doubt and lead them to His unfailing guidance.

XVIII. Obligatory prayers and supplications are the very water of life. They are the cause of existence, of the refinement of souls, and of their attainment to the utmost joy.

('Abdu'l-Bahá, *Compilation on the Importance of Obligatory Prayer*, Section 2)

LESSON #4

What is a Human Being?

*Teachers may wish to study the following references in order to
gain a deeper understanding of the material presented in each lesson.*

Mankind Created by God for a Purpose

O Son of Bounty! Out of the wastes of nothingness, with the clay of My command I made thee to appear, and have ordained for thy training every atom in existence and the essence of all created things.

    (Bahá'u'lláh, *Persian Hidden Words* #29)

The purpose of God in creating man hath been, and will ever be, to enable him to know his Creator and to attain His Presence.

    (Bahá'u'lláh, *Gleanings from the Writings of Bahá'u'lláh,* p. 70)

The All-loving God created man to radiate the Divine light and to illumine the world by his words, action and life.

    ('Abdu'l-Bahá, *Paris Talks,* p. 113)

God, the Almighty, has created all mankind from the dust of earth. He has fashioned them all from the same elements; they are descended from the same race and live upon the same globe. He has created them to dwell beneath the one heaven. As members of the human family and His children He has endowed them with equal susceptibilities. He maintains, protects and is kind to all.

    ('Abdu'l-Bahá, *The Promulgation of Universal Peace,* p. 297)

Man Contains the Lower Kingdoms

The mineral kingdom possesses the power of existing. The plant has the power of existing and growing. The animal, in addition to existence and growth, has the capacity of moving about, and the use of the faculties of the senses. In the human kingdom we find all the attributes of the lower worlds, with much more added thereto. Man is the sum of every previous creation, for he contains them all.

    ('Abdu'l-Bahá, *Paris Talks,* p. 26)

Unique Distinction and Capacity to Know and Love God

Having created the world and all that liveth and moveth therein, He, through the direct operation of His unconstrained and sovereign Will, chose to confer upon man the unique distinction and capacity to know Him and to love Him – a capacity that must needs be regarded as the generating impulse and the primary purpose underlying the whole of creation.... Upon the inmost reality of each and every created thing He hath shed the light of one of His names, and made it a recipient of the glory of one of His attributes. Upon the reality of man, however, He hath focused the radiance of all of His names and attributes, and made it a mirror of His own Self. Alone of all created things man hath been singled out for so great a favor, so enduring a bounty.

(Bahá'u'lláh, *Gleanings from the Writings of Bahá'u'lláh,* p. 65)

Human Capacities Latent; Obscured by Worldly Desires

These energies with which the Day Star of Divine bounty and Source of heavenly guidance hath endowed the reality of man lie, however, latent within him, even as the flame is hidden within the candle and the rays of light are potentially present in the lamp. The radiance of these energies may be obscured by worldly desires even as the light of the sun can be concealed beneath the dust and dross which cover the mirror. Neither the candle nor the lamp can be lighted through their own unaided efforts, nor can it ever be possible for the mirror to free itself from its dross. It is clear and evident that until a fire is kindled the lamp will never be ignited, and unless the dross is blotted out from the face of the mirror it can never represent the image of the sun nor reflect its light and glory.

(Bahá'u'lláh, *Gleanings from the Writings of Bahá'u'lláh,* p. 65-66)

Yet if man remain content in an undeveloped state viewed from the point of capacity he is the lowest of creatures. If he attains unto his heritage through divine wisdom, then he becomes a clear mirror in which the beauty of God is reflected; he has eternal life and becomes a participator of the sun of truth.

('Abdu'l-Bahá, *Divine Philosophy,* p. 110)

Qualities Manifested As a Result of Own Volition

All that which ye potentially possess can, however, be manifested only as a result of your own volition. Your own acts testify to this truth. Consider, for instance, that which hath been forbidden, in the Bayán, unto men. God hath in that Book, and by His behest, decreed as lawful whatsoever He hath pleased to decree, and hath, through the power of His sovereign might, forbidden whatsoever He elected to forbid. To this testifieth the text of that Book. Will ye not bear witness? Men, however, have wittingly broken His law. Is such a behavior to be attributed to God, or to their proper selves? Be fair in your judgment.

(Bahá'u'lláh, *Gleanings from the Writings of Bahá'u'lláh,* p. 149)

Human Beings Created in the Image of God

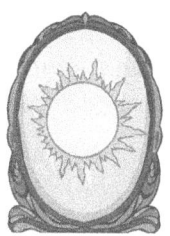

O ye young Bahá'í children, ye seekers after true understanding and knowledge! A human being is distinguished from an animal in a number of ways. First of all, he is made in the image of God...

('Abdu'l-Bahá, *Selections from the Writings of 'Abdu'l-Bahá,* p. 140)

According to the words of the Old Testament God has said, "Let us make man in our image, after our likeness." This indicates that man is of the image and likeness of God -- that is to say, the perfections of God, the divine virtues, are reflected or revealed in the human reality. Just as the light and effulgence of the sun when cast upon a polished mirror are reflected fully, gloriously, so, likewise, the qualities and attributes of Divinity are radiated from the depths of a pure human heart. This is an evidence that man is the most noble of God's creatures.

...The human kingdom is replete with the perfections of all the kingdoms below it with the addition of powers peculiar to man alone. Man is, therefore, superior to all the creatures below him, the loftiest and most glorious being of creation...

Let us now discover more specifically how he is the image and likeness of God and what is the standard or criterion by which he can be measured and estimated. This standard can be no other than the divine virtues which are revealed in him. Therefore, every man imbued with divine qualities, who reflects heavenly moralities and perfections, who is the expression of ideal and praiseworthy attributes, is, verily, in the image and likeness of God. If a man possesses wealth, can we call him an image and likeness of God? Or is human honor and notoriety the criterion of divine nearness? Can we apply the test of racial color and say that man of a certain hue -- white, black, brown, yellow, red -- is the true image of his Creator? We must conclude that color is not the standard and estimate of judgment and that it is of no importance, for color is accidental in nature. The spirit and intelligence of man is essential, and that is the manifestation of divine virtues, the merciful bestowals of God, the eternal life and baptism through the Holy Spirit. Therefore, be it known that color or race is of no importance. He who is the image and likeness of God, who is the manifestation of the bestowals of God, is acceptable at the threshold of God -- whether his color be white, black or brown; it matters not. Man is not man simply because of bodily attributes. The standard of divine measure and judgment is his intelligence and spirit.

('Abdu'l-Bahá, *The Promulgation of Universal Peace,* p. 69-70)

It is recorded in the Holy Bible that God said, "Let us make man in our image, after our likeness." It is self-evident that the image and likeness mentioned do not apply to the form and semblance of a human being because the reality of divinity is not limited to any form or figure. Nay, rather the attributes and characteristics of God are intended. Even as God is pronounced to be just, man must likewise be just. As God is loving and kind to all men, man must likewise manifest loving-kindness to all humanity. As God is loyal and truthful, man must show forth the same attributes in the human world. Even as God exercises mercy toward all, man must prove himself to be the manifestation of mercy. In a word, the "image and likeness of God" constitute the virtues of God...

('Abdu'l-Bahá, *Foundations of World Unity,* p. 92)

Consequently man must learn the lesson of kindness and beneficence from God Himself. Just as God is kind to all humanity, man also must be kind to his fellow creatures. If his attitude is just and loving toward his fellow men, toward all creation, then indeed is he worthy of being pronounced the image and likeness of God.

('Abdu'l-Bahá, *Foundations of World Unity,* p. 79)

The Perfect Man is as a polished mirror reflecting the Sun of Truth, manifesting the attributes of God.

('Abdu'l-Bahá, *Paris Talks,* p. 25)

Until man reaches this high station, the world of humanity shall not find rest, and eternal felicity shall not be attained. But if man lives up to these divine commandments, this world of earth shall be transformed into the world of heaven, and this material sphere shall be converted into a paradise of glory. It is my hope that you may become successful in this high calling so that like brilliant lamps you may cast light upon the world of humanity and quicken and stir the body of existence like unto a spirit of life. This is eternal glory. This is everlasting felicity. This is immortal life. This is heavenly attainment. This is being created in the image and likeness of God.

('Abdu'l-Bahá, *The Promulgation of Universal Peace,* p. 470)

Know thou, O handmaid, that in the sight of Bahá, women are accounted the same as men, and God hath created all humankind in His own image, and after His own likeness. That is, men and women alike are the revealers of His names and attributes, and from the spiritual viewpoint there is no difference between them.

('Abdu'l-Bahá, *Selections from the Writings of 'Abdu'l-Bahá,* p. 79-80)

All Things Captives of Nature Except Man

The stars and suns swinging through infinite space, all earthly forms of life and existence whether mineral, vegetable or animal come under the dominion and control of natural law. Man through scientific knowledge and power rules nature and utilizes her laws to do his bidding.

('Abdu'l-Bahá, *Foundations of World Unity,* p. 61)

All things are captives of nature except man. Man is the sovereign of nature; he breaks nature's laws. Though an animal fitted by nature to live upon the surface of the earth he flies in the air like a bird, sails upon the ocean and dives deep beneath its waves in submarines. Man is gifted with a power whereby he penetrates and discovers the laws of nature, brings them forth from the world of invisibility into the plane of visibility. Electricity was once a latent force of nature. According to nature's laws it should remain a hidden secret, but the spirit of man discovered it, brought it forth from its secret depository and made its phenomena visible. It is evident and manifest that man is capable of breaking nature's laws. How does he accomplish it? Through a spirit with which God has endowed him at creation. This is a proof that the spirit of man differentiates and distinguishes him above all the lower kingdoms.

('Abdu'l-Bahá, *Foundations of World Unity,* p. 90-91)

God and the Universe – References

The sun, that colossal center of our solar system, the giant stars and planets, the towering mountains, the earth itself and its kingdoms of life lower than the human, -- all are captives of nature except man. No other created thing can deviate in the slightest degree from obedience to natural law. The sun in its glory and greatness millions of miles away is held prisoner in its orbit of universal revolution, captive of universal natural control. Man is the ruler of nature. According to natural law and limitation he should remain upon the earth, but behold how he violates this command and soars above the mountains in aeroplanes. He sails in ships upon the surface of the ocean and dives into its depths in submarines. Man makes nature his servant; harnesses the mighty energy of electricity for instance and imprisons it in a small lamp for his uses and conveniences. He speaks from the East to the West through a wire. He is able to store and preserve his voice in a phonograph. Though he is a dweller upon earth he penetrates the mysteries of starry worlds inconceivably distant. He discovers latent realities within the bosom of the earth, uncovers treasures, penetrates secrets and mysteries of the phenomenal world and brings to light that which according to nature's jealous laws should remain hidden, unknown and unfathomable. Through an ideal inner power man brings these realities forth from the invisible plane to the visible. This is contrary to nature's law.

It is evident therefore that man is ruler over nature's sphere and province. Nature is inert, man is progressive. Nature has no consciousness, man is endowed with it. Nature is without volition and acts perforce whereas man possesses a mighty will. Nature is incapable of discovering mysteries or realities whereas man is especially fitted to do so. Nature is not in touch with the realm of God, man is attuned to its evidences. Nature is uninformed of God, man is conscious of Him. Man acquires divine virtues, nature is denied them. Man can voluntarily discontinue vices, nature has no power to modify the influence of its instincts. Altogether it is evident that man is more noble and superior; that in him there is an ideal power surpassing nature. He has consciousness, volition, memory, intelligent power, divine attributes and virtues of which nature is completely deprived, bereft and minus; therefore man is higher and nobler by reason of the ideal and heavenly force latent and manifest in him.

('Abdu'l-Bahá, *Foundations of World Unity*, p. 69-70)

Power of Understanding, God's Greatest Gift to Man

God's greatest gift to man is that of intellect, or understanding…How grievous it is to see how man has used his God-given gift to frame instruments of war, for breaking the Commandment of God 'Thou shalt not kill', and for defying Christ's injunction to 'Love one another'.

God gave this power to man that it might be used for the advancement of civilization, for the good of humanity, to increase love and concord and peace. But man prefers to use this gift to destroy instead of to build, for injustice and oppression, for hatred and discord and devastation, for the destruction of his fellow-creatures, whom Christ has commanded that he should love as himself!

I hope that you will use your understanding to promote the unity and tranquility of mankind, to give enlightenment and civilization to the people, to produce love in all around you, and to bring about the universal peace.

('Abdu'l-Bahá, *Paris Talks,* p. 41-43)

This supreme emblem of God stands first in the order of creation and first in rank, taking precedence over all created things. Witness to it is the Holy Tradition, "Before all else, God created the mind." From the dawn of creation, it was made to be revealed in the temple of man.

('Abdu'l-Bahá, *Secret of Divine Civilization,* p. 1)

The animal is perfect when its body is healthy and its physical senses are whole…when food and surrounding conditions minister to its needs, it has attained the ultimate perfection of its kingdom. But man does not depend upon these things for his virtues. No matter how perfect his health and physical powers, if that is all, he has not yet risen above the degree of a perfect animal. Beyond and above this, God has opened the doors of ideal virtues and attainments before the face of man. He has created in his being the mysteries of the divine Kingdom. He has bestowed upon him the power of intellect so that through the attribute of reason, when fortified by the Holy Spirit, he may penetrate and discover ideal realities and become informed of the mysteries of the world of significances.

('Abdu'l-Bahá, *Promulgation of Universal Peace,* p. 302)

The Inner Reality of Man

It is manifest that beyond this body man is endowed with another reality…At the time of speech man says: "I said," "I saw." Who is this "I"? It is obvious that this "I" is different from this body. It is clear that when man is thinking, it is as though he were consulting with some other person. Whom is he consulting with? It is evident that it is another reality or one aside from this body with whom he enters into consultation…

('Abdu'l-Bahá, *Bahá'í Scriptures,* p. 294)

Furthermore, in the world of dreams man sees things. He travels in the East, he travels in the West, although his body is stationary. His body is here, yet it is that reality in him which makes the journey to the West while the body sleeps. There is no doubt that a reality is there other than the outward, physical reality. For instance, a person is dead, is buried in the ground. We see him in the world of dreams, we speak with him. While that person's body is interred in the ground, who then is the person whom you see in your dreams, talk to, and who also speaks to you? Therefore, this again proves that there is another reality, different from this physical one which dies and is buried. Thus it is evident that in man there is a reality other than this physical one which is not his body… For instance, the body of man may lose one arm, but the reality of man, which is not visible, loses nothing and is in its own normal state. This body goes to sleep, becomes as one dead, but that reality in that body which is asleep is moving about, is comprehending things, is expressing them, is discovering the realities of things.

…That reality grasps the mysteries of existence. It discovers scientific facts. It discovers technical points. It discovers electricity, telegraphy, the telephone, and so on, discovering all the arts -- and yet the reality which makes all these discoveries is other than this body, for, were it this body, then the animal would likewise be able to make these scientific and wonderful discoveries, for the animal shares with man all physical limitation and physical powers. What then is that power which discovers the realities of things which is not to be found in the animal? There is no doubt that it is the inner reality of man…

('Abdu'l-Bahá, *Bahá'í Scriptures*, p. 295)

Nature of the Soul

Thou hast asked Me concerning the nature of the soul. Know, verily, that the soul is a sign of God, a heavenly gem whose reality the most learned of men hath failed to grasp, and whose mystery no mind, however acute, can ever hope to unravel. It is the first among all created things to declare the excellence of its Creator, the first to recognize His glory, to cleave to His truth, and to bow down in adoration before Him. If it be faithful to God, it will reflect His light, and will, eventually, return unto Him. If it fail, however, in its allegiance to its Creator, it will become a victim to self and passion, and will, in the end, sink in their depths.

(Bahá'u'lláh, *Gleanings from the Writings of Bahá'u'lláh*, p. 158-159)

Life After Death

And now concerning thy question regarding the soul of man and its survival after death. Know thou of a truth that the soul, after its separation from the body, will continue to progress until it attaineth the presence of God, in a state and condition which neither the revolution of ages and centuries, nor the changes and chances of this world, can alter. It will endure as long as the Kingdom of God, His sovereignty, His dominion and power will endure. It will manifest the signs of God and His attributes, and will reveal His loving kindness and bounty. The movement of My Pen is stilled when it attempteth to befittingly describe the loftiness and glory of so exalted a station. The honor with which the Hand of Mercy will invest the soul is such as no tongue can adequately reveal, nor any other earthly agency describe.

(Bahá'u'lláh, *Gleanings from the Writings of Bahá'u'lláh*, p. 155-156)

Additional References on God and the Universe

Meditation

Do thou meditate on that which We have revealed unto thee, that thou mayest discover the purpose of God, thy Lord, and the Lord of all worlds.

   (Bahá'u'lláh, *Gleanings from the Writings of Bahá'u'lláh,* p. 152)

   Bahá'u'lláh says there is a sign (from God) in every phenomenon: the sign of the intellect is contemplation and the sign of contemplation is silence, because it is impossible for a man to do two things at one time -- he cannot both speak and meditate.

   It is an axiomatic fact that while you meditate you are speaking with your own spirit. In that state of mind you put certain questions to your spirit and the spirit answers: the light breaks forth and the reality is revealed.

   You cannot apply the name 'man' to any being void of this faculty of meditation; without it he would be a mere animal, lower than the beasts.

   Through the faculty of meditation man attains to eternal life; through it he receives the breath of the Holy Spirit -- the bestowal of the Spirit is given in reflection and meditation.

   The spirit of man is itself informed and strengthened during meditation; through it affairs of which man knew nothing are unfolded before his view. Through it he receives Divine inspiration, through it he receives heavenly food.

   Meditation is the key for opening the doors of mysteries. In that state man abstracts himself: in that state man withdraws himself from all outside objects; in that subjective mood he is immersed in the ocean of spiritual life and can unfold the secrets of things-in-themselves. To illustrate this, think of man as endowed with two kinds of sight; when the power of insight is being used the outward power of vision does not see.

   This faculty of meditation frees man from the animal nature, discerns the reality of things, puts man in touch with God.

   This faculty brings forth from the invisible plane the sciences and arts. Through the meditative faculty inventions are made possible, colossal undertakings are carried out; through it governments can run smoothly. Through this faculty man enters into the very Kingdom of God…

   The meditative faculty is akin to the mirror; if you put it before earthly objects it will reflect them. Therefore if the spirit of man is contemplating earthly subjects he will be informed of these.

   But if you turn the mirror of your spirits heavenwards, the heavenly constellations and the rays of the Sun of Reality will be reflected in your hearts, and the virtues of the Kingdom will be obtained.

   Therefore let us keep this faculty rightly directed -- turning it to the heavenly Sun and not to earthly objects -- so that we may discover the secrets of the Kingdom, and comprehend the allegories of the Bible and the mysteries of the spirit.

   ('Abdu'l-Bahá, *Paris Talks,* p. 174-176)

God and the Universe – References

Creation and Evolution

For man, from the beginning of the embryonic period till he reaches the degree of maturity, goes through different forms and appearances. His aspect, his form, his appearance, and color change; he passes from one form to another, and from one appearance to another. Nevertheless, from the beginning of the embryonic period he is of the species of man; that is to say, an embryo of a man, and not of an animal; but this is not at first apparent but later it becomes visible and evident. For example, let us suppose that man once resembled the animal, and that now he has progressed and changed; supposing this to be true, it is still not a proof of the change of species…We will state it more clearly: let us suppose that there was a time when man walked on his hands and feet, or had a tail; this change and alteration is like that of the fetus in the womb of the mother….

….as man in the womb of the mother passes from form to form, from shape to shape, changes and develops, and is still the human species from the beginning of the embryonic period -- in the same way man, from the beginning of his existence in the matrix of the world, is also a distinct species -- that is, man -- and has gradually evolved from one form to another. Therefore, this change of appearance, this evolution of members, this development and growth, even though we admit the reality of growth and progress, does not prevent the species from being original. Man from the beginning was in this perfect form and composition, and possessed capacity and aptitude for acquiring material and spiritual perfections, and was the manifestation of these words, "We will make man in Our image and likeness." He has only become more pleasing, more beautiful, and more graceful. Civilization has brought him out of his wild state, just as the wild fruits which are cultivated by a gardener became finer, sweeter, and acquire more freshness and delicacy.

The gardeners of the world of humanity are the Prophets of God.

('Abdu'l-Bahá: *Some Answered Questions,* p. 193-194)

…ye can see that this endless creation carrieth out its functions in perfect order, every separate part of it performing its own task with complete reliability, nor is there any flaw to be found in all its workings. Thus it is clear that a Universal Power existeth, directing and regulating this infinite universe.

('Abdu'l-Bahá, *Selections from the Writings of 'Abdu'l-Bahá,* p. 48-49)

So you will find the smallest atoms in the universal system are similar to the greatest beings of the universe. It is clear that they come into existence from one laboratory of might under one natural system and one universal law…

('Abdu'l-Bahá, *Some Answered Questions*, p. 182-185)

The suckling babe passeth through various physical stages, growing and developing at every stage, until its body reacheth the age of maturity…Similarly, in the contingent world, the human species hath undergone progressive physical changes and, by a slow process, hath scaled the ladder of civilization… until it gained the capacity to express the splendours of spiritual perfections…and became capable of hearkening to the call of God.

('Abdu'l-Bahá, *Selections from the Writings of 'Abdu'l-Bahá,* p. 285-286)

God and the Universe – References

In the same way, the embryo of man in the womb of the mother was at first in a strange form; then this body passes from shape to shape, from state to state, from form to form, until it appears in utmost beauty and perfection. But even when in the womb of the mother...and in this strange form...his species and essence undergo no change...Man was always a distinct species, a man, not an animal.

('Abdu'l-Bahá, *Some Answered Questions,* p. 182-185]

But at all times, even when the embryo resembled a worm, it was human in potentiality and character... Realizing this we may acknowledge the fact that at one time man was an inmate of the sea, at another period an invertebrate, then a vertebrate and finally a human being standing erect.

('Abdu'l-Bahá, *Promulgation of Universal Peace,* p. 359)

All beings, whether large or small, were created perfect and complete from the first, but their perfections appear in them by degrees... Each seed has in it from the first all the vegetable perfections... So it is first the shoot which appears from the seed, then the branches, leaves, blossoms and fruits; but from the beginning of its existence all these things are in the seed, potentially though not apparently.

In the same way, the embryo possesses from the first all perfections, such as the spirit, the mind, the sight, the smell, the taste -- in one word, all the powers -- but they are not visible and become so only by degrees.

Similarly, the terrestrial globe from the beginning was created with all its elements, substances, minerals, atoms and organisms; but these only appeared by degrees: first the mineral, then the plant, afterward the animal, and finally man. But from the first these kinds and species existed, but were undeveloped in the terrestrial globe, and then appeared only gradually. For the supreme organization of God, and the universal natural system, surround all beings, and all are subject to this rule.

("Abdu'l-Bahá, *Some Answered Questions,* p. 199-200)

From this it is evident that it is the creation of God, and is not a fortuitous composition and arrangement....For example, if a man of his own mind and intelligence collects some elements and combines them, a living being will not be brought into existence... It is God Who makes the combination.

('Abdu'l-Bahá, *Some Answered Questions,* p. 181-182)

Again, there are men whose eyes are only open to physical progress and to the evolution in the world of matter. These men prefer to study the resemblance between their own physical body and that of the ape, rather than to contemplate the glorious affiliation between their spirit and that of God. This is indeed strange, for it is only physically that man resembles the lower creation...

As for the spiritual perfections they are man's birthright and belong to him alone of all creation. Man is, in reality, a spiritual being, and only when he lives in the spirit is he truly happy.

('Abdu'l-Bahá, *Paris Talks,* p. 71-72)

Educational Strategy

Think-Pair-Share

Think-Pair-Share is a cooperative discussion strategy formalized by Professor Frank Lyman at the University of Maryland in 1981. Its name derives from the three steps of student action:

1) Think: The teacher poses an open-ended, thought-provoking question (not something with a simple *yes* or *no* answer). Students are given a brief period (anywhere from 10 seconds to about 5 minutes, depending on the complexity of the topic) to think individually about their responses.

2) Pair: Students pair up with a partner to discuss their answers, and based on their collective insights, identify the ones they think are best. This interaction also provides an opportunity to clarify difficult words and challenging concepts. Students are given 1 to 10 minutes to work, depending on the difficulty of the question. More time will be needed if students are asked to produce a chart or diagram of their thinking. With a large class and a complex topic, the teacher may wish to add an additional step: Ask the pairs to regroup into fours in order to further refine their thoughts before sharing with the entire class.

If there are an odd number of students, one of them can partner with a teacher's assistant, or join one of the pairs.

3) Share: The teacher asks each pair to share its thinking with the class. With a large group, the teacher might only call on some of the pairs. Responses can be noted on the board. If desired, one or two students can also be called upon to summarize the entire discussion. The quality of the activity will depend upon the quality of the question posed in step one.

Some Benefits of Think-Pair-Share

Think-Pair-Share has many advantages over the traditional classroom practice of the teacher asking a question, then calling on one or two students to answer. In the traditional classroom, as soon as the first individual is called upon, the others often stop thinking about the question. Think-Pair-Share is a valuable educational strategy for the following reasons:

- It allows everyone to participate equally, including those who never volunteer in class or who might be slower to respond. Increased student participation leads to improved learning and retention of information.

- It structures the discussion, promoting focused student conversations and limiting off-task behavior.

- It develops thinking and communication skills through speaking, listening, asking questions, analyzing and summarizing others' ideas.

- It allows concepts to be presented in the language of the students, rather than the language of the textbook or teacher.

- It improves the quality of class discussions by giving students a chance to think about and discuss their answers, rather than blurting out the first thing that comes to mind. Teachers often wait less than a second before calling on students. With silent "wait time" built in, responses will have better explanations and greater detail.

- It is a low-risk strategy, allowing students to try out ideas on a partner and refine their thoughts before sharing with the group at large. This is less threatening than speaking in front of the entire class with an untested answer.

- It allows students to learn from each other, and to see the same concepts expressed in a variety of ways, as different individuals develop answers to the same question.

- It ensures a high level of student engagement in a cooperative process.

- It is an effective strategy for children, youth and adults, in classes of any size.

BIBLIOGRAPHY

Ancient Goddess Religions. The Universal House of Justice. Bahá'í World Centre: Haifa, Israel, 23 February 1992.

Bahá'í Education: A Compilation. Compiled by the Research Department of the Universal House of Justice. Bahá'í Publishing Trust: Wilmette, Illinois, 1978.

Bahá'í Prayers: A Selection of Prayers Revealed by Bahá'u'lláh, The Báb and 'Abdu'l-Bahá. Bahá'í Publishing Trust: Wilmette, Illinois, 1954; 1991 edition.

Bahá'í Scriptures: Selections from the Utterances of Bahá'u'lláh and 'Abdu'l-Bahá. Horace Holley, ed. Bahá'í Publishing Committee: New York, 1928 edition.

Bahá'í World Faith: A Selection of Writings from Bahá'u'lláh and 'Abdu'l-Bahá. Bahá'í Publishing Trust: Wilmette, Illinois, 1943, 1976.

Bahá'í Year Book [The Bahá'í World], vol. 1, 1925-1926. Bahá'í Publishing Committee: New York, 1926.

The Bible. King James Version. World Publishing Company: Cleveland, Ohio, conformable to the edition of 1611.

Compilation on the Importance of Obligatory Prayer and Fasting: Selection of Extracts and Prayers from the Bahá'í Writings. Compiled by the Research Department of the Universal House of Justice, May 2000.

Developing Distinctive Bahá'í Communities. National Spiritual Assembly of the Bahá'ís of the U.S. Office of Assembly Development, Evanston, Illinois, 1998.

Divine Philosophy. Compiled from the talks of 'Abdu'l-Bahá and published by Isabel Fraser Chamberlain. Cited in Ocean (http://bahai-education.org/ocean)

Epistle to the Son of the Wolf. Bahá'u'lláh. Translated by Shoghi Effendi, Bahá'í Publishing Trust, Wilmette, Illinois, 1941; 1988 edition.

Foundations of World Unity. 'Abdu'l-Bahá. Bahá'í Publishing Trust: Wilmette, Illinois, 1945; 1968 edition.

Gleanings from the Writings of Bahá'u'lláh. Bahá'u'lláh. Translated by Shoghi Effendi. Bahá'í Publishing Trust: Wilmette, Illinois, 1952; 1983 edition.

God and the Universe

The Hidden Words. Bahá'u'lláh. Translated by Shoghi Effendi with the assistance of some English friends. Bahá'í Publishing Trust: Wilmette, Illinois, 1954.

Journey to the Father: New Perspectives on Gender and the Bahá'í Revelation. Joell Ann Vanderwagen, Journey Publications, Toronto, 2004.

Letter to the Continental Boards of Counsellors. International Teaching Centre. Bahá'í World Centre: Haifa, Israel, 5 December 1988.

Paris Talks. 'Abdu'l-Bahá. Bahá'í Publishing Trust: London, 1995 edition.

Prayers and Meditations by Bahá'u'lláh. Bahá'u'lláh. Translated by Shoghi Effendi. Bahá'í Publishing Trust: Wilmette, Illinois, 1987 edition.

The Promulgation of Universal Peace. Talks by 'Abdu'l-Bahá during His visit to the United States and Canada in 1912. Bahá'í Publishing Trust: Wilmette, Illinois, 1982 edition.

Ridván 2000 Message to the Bahá'ís of the World. The Universal House of Justice. Bahá'í World Centre: Haifa, Israel, 2000.

The Secret of Divine Civilization. 'Abdu'l-Bahá. Translated from the original Persian by Marzieh Gail. Bahá'í Publishing Trust: Wilmette, Illinois, 1990 edition.

Selections from the Writings of 'Abdu'l-Bahá. Translated by a Committee at the Bahá'í World Centre & Marzieh Gail. Bahá'í World Centre: Haifa, Israel, 1978, 1982 printing.

Selections from the Writings of the Báb. Translated by Habib Taherzadeh with the assistance of a committee at the Bahá'í World Centre. Bahá'í World Centre: Haifa, Israel, 1978 edition.

The Seven Valleys and the Four Valleys. Bahá'u'lláh. Translated by Marzieh Gail in consultation with Ali Quli Khan. Bahá'í Publishing Trust: Wilmette, Illinois, 1986 edition.

Some Answered Questions. 'Abdu'l-Bahá. Collected and translated by Laura Clifford Barney. Bahá'í Publishing Trust: Wilmette, Illinois, 1987 edition.

Tablets of 'Abdu'l-Bahá Abbás, volume 1. Translated by Edward G. Browne. Bahá'í Publishing Committee: New York, 1930 edition.

Tablets of Bahá'u'lláh Revealed After the Kitáb-i-Aqdas. Translated by Habíb Taherzadeh with assistance of a Committee at the Bahá'í World Centre. Bahá'í World Centre: Haifa, Israel, 1978.

Vignettes from the Life of 'Abdu'l-Bahá. Collected and edited by Annamarie Honnold. George Ronald: Oxford, 1982. Original story by Dorothy Baker, in *The Path to God.* Bahá'í Publishing Committee: New York, 1937.

Will and Testament of 'Abdu'l-Bahá. 'Abdu'l-Bahá. Bahá'í Publishing Trust: Wilmette, IL, 1968 edition.

WORKS BY THE SAME AUTHOR

www.UnityWorksStore.com

Some books also available from: www.BahaiBookStore.com, (800) 999-9019
and Special Ideas: www.bahairesources.com, (800) 326-1197

> Check our website for high-quality, low-cost, easy-to-use Bahá'í resources. Download PowerPoint firesides, Five Year Plan study guides, children's class materials, Bahá'í mini ads, and much more!

Activity Books for Bahá'í Children's Classes

This series of easy-to-use teacher's guides is filled with fun, hands-on, kid-tested learning activities designed for ages 8-12. A useful resource for Bahá'í summer and winter schools, Holy Day programs, academic classes and weekend retreats. The activities were developed and tested in the field, in response to the needs of teachers and children, and have been used successfully in multiple settings over many years. Each book includes detailed lessons, copy-ready student handouts, song sheets, craft instructions and more!

"Your curriculum is the best I've seen to teach kids about the Faith. I love it!! They aren't being taught principles, they are investigating, exploring, and owning the principles."
— **Sue Walker, PhD**

Bahá'í Children's Retreats (A Complete Planning Guide)

Want to plan an unforgettable Bahá'í activity for children ages 8-12, but don't know where to begin? This retreat planning guide covers the following topics:

- Sponsorship, Schedules, Forms
- Teachers, Facility, Finances, Publicity
- Registration, Materials, Menus
- Orientation, Children's Performance
- Outdoor Activities and more!

Also included are medical release forms, recipes, a planning checklist and a graduation certificate—everything you need to organize a successful children's retreat. This planning guide is the perfect companion to the activity books on each theme.

"This retreat was life changing. You feel a renewal of passion for educating children!"
— **Lynn Haug, parent**

Bahá'í Public Speaking (Teacher's Guide with Nine Workshops)

This practical, easy-to-use teacher's guide contains nine hands-on workshops on Bahá'í public speaking. It is designed to equip youth, adults and children with the skills and confidence needed to become more effective teachers of the Faith. Participants will learn to speak with clarity and conviction—from the kitchen table to the conference hall. Be prepared for home visits, devotional meetings, fireside talks, direct teaching campaigns and public discourse. Great for junior youth groups, youth workshops and campus clubs!

This training manual can be used in conjunction with Ruhi Book 6.
It comes complete with copy-ready student handouts. Each lesson includes:

- Warm-up activities
- Speaking tips
- Practice exercises
- Homework assignment

"Fabulous! I'm very glad that you're publishing this, and I hope it is widely circulated!"
– Erica Toussaint

Once to Every Man and Nation (Stories About Becoming a Bahá'í)

A great gift for seekers, this book brings together 37 heartwarming stories of how people became Bahá'ís. The contributors to *Once to Every Man and Nation* come from all over North America and represent a wide variety of cultural, racial, social and ethnic backgrounds. Young and old, black and white, each with a different experience of life, their very diversity demonstrates the universal appeal of the Bahá'í teachings.

"Will be enjoyed by many believers...thoroughly recommend it."
– Bahá'í Reviewing Panel of the United Kingdom

Bahá'í Mini Ads

Thirty small print ads for use with local media campaigns. The series is designed to complement our Bahá'í teaching efforts by creating greater awareness and positive interest in the Faith. It includes basic Bahá'í beliefs and principles, short quotations from the Bahá'í Writings, offers of free literature, an invitation to the core activities, and an invitation to join the Bahá'í community. The file is in Microsoft Word format so it is easy to insert local contact information.

"These will surely boost teaching efforts in all communities that use them!"
– Dale Eng

PowerPoint Firesides on the Bahá'í Faith

(1)
The Bahá'í Faith:
An Introduction*

(2)
Central Figures
of the Bahá'í Faith

(3)
The Proclamation
of Bahá'u'lláh

(4)
The Power
of Unity

These colorful slide shows are designed to introduce the Bahá'í Faith. They offer an overview of the Faith: its Central Figures, purpose, core beliefs and teachings, photographs of its World Center, Houses of Worship, and scenes from Bahá'í community life. The programs have been used to effectively share the Bahá'í teachings in churches, classrooms, public libraries and community firesides.

- Perfect for high school and university students
- Ideal for projecting in large group settings
- Can also be used with a laptop one-on-one

* Also available in French and Spanish

What People Are Saying

"I don't know if the presentation could have gone any better!...This was one of the most amazing teaching experiences I've ever had!" — **Charisse Johnson, student**

"... a wonderful conclusion to our study of world faiths...it makes for a great end of semester presentation." — **Steve Deligan, high school religion teacher**

"...a fantastic presentation...very understandable...excellent to use for youth."
— **Seth Walker, youth**

"A wonderful trilogy for humans everywhere to learn from." — **Beth Shevin, seeker**

"...a great success tonight in Australia...the Baha'is were very pleased with their professional quality." — **Nancy Watters, traveling teacher**

"...straight-forward...high-quality...a wonderful introduction to the Teachings"
— **Shannon Javid, Regional Bahá'í Council member**

"Very respectful and professional. Job well done!" — **Warren Odess-Gillett**

 **Download from: www.UnityWorksStore.com**

Starting a Bahá'í-Inspired Academic School

This booklet presents basic guidelines and suggestions for those considering the establishment of a Bahá'í-inspired academic school. It provides a useful framework for organizing critical tasks and decisions, utilizing a detailed checklist with hundreds of practical tips.

Escuela de las Naciones (School of the Nations)

Description with color photographs of a Bahá'í-inspired K-6 elementary school established in Puerto Rico in 1991. This monograph provides an overview of the establishment and functioning of the private, non-profit, competency-based school, including the students, facilities, classroom design, curriculum, instructional methods and materials, system of evaluation, schedule, integration of the arts, and service.

Service: Heart of the Curriculum for a Global Civilization

This monograph considers the significance of service to mankind as a central organizing principle for our educational endeavors, and recommends practical strategies for systematically integrating service into the daily life and culture of our schools.

Principles into Practice

Workshop and compilation of Bahá'í Writings on education. This resource is offered as a tool for educators who wish to put Bahá'í principles into practice in their classrooms. Detailed step-by-step instructions for conducting the workshop are presented, and copy-ready student handouts are included. The workshop complements Ruhi Book 3 training and is appropriate for Bahá'ís and friends of the Faith.

Needs Assessment Survey to Determine the Training Requirements of International Bahá'í Traveling Teachers

This doctoral thesis details the training needs of personnel on international service projects. The survey of 200 returned volunteers and Bahá'í Institutions in the 81 countries they visited, was done under the auspices of the U.S. Bahá'í International Goals Committee. The study focuses on cross-cultural communication, critical incidents, training and materials design.

God and the Universe

List of Activities by Chapter

Opening Activities   Page
1. Unity Bingo (ice breaker) 14
2. Thinking about God (write, exchange, share) 14
3. Who Am I? (20 questions strategy game, in pairs) 14-15
4. Cosmic Voyage (video on the universe – from galaxies to atoms) 15
5. Group singing (instructions, song sheets, musical scores) 177-191

Lesson 1: The Kingdoms of Creation
1. Introduction: Creator or created (differentiating cause and effect) 8, 27-32
2. Kingdoms of creation (picture sorting) 18, 38
3. Kingdom questions (whole class discussion) 19, 34
4. Kingdom categories (brainstorming) 20
5. Kingdom comparisons (small group discussion) 20, 26, 35
6. Kingdoms of creation (felt lesson) 21, 36-42
7. Additional activities 21, 121-134
8. Closing questions (review and feedback) 21
9. Kingdoms of God (song) 21
10. Craft Activities 21-25
    A. God is the Creator (freehand drawing and coloring page) 22-23
    B. Kingdoms of creation (collage booklet) 24
    C. Kingdoms of creation (wall mural) 25
11. Galaxy maps and photos (individual study) 44

Lesson 2: God, the Creator
1. Review 46
2. O God, Guide Me (song) 46
3. Introduction to the theme 46
4. God, the Creator (reading with student questions and discussion) 46, 52, 166
5. Kids' questions about God (small group discussion) 47, 53
6. The Universe (demonstration of causality using building blocks) 48, 54
7. Creation meditation (meditation exercise) 48-49
8. O Son of Being (memory quote, Arabic Hidden Word #12) 50, 51
9. God's eye (yarn weaving) 51, 55-57

Lesson 3: Prayer, Our Connection with God

1. Review 60
2. Pray to God; O God, Guide Me (songs) 60
3. Introduction to the theme 60
4. Prayer questions (student-led discussion) 60-61, 66, 172
5. Reverence (prayer postures demonstration) 62, 67-76, 167
6. Prayer, our connection with God (reading and discussion) 63, 77, 168
7. The Prayer Lesson (story about 'Abdu'l-Bahá with questions) 63, 78, 169
8. Prayer connection (lamp demonstration) 64
9. Personal stories (small group sharing about prayer) 64
10. Prayer maps (add stars to show where prayers were said) 64, 79-83
11. Blessed is the Spot (song) 65
12. Craft Activities...65, 84-94
    A. Prayer pouch (leather craft)..85-87
    B. Blessed is the spot (coloring booklet and posters) 88-94, 170-171

Lesson 4: What Is a Human Being?

1. Review of lessons 1-3 98
2. What is a human being? (pairs discussion) 99
3. Who am I? (self reflection and sharing) 99
4. What is a human being? (felt lesson) 100, 103-107
5. In the image of God (reading and discussion).................................... 100, 108, 173
6. The purpose of life (small group discussion) 100-101, 109
7. Memory quotes (student choice) 101, 110-111, 161-162
8. A human being is (reflection and review) 102, 112, 175
9. Song of Love (song) 102
10. Spirit banners (felt craft) 102, 113-117
11. The universe is amazing (bonus maze) 174

Additional Activities

1. Kingdoms of Creation 121
    A. Four kingdoms (dramatic movement) 121
    B. Twenty questions (strategy game)... 122
    C. Outdoor kingdom hunt (outdoor walk) 122
    D. Who created it? (brainstorming) 122
    E. Origami (paper folding craft).. 123
    F. Creation Boxes (categorizing and sorting)... 124

2. Prayer Activities 125
    A. Prayer tree (cut out leaves) 125-126
    B. Personal prayer book (make a booklet for adding memorized prayers) 127
    C. Prayer station (to learn, copy, decorate and memorize prayers) 127

 3. Word Puzzles 128
    A. Word Search 129
    B. Word Search with a Hidden Message 130
    C. Double Puzzle 131
    D. Letter Tiles 132
    E. Puzzle Solutions 133-134

Children's Performance

 1. Instructions, materials, agenda and program 135-139, 155
 2. American Indian prayer (opening prayer) 140
 3. Kingdoms of creation (felt lesson) 141
 4. True understanding (reading with pictures) 142-146
 5. Kids' questions about God (brainstorming results) 147
 6. The universe (demonstration of causality using building blocks) 148
 7. Some divine humor (jokes) 149
 8. The names of God (devotional reading) 150-151
 9. Prayer connection (lamp demonstration) 152
 10. Prayer postures (demonstration) 153
 11. Quiz show on prayer (with host and panelists) 154

Music

 1. Instructions for group singing 177-179
 2. Song sheets 159-160, 180-181
 3. Musical scores 182-191
    A. Blessed Is the Spot / Bendito Es el Sitio 183
    B. Day by Day 184
    C. Glorious Day 185
    D. God Is One / Dios es Uno 186
    E. Kingdoms of God 187
    F. Love Me That I May Love Thee 188
    G. O God, Guide Me 189
    H. Pray to God 190
    I. Song of Love 191

Closing and Follow-up Activities 193-196

God and the Universe – Index

Index of Activities by Category

(Note: Some items are listed in more than one category.)

Arts and Crafts   Page

Blessed is the spot (coloring booklet and posters) 88-94, 170-171
Children's performance (project presentations) 137-139
Creation Boxes (categorizing and sorting).. 124
Folder decorations (drawing, cut-and-paste).. 13
God's eye (yarn weaving) 51, 55-57
Kingdoms of creation (collage booklet)... 24
God is the Creator (freehand drawing and coloring page) 22-23
Kingdoms of creation (wall mural) 25
Origami (paper folding craft).. 123
Personal prayer book (make a booklet for adding memorized prayers) 127
Prayer pouch (leather craft)...85-87
Prayer station (to learn, copy, decorate and memorize prayers) 127
Prayer tree (cut out leaves) 125-126
Spirit banners (felt craft) 102, 113-117

Demonstrations and Felt Lessons

Children's performance (presentations to an audience) 135-156
Kingdoms of creation (felt lesson)... 21, 36-42, 141
Prayer connection (lamp demonstration) 64
Reverence (prayer postures demonstration) 62, 67-76, 167
The universe (demonstration of causality using building blocks) 148
What is a human being? (felt lesson) 100, 103-107

Discussion

Creator or created (differentiating cause and effect) 8, 27-32
God, the Creator (reading with student questions and discussion)...................... 46, 52, 166
In the image of God (reading and discussion) 100, 108, 173
Kids' questions about God (brainstorming) 147
Kingdom comparisons (small group discussion) 20, 26, 35
Kingdom questions (whole class discussion) 19, 34
Personal stories (small group sharing about prayer)... 64
The Prayer Lesson (story about 'Abdu'l-Bahá with questions) 63, 78, 169
Prayer, our connection with God (reading and discussion) 63, 77, 168

Bahá'í Children's Classes and Retreats: Theme 1, p. 233

God and the Universe – Index

    Prayer questions (student-led discussion) 60-61, 66, 172
    The purpose of life (small group discussion) 100-101, 109
    What is a human being? (pairs discussion) 99

Games and Puzzles

    Quiz show on prayer (with host and panelists) 154
    Twenty questions (strategy game) 122
    Who Am I? (20 questions strategy game, in pairs) 14-15
    Word Puzzles 128-134
    1. O God, guide me (word search) 129
    2. God is the greatest mystery of all (word search with a hidden message) 130
    3. Kingdoms of creation (scrambled word double puzzle) 131
    4. Prayer is talking with God; Blessed is the spot (letter tiles) 132
    5. Puzzle solutions 133-134
    The universe is amazing (maze) 174

Memory Quotes and Prayers

    Quotations from the Bahá'í Writings (handout) 101, 110-111, 161-162
    American Indian prayer (opening prayer) 140
    Children's performance (recitation of memory quotes) 138-139
    Memorization activity (student choice of quotes) 101
    O Son of Being (Arabic Hidden Word #12) 50, 51
    Personal prayer book (make a booklet for adding memorized prayers) 127
    Prayer station (to learn, copy, decorate and memorize prayers) 127
    Prayer tree (cut out leaves) 125-126

Miscellaneous and Audio-Visual

    Cosmic Voyage (DVD/video on the universe – from galaxies to atoms) 15
    Follow-up ideas 195
    Prayer maps (add stars to show where prayers were said) 64, 79-83
    Quiz show on prayer (with host and panelists) 154
    Some divine humor (jokes) 149

Music

    Children's performance 138-139
    Instructions for group singing 178-179
    List of songs 182
    1. Blessed Is the Spot / Bendito Es el Sitio 65, 183
    2. Day by Day 184

3. Glorious Day 185
4. God Is One / Dios Es Uno 186
5. Kingdoms of God 21, 187
6. Love Me That I May Love Thee 188
7. O God, Guide Me 189
8. Pray to God 60, 190
9. Song of Love 191
Musical scores 183-191
Song sheets 159-160, 180-181

Outdoor and Movement Activities

Kingdom hunt (outdoor walk to find examples of minerals, plants and animals) 122
Kingdoms of creation (dramatic movement) 121
Who created it? (brainstorming) 122

Readings and Stories

God, the Creator (reading with student questions and discussion) 46, 52, 166
Handout packet (readings and stories for all four lessons) 157-175
In the image of God (reading and discussion) 100, 108, 173
Prayer lesson (story about 'Abdu'l-Bahá with questions) 63, 78, 169
Prayer, our connection with God (reading and discussion) 63, 77, 168
Names of God (devotional reading) 150-151
True understanding (reading with pictures about God, the unknowable essence) 142-146

Thinking Exercises and Quiet Time

Creation meditation (meditation exercise) 48-49
Galaxy maps and photos (individual study) 44
Kingdom categories (brainstorming) 20
Kingdom hunt (outdoor walk to find examples of minerals, plants and animals) 122
Kingdoms of creation (picture sorting) 18, 38
Thinking about God (write, exchange, share) 14
Who am I? (self reflection and sharing) 99
Who created it? (brainstorming) 122
Word Puzzles 128-134
The universe is amazing (maze) 174

* * * * *

www.ingramcontent.com/pod-product-compliance
Lightning Source LLC
Chambersburg PA
CBHW080537170426
43195CB00016B/2590